P9-CMR-443

Ways of Knowing in Science and Mathematics Series
RICHARD DUSCHL, SERIES EDITOR

ADVISORY BOARD: Charles W. Anderson, Raffaella Borasi, Nancy Brickhouse, Marvin Druger, Eleanor Duckworth, Peter Fensham, William Kyle, Roy Pea, Edward Silver, Russell Yeany

Standards-Based Mathematics Assessment in Middle School

Rethinking Classroom Practice

THOMAS A. ROMBERG

EDITOR

Teachers College, Columbia University
New York and London

Published by Teachers College Press, 1234 Amsterdam Avenue, New York, NY 10027

Library of Congress Cataloging-in-Publication Data

Standards-based mathematics assessment in middle school : rethinking classroom
   practice / edited by Thomas A. Romberg.
      p. cm. — (Ways of knowing in science and mathematics series)
   Includes bibliographical references and index.
   ISBN 0-8077-4482-4 (acid-free paper)—ISBN 0-8077-4481-6 (pbk. : acid-free paper)
   1. Mathematics—Study and teaching (Middle school)—United States—Evaluation.
2. Educational evaluation—United States.   I. Romberg, Thomas A.   II. Series.

QA13.S7 2004
510'.71'273—dc22

                                                                    2004046080

ISBN 0-8077-4481-6 (paper)
ISBN 0-8077-4482-4 (cloth)

Printed on acid-free paper

Manufactured in the United States of America

11   10   09   08   07   06   05   04   8   7   6   5   4   3   2   1

Contents

Introduction   1

**PART I   Overview and Background
of Reform in Assessment Practices   3**

1 Monitoring Student Progress   5
       Jan de Lange and Thomas A. Romberg

**PART II   Teaching and Assessment Under
a Reform Curriculum   23**

2 Instructional Innovation and Changing Assessments   25
       M. Elizabeth Graue and Stephanie Z. Smith

3 Expanding Classroom Practices   45
       Mary C. Shafer

4 Practices in Transition: A Case Study
       of Classroom Assessment   60
       Marvin E. Smith

**Part III   The Design of New
Assessment Tasks   81**

5 Developing Assessment Problems on Percentage   83
       Marja van den Heuvel-Panhuizen

6 Analysis of an End-of-Unit Test   100
       Monica Wijers

7 The Design of Open—Open Assessment Tasks   122
       Els Feijs and Jan de Lange

8 Investigations as Thought-Revealing Assessment Problems   137
     Martin van Reeuwijk and Monica Wijers

**PART IV   Embedding Assessment
in Instructional Practice   153**

 9 Making Instructional Decisions: Assessment to
     Inform the Teacher   155
     Martin van Reeuwijk

10 Enriching Assessment Opportunities Through
     Classroom Discourse   169
     David C. Webb

11 Collaborative Partnership: Staff Development
     That Works   188
     Ann Frederickson and Michael Ford

12 Retracing a Path to Assessing for Understanding   200
     Teresa Her and David C. Webb

PART V   Generalizing the Approach   221

13 Classroom Assessment as a Basis for Teacher Change   223
     David C. Webb, Thomas A. Romberg, Truus Dekker,
     Jan de Lange, and Mieke Abels

References   237
About the Contributors   245
Index   251

Introduction

Standards-Based Mathematics Assessment in Middle School takes an in-depth look at the problems and practices involved in conducting formative assessments in reform mathematics classrooms. In the chapters, researchers and teachers identify the problems teachers face as they attempt to implement new assessment procedures in conjunction with their use of the *Mathematics in Context* (MiC) curriculum materials (National Center for Research in Mathematical Sciences Education & Freudenthal Institute, 1997-1998). These materials were developed from 1992 to 1997 by the staff of the Freudenthal Institute at the University of Utrecht and adapted for use in U.S. schools by the staff of the National Center for Research in Mathematical Sciences Education (NCRMSE) at the University of Wisconsin–Madison. The comprehensive mathematics curriculum for grades 5–8 includes 40 units (10 at each grade level), teacher guides, supporting materials, and a variety of assessment materials. Furthermore, the materials were designed to reflect the National Council of Teachers of Mathematics (NCTM; 1989, 1991, 1995) content, teaching, and assessment standards. The curriculum—grounded in quantitative and spatial situations and based in the domains of number, algebra, geometry, and statistics and probability—emphasizes making connections among mathematical topics and domains, and between mathematics and real-world problem solving.

Each chapter tells a story of one or more teachers who discovered the need and developed methods for changing the way they judge student performance. Each chapter is a product of the collaborative research on formative assessment practices carried out by the staffs of the Freudenthal Institute and the National Center for Improving Student Learning and Achievement in Mathematics and Science (NCISLA) and its predecessor, NCRMSE, both at the University of Wisconsin–Madison, with help from a group of dedicated professional mathematics teachers. The set of studies involved five sites: Madison, Stoughton, and Verona, WI; Culver City, CA; and Providence, RI. As teachers and their students implemented the MiC middle school mathematics materials at these sites, data were gathered on teachers' assessment practices through classroom observations, teacher interviews, and student work. Pseudonyms are used for all teachers (except Anne Frederickson and Teresa Her, who are chapter authors) and for all students.

Chapters 1 and 13 are products of the NCRSME Classroom Assessment as a Basis for Teacher Change project (funded by the U.S. Department of Education). Chapters 2 and 5 are products of the NCRMSE Achieved Curriculum project (funded by the National Science Foundation). Chapters 3 and 4 are products of the NCRMSE Assessment project. Chapters 6, 7, 8, 9, and 10 are products of the NCISLA Research on Assessment Practices project. Chapters 11 and 12 are products of the NCISLA Middle School Design Collaborative. Even though the chapters are products of different funded projects, the authors were all part of the same research group.

The book is divided into five parts. Part I, Overview and Background of Reform in Assessment Practices, contains a single overview chapter. Part II, Teaching and Assessment Under a Reform Curriculum, contains three chapters that describe the struggle teachers encountered in assessing student performance as they taught units from *Mathematics in Context*.

Part III, The Design of New Assessment Tasks, contains four chapters about the development and use of new test items (assessment tasks) designed to yield information beyond whether an answer is correct (e.g., information about student strategies and thought processes). These four chapters are brief stories that provide insight into the problems of developing and using new assessment tasks.

Part IV, Embedding Assessment in Instructional Practice, contains four "insight stories" about how teachers, as a consequence of teaching MiC units, gradually changed their views about their students and how to assess their progress. The teachers also began to see the importance of such information as they planned and carried out daily instruction in their classrooms.

Part V, Generalizing the Approach, contains the final chapter that summarizes both the need for a good professional development program focused on formative classroom assessment and some of the components of such a program.

PART I

OVERVIEW AND
BACKGROUND OF REFORM
IN ASSESSMENT PRACTICES

This part contains background information that underlies all of the research studies reported in the following chapters. In Chapter 1, Monitoring Student Progress, Jan de Lange and Thomas A. Romberg first describe *Mathematics in Context* and give an example of what instruction in an MiC classroom is like. This is followed by a brief overview of the Dutch conception of mathematics instruction, referred to as "Realistic Mathematics Education" (RME). This conceptual framework provided the basis upon which the MiC units were created. Finally, the authors explain the principles and features of a classroom assessment system consistent with the RME framework.

Chapter 1

Monitoring Student Progress

Jan de Lange
FREUDENTHAL INSTITUTE, UNIVERSITY OF UTRECHT

Thomas A. Romberg
UNIVERSITY OF WISCONSIN–MADISON

Today many teachers are implementing a standards-based reform curriculum in their mathematics classrooms. In so doing, they are finding that the instructional approach to mathematics teaching characterized, for example, in *Mathematics in Context* (MiC; National Center for Research in Mathematical Sciences Education & Freudenthal Institute, 1997–1998) represents a substantial departure from their prior experience, established beliefs, and present practice. This book focuses on how teachers responded to the challenge of changing their classroom assessment practices when implementing the MiC reform materials.

To understand the approach to the development of a new formative assessment system, a brief overview of the MiC curriculum is given. This is followed by a description of the Dutch theory of instruction called "Realistic Mathematics Education" (RME) that underlies both the MiC materials and the assessment system that is being developed. Then, to exemplify this approach to instruction, the types of problems students are expected to work in the units in the statistics and probability strand of MiC are summarized. The chapter concludes with a set of assessment principles and a description of the key steps toward a new classroom assessment system.

OVERVIEW OF *MATHEMATICS IN CONTEXT*

MiC is one of the reform curricula for middle school mathematics funded by the National Science Foundation (NSF). Using the MiC materials, students are expected to make sense of a real-world situation by seeing and extracting the mathematics embedded within it. The instructional activities in MiC involve contexts that can be mathematized. Students learn to represent quantitative and spatial relationships in a broad range of situations; to express those relations using the terms, signs, and symbols of mathematics; to use procedures with those signs and symbols, following understood rules, to carry out numerical and symbolic calculations; and to make predictions and interpret results based on the use of those procedures. They come to understand the rationale for and use of mathematical terms, signs, symbols, and rules—notions useful for purposes that include solving problems in engineering and science, understanding the human condition, and creating new and abstract mathematics. The sequence of contextual activities permits students to gradually develop methods for symbolizing problem situations.

Instruction in MiC classrooms does not begin by presenting students with the formal terms, signs, symbols, and rules, along with the expectation that students then will appropriately use these formal ideas to solve problems. Instead, instruction in MiC classrooms leads students to value and understand the need for mathematics through the gradual development of their ability to mathematically represent complex problems, a process called "progressive formalization."

Each unit includes tasks and questions designed to engage students in mathematical thinking and discourse. Students explore mathematical relationships, develop their own strategies for solving problems, use appropriate problem-solving tools, work together cooperatively, and value one another's strategies. They are encouraged to explain their thinking as well as their solutions. Teachers are expected to help students develop common understanding and usage of the terms, signs, symbols, and rules of mathematics, which the students then attempt to use in articulating their thinking. Other activities have been designed so that students can extend their ideas to new problem situations.

REALISTIC MATHEMATICS EDUCATION

The Dutch "Realistic Mathematics Education" instructional framework underlies the creation of MiC. RME is based on an epistemological view of mathematics as a human activity that reflects the work of mathematicians—finding out why given techniques work, inventing new techniques, justifying assertions, and so forth. It also reflects how users of mathematics investigate a problem situation, decide on variables, build models relating the variables, decide how to use mathematics to quantify and relate the variables, carry out calculations, make predictions, and verify the utility of the predictions. This perspective is based on the ideas of the mathematician Hans Freudenthal (1983), who believed that "students are entitled to recapitulate in a fashion the learning process of mankind" (p. ix). He stated that "mathematical structures are not presented to the learner so that they might be filled with realities. . . . They arise, instead, from reality itself, which is not a fixed datum, but expands continuously in individual and collective learning process" (Freudenthal, 1987, p. 280). Freudenthal's beliefs about what types of mathematics students should learn and how they should learn them have been made operational in MiC.

RME's set of philosophic tenets transfer into an instructional approach with four components: (1) goals that reflect Freudenthal's notions of students recapitulating the creation of the discipline, (2) the design of structured sets of activities in mathematical domains that reflect those goals, (3) the provision to teachers of a guide to strategies that support students' collective investigation of reality, and (4) the development of an assessment system that monitors both group and individual student progress in those domains.

MIC APPROACH TO STATISTICS AND PROBABILITY

To illustrate how the four tenets are realized in the MiC units, an overview of the eight units in the domain of statistics and probability appropriate for middle school students is presented in relationship to each tenet.

Goals for Students: Reinventing Math

For school mathematics, this RME tenet emphasizes the notion that mathematics is a plural noun that comprises several intertwined strands or domains, each an assemblage of ideas defined by the community of mathematicians, mathematics educators, and users of mathematics. This domain view of mathematics differs from current perspectives about mathematics in at least three important ways. First, the emphasis in this approach is not with the "parts" of mathematics (the concepts and skills in the domain) but with the whole of which these are the parts, and in turn how those parts are related to other parts, other domains, and ideas in other disciplines. Second, this conception rests on the signs, symbols, terms, and rules for use—the language that humans have invented to communicate with each other about the ideas in the domains. As a consequence, teachers must introduce and negotiate with students the meanings and use of those elements. Finally, the choice of mathematical methods and representations is often dependent on the situations in which problems are presented.

Units in MiC are organized with respect to four domains: number, geometry, algebra, and statistics and probability. The goal for students for the content domain of statistics and probability is that they acquire a "critical attitude" toward the role of statistics in contemporary society. To accomplish this goal, several conceptual themes are developed across the grades. These themes form the basis for the construction of each unit within the strand and for the connections with other strands. The major themes in the statistics and probability strand are data collection, data visualization, numerical characteristics, reflections and conclusions, dealing with data, developing an understanding of chance and probability, using probability in situations connected to statistics, and developing critical thinking skills.

Structured Sets of Instructional Activities

In the RME approach to instruction, the starting point should be justifiable in terms of the potential end point of a potential learning sequence. To accomplish this, the domain needs to be well mapped. This involves identifying the key features and resources of the domain that are important for students to find, discover, use, or even invent for themselves, and then relating them via a possible hypothetical learning trajectory. The starting points, end points, and a map of the domain are necessary for the development of a structured set of instructional activities to help students move over time from informal to formal reasoning in a particular domain.

In the MiC statistics and probability strand there are eight units organized into two substrands: statistics and probability (see Figure 1.1). In most of these units, one central theme is used to organize a set of concepts. For example, the initial unit, Picturing Numbers, does just that—it pictures numbers. Experiences in reading and making statistical pictures or graphs are closely connected to experiences students might have with statistics in newspapers and other media.

Figure 1.1. Organization map for the statistics strand of *Mathematics in Context*. From *Mathematics in Context: Teacher Resource and Implementation Guide* (p. 59) by T. A. Romberg & J. de Lange, 1998, Chicago: Encyclopædia Britannica. Copyright © 1998 by Encyclopædia Britannica. Reprinted with permission.

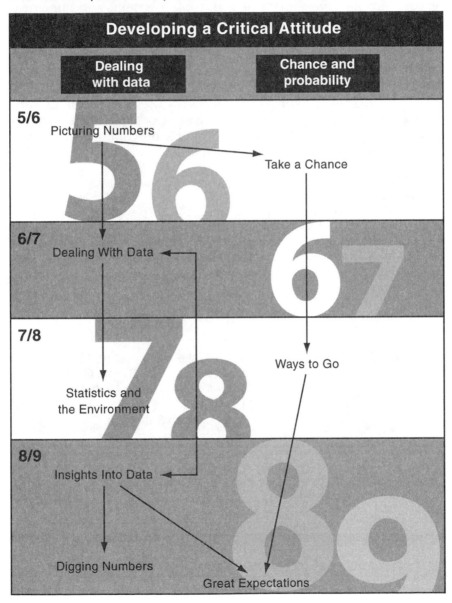

Next, students confront fair and unfair situations in the Take a Chance unit and learn how to quantify chance and design strategies to produce fair outcomes. A typical problem in this unit (presented after students have discussed fair decision-making methods) is shown in Figure 1.2.

In the third unit, Dealing With Data, making sense of a large data set leads to the development of such tools as graphs and numerical measures. The advantages and disadvantages of each tool get attention. Statistics and the Environment, a thematic unit, follows. Students have the opportunity to apply, in an environmental context, the statistics they have learned. They decide which representations and character-istics to use to make sense of different data sets, some of which they are given and some of which they collect themselves. Probability con-cepts are reinforced and extended in Ways to Go, where students begin to formalize procedures for counting possible outcomes. Consider the following example from Ways to Go:

> Suppose that a restaurant serves mushroom, sausage, or pepperoni pizzas and iced tea, root beer, or water.
> a. How many different meal combinations are possible if you order one pizza with one topping and one drink?
> b. How would the number of possible meal combinations change if you could have more than one topping on your pizza?
> (de Jong, de Lange, Pligge, & Spence, 1998, p. 40)

The next two units bring together the concepts that students have learned about probability and statistics. In Insights Into Data, the focus

Figure 1.2. Making a fair decision. From "Take a Chance" (p. 10) by V. Jonker, F. van Galen, N. Boswinkel, M. Wijers, A. N. Simon, G. Burrill, & J. A. Middleton, 1997, in National Center for Research in Mathematical Sciences Education & Freudenthal Institute (Eds.) (1997–1998), *Mathematics in Context*, Chicago: Encyclopædia Britannica. Copyright © 1997 by Encyclopædia Britannica. Reprinted with permission.

a. Can you toss a pencil to make a fair decision? How might you find out?

b. Can you toss a thumbtack to make a fair decision? How might you find out?

is on thinking critically about situations, using tools studied earlier, and adding new tools such as correlation and sampling. Next, in Great Expectations, students confront the issue of making inferences, or having expectations, about a population sample.

> Bora Middle School has a total of 250 students. A survey about pets was conducted at the school. Sixty percent of the students have one or more pets.
> 1. How many students in Bora Middle School have one or more pets? Claire asked 20 students in her sixth-grade science class if they have any pets.
> 2. How many of the 20 students do you expect answered *yes*? Explain.
> 3. It turned out that 16 out of the 20 students that Claire surveyed have one or more pets.
>   a. Does this result surprise you? Why or why not?
>   b. Why do you think so many students in Claire's science class have pets?
> (Roodhardt, Wijers, Cole, & Burrill, 1998, p. 50)

In a final thematic unit, Digging Numbers, students again have the opportunity to use all they have learned to resolve problems.

The units in the data visualization theme exemplify how "progressive formalization" proceeds in MiC. Students begin to use graphic representations for data in Picturing Numbers. They construct and interpret bar graphs, pictograms, and number line plots. Students learn to label axes and choose appropriate scales. The connection between the graphs and the situations from which the data are collected is critical, and students are asked to think about a graph only as a way to understand the situation, not as an end in itself. In Dealing With Data, students add scatter plots, box plots, histograms, and stem-and-leaf plots to their collection of graphic tools. These become part of the students' repertoire for working with data in later units when they begin to learn regression and correlation.

At every level, graphs are analyzed for advantages and disadvantages, and different displays are examined to see what information can be obtained from them. Conclusions based on data and graphs are examined, and several activities focus on analyzing the way graphic representations are used in the media. Misuse of graphs is revisited in a more formal way in Insights Into Data. In the final unit, Digging Numbers, students are given an archeological problem that allows them to choose from the statistical techniques they have learned.

> Archaeologists have discovered the jawbones of approximately 70 ancient pike in an old lakebed. They want to know whether there is a similarity

between ancient and contemporary pike and try to estimate how large
the ancient pike might have been. From a nearby lake, data are collected
about the length and width measurements of contemporary pike. (de Lange,
Roodhardt, Pligge, Simon, Middleton, & Cole, 1998, pp. 23–24)

These data are given to students, who are asked to use them to resolve
several problems. Students can organize the information by using a
stem-and-leaf plot or a number line plot. When the jawbone lengths
are displayed in side-by-side box plots or corresponding histograms,
the answer to the first question is quite clear: The ancient pike are
smaller than contemporary pike. A scatter plot of the body and jawbone lengths of the contemporary pike reveals a linear pattern that can
be summarized by an equation, which in turn can be used to estimate
the length of the ancient pike. The focus of the activity, however, is to
see which tools students choose when they are not told to "do" statistics and whether, and how well, they can build an argument based on
the application of these tools.

Classroom Instruction: Keeping Instruction Interactive

RME's philosophic tenet is that the learning process in classrooms
can be effective only when it occurs within the context of interactive
instruction (where, for example, students explain and justify solutions,
work to understand other students' solutions, agree and disagree openly,
question alternatives, reflect on what they have discussed and learned,
and so on, as in the "ancient pike" problem). In order to accomplish
this, the initial instructional activity should be experientially real to
students so they can engage in personally meaningful mathematical
work (Gravemeijer, 1990). Such problems often involve everyday life
settings such as "students with pets" or fictitious scenarios such as
judging the fairness of "tossing a thumbtack"; with experience, however, parts of mathematics become experientially real to students. Because, as Freudenthal (1983) put it, "mathematical concepts, structures,
ideas have been invented as tools to organize the phenomena of the
physical, social, and mental world" (p. ix), initial student activities need
to be authentic, or realistic. Such activities should reflect the real phenomena from which mathematics developed, or actual situations and
phenomena, the interpretation of which requires the use of mathematics, again, as used by archeologists in the "ancient pike" problem.

For teachers first teaching a MiC unit, the initial change involved a
shift in the daily pattern of instruction. In de Lange, Burrill, Romberg,
and van Reeuwijk (1993), co-author Burrill reflected on this challenge.

> The surprise came when we tried to teach the first lesson. There was little to "teach"; rather, the students had to read the map, read the keys, read the questions, determine what they were being asked to do, decide which piece of information from the map could be used to help them do this, and finally, decide what mathematics skills they needed, if any, in answering the question. There was no way the teacher could set the stage by demonstrating two examples (one of each kind), or by assigning five "seat work" problems and then turning students loose on their homework with a model firmly (for the moment) in place. (p. 154)

The changes in the pattern of instruction forced some teachers to reconsider how they interacted with their students. In particular, authority in the traditional classroom resides with the teacher or with the textbook author. Because the student booklets contained tasks for students to read and make sense of, such as the "ancient pike" problem in Digging Numbers, authority shifted from the text and teacher to the students. This changed the work environment for both teachers and students from well-rehearsed routines to a variety of nonroutine activities. For most teachers, the adjustments in what they and their students were regularly expected to do, were unsettling.

Given such problems, students need to identify information necessary to answer the questions. In the statistics units, this often involves specifying variables, describing a model to indicate the relationships between variables, and either searching for existing data or collecting new data about the variables. Then the batches of data need to be organized. The differences between categorical data and numerical data need to be identified. Only then does one use a variety of descriptive and quantitative techniques to make sense of the data. As illustrated in the statistics and probability units, these include a variety of procedures for visualizing the data, calculating data summaries for central tendency and dispersion, producing tables and scatter plots for pairs of data, and so forth. Following such descriptions of data, often one uses inferential techniques to make decisions or predictions based on the data. It is at this point that the importance of probabilistic reasoning becomes apparent. However, the role of probability in making rational decisions is problematic unless sampling and design issues are addressed. Finally, one needs to build a coherent case to answer the questions originally raised, based on the information and its analysis.

Throughout this sequence, MiC emphasizes that the statistical concepts are connected to situations where they make sense in a "natural" way. Statistical and probability tools and concepts are not presented and learned as a long list of separate items, but rather as items connected to one another and to their applications in given situations. For example, measures of central tendency are connected to different graphic representations. The ability to think critically about a situation is emphasized throughout the entire development of the strand.

Creating a classroom that fosters such interaction involves shifts in the teacher's role: from transmitting prescribed knowledge via a routine instructional sequence, to orchestrating activities situated in learning trajectories, wherein ideas emerge and develop in the social setting of the classroom, to creating discourse communities that support and encourage conjectures, modeling, re-modeling, argumentation, and so on. Central to this interactive classroom is the development of students' abilities to use mathematical argumentation to support their own conjectures. For teachers, this means establishing shared norms of behavior conducive to achieving consensus through comparing solutions, challenging explanations, and requiring others to defend their positions.

Assessment: Monitoring What Students Understand

The RME approach to classroom assessment is closely aligned with instruction and is seen as part of daily instructional practice (de Lange, 1987; van den Heuvel-Panhuizen, 1996). In this approach, ascertaining how many concepts and skills of the domain a student can identify, is not sufficient. Instead, assessment should focus on the ways in which students identify and use such concepts and skills to model, solve, and defend their solutions with respect to increasingly complex tasks. Monitoring student progress, therefore, involves the use of open tasks, through which students relate concepts and procedures and use them to solve nonroutine problems, in contrast to conventional tasks that require the reiteration of procedures "learned" to solve problems that merely mimic the content covered. Responses to open tasks should provide reliable evidence of what a student is able to do in any domain at a point in time. With additional work on a variety of problem situations (often over the course of several years), growth is expected in the complexity of tasks a given student is able to solve.

The monitoring of students' progress has always been a key aspect of the job of teaching. Mathematics teachers traditionally have monitored progress by giving quizzes and chapter tests, scoring and counting the number of correct answers on each, and periodically summarizing student performance in terms of a letter grade. The need to consider alternative ways of assessing students' classroom performance grew as a consequence of teachers' use of MiC in their classrooms. For teachers, one consequence of this shift in authority was a changed view of their students and their students' capabilities. All of these teachers were surprised by the work their students were able to do. A common comment was, "Kids get things that we thought might be hard for them." Burrill wrote, "The students were excited about ideas—they were thinking and interpreting problems that were real and not contrived. No one said, 'When will I ever need this?'" (de Lange et al., 1993, p. 158).

As teachers observed the work that students were able to do, they "needed ways of finding out what students had learned" (D. M. Clarke, 1993, p. 222). Teachers in another study (B. A. Clarke, 1995) quickly realized that

> Students' correct solutions also represented different levels of sophistica-
> tion. Teachers were faced with valuing all genuine attempts at problems,
> while seeking to move students towards increasingly mathematically ele-
> gant methods. . . . [These teachers also found that] although incorrect
> solutions are a common occurrence in a traditional classroom, the im-
> portance placed on the value of student thinking and the de-emphasis
> on the one appropriate solution placed extra demands on the teachers in
> this study, as they struggled to both understand and build on student
> thinking. (pp. 156–157)

ASSESSMENT PRINCIPLES AND FEATURES
OF A CLASSROOM ASSESSMENT SYSTEM

The first step in the change process involves using MiC units to motivate teachers to see the need to change their assessment practices. This usually comes as a consequence of changing their instructional practices and seeing the quality of the work their students are doing. Recognizing that a need exists does not lead automatically to ways of alleviating that need. Teachers need help.

The second step in bringing about change involves providing teachers with information about alternatives and with examples of assessment tasks and scoring rubrics. For the teachers in the studies reported in this book, de Lange and the staff of the Freudenthal Institute developed a *Framework for Classroom Assessment in Mathematics* (1999), which reflects both RME's approach to assessment and NCTM's (1995) assessment standards. The intent of this framework was to generalize what had been learned about classroom assessment into a set of principles, with examples, so that teachers could use the ideas at all levels, using any curricular materials. The researchers developed the following principles for classroom assessment:

1. The main purpose of classroom assessment is to improve learning.
2. The mathematics are embedded in worthwhile (engaging, educative, authentic) problems that are part of the students' real world.
3. Methods of assessment enable students to show what they know rather than what they do not know.
4. Assessments include multiple and varied opportunities (formats) for students to display and document their achievement.
5. Tasks make operational all the goals of a curriculum (not just the "lower" ones). Performance standards, including indications of the different levels of mathematical thinking, are helpful tools in this process.
6. Grading criteria, including examples of exemplary and less-than-exemplary work, are published and consistently applied.
7. Testing and grading involve minimal secrecy.
8. Feedback given to students is genuine.
9. The quality of a task is not defined by its accessibility to objective scoring, reliability, or validity in the traditional sense, but by its authenticity, fairness, and exemplification of the above principles.

These principles form a "checklist" for teachers who take classroom assessment seriously. But from principles to practice can be a long road. Many skills are drawn on simultaneously in doing real mathematics.

The third step is to create assessment tasks. The pyramid shown in Figure 1.3 has proven useful both in developing assessment tasks and documenting student achievement. For use with MiC units, the pyramid has three aspects: (1) the domains of mathematics: number, geometry, algebra, and statistics and probability; (2) three levels of mathematical thinking and understanding: reproduction, connections, and mathematization; and (3) the complexity of expected student responses (i.e., gauged both by the degree of formality or informality of strategies needed and by the complexity or ease of the task). All test questions can be located in the pyramid according to the mathematical content, the level of thinking called for, and the difficulty of task linked with the richness of expected response.

The three levels of student performance are described next.

Level 1: Reproduction, Procedures, Concepts, and Definition

This level deals with knowing facts, representing, recognizing equivalents, recalling mathematical objects and properties, performing routine

Figure 1.3. Assessment pyramid. From "Enquiry Project: Assessing Realistic Mathematics Education" (p. 4) by T. Dekker, 1997, Utrecht, The Netherlands: Freudenthal Institute. (Figure reprinted in "Mathematics Education and Assessment" by H. Verhage & J. de Lange, 1997, *Pythagoras, 42*, p. 16.) Copyright © 1997 by T. Dekker. Adapted and reprinted with permission.

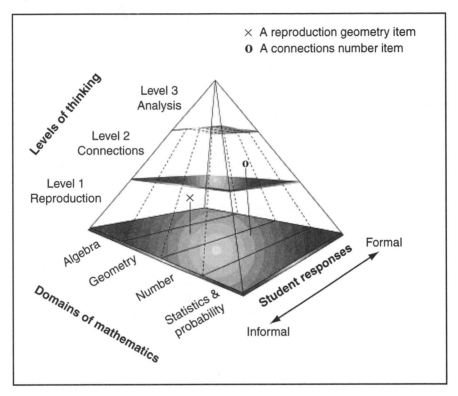

procedures, applying standard algorithms, and developing technical skills, as well as dealing and operating with statements and expressions that contain symbols and formulas in "standard" form. Test items at this level are often similar to those on standardized tests and on chapter tests related to conventional curricula. These are familiar tasks for teachers and tend to be the types of tasks they are able to create. Consider the following example:

Calculate the probability of flipping a coin twice and getting two heads.

$$P(H, H) = \text{———}$$

Level 2: Connections and Integration for Problem Solving

At this level, students start making connections within and between the different domains in mathematics, integrate information
in order to solve simple problems, have a choice of strategies, and
have a choice in the use of mathematical tools. At this level, students
also are expected to handle representations according to situation and
purpose, and need to be able to distinguish and relate a variety of
statements (e.g., definitions, claims, examples, conditioned assertions,
proofs). Items at this level often are placed within a context and engage students in mathematical decision making. These tasks tend to
be open and similar to instructional activities. Teachers need help
creating and using such tasks. An example of a Level 2 task is shown
in Figure 1.4.

Level 3: Mathematization, Mathematical Thinking, Generalization, and Insight

At this level, students are asked to mathematize situations: recognize and extract the mathematics embedded in the situation and use
mathematics to solve the problem; analyze; interpret; develop models
and strategies; and make mathematical arguments, proofs, and gener-
alizations. Items at this level involve extended-response questions with
multiple answers (involving questions with or without increasing levels of complexity). The "floor covering problem" discussed in Chapter
8 (on page 139) is an example of an item at this level.

The dimensions of the pyramid are not meant to be orthogonal, and
the "area" of a given level indicates the relative number of items required
to give a fair image of a student's understanding of mathematics. Because the items used to assess the lower levels are simple in format and
require little time to "solve," more items are needed to assess students'
knowledge. At the higher levels, the open tasks are quite complex, are
time-consuming to solve, and draw on students' integrated knowledge;
as a result, only a few items are needed to assess students' understanding. The third dimension accounts for the variation from informal to
formal use of terms and symbols. For a complete assessment program,
there should be questions at all levels of thinking, of varying degrees of
difficulty, and in all content domains.

The final and culminating step in the change process involves

Figure 1.4. Example of a Level 2 task.

Use the circle graph, which shows the ages of runners in a local July 4th 10-kilometer race.

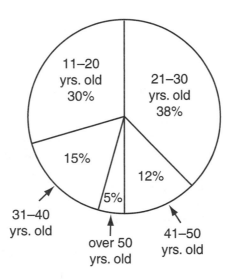

What is the largest group of runners?

What is the smallest group of runners?

By what percentage is the 31–40-year-old age group larger than the 41–50-year-old age group?

What percent of the runners are over 20 years old?

What percent of the runners are over 30 years old?

expanding teachers' notions of classroom assessment. The RME approach sees assessment as embedded in daily instructional practices. In fact, in this approach, the usual distinctions between assessment and instruction are viewed as artificial, and information from many sources (e.g., hearing what students say, observing their individual efforts and groupwork) can be used both to assess student performance and growth and to make instructional decisions.

SUMMARY

Several studies have documented how teachers have coped with the transition from traditional instruction when implementing MiC (Romberg, 1997). As Sarason (1971) in his examination of the culture of schools argued, "Any attempt to introduce a change into the school involves [challenging] some existing regular, behavioral, or programmatic features of schooling" (p. 3). One regular feature that needs to be changed, is the way teachers assess their students' performance.

In the earlier set of studies on using MiC, all of the teachers who participated were experienced, fully certified, confident in their ability to teach, and committed to reform. Thus, no claim is made that they were typical teachers. To these teachers, teaching a new unit sounded relatively easy. They believed they would "gain a few new ideas that we could use in our classes once the project was over" (de Lange et al., 1993, p. 153). Instead, as they taught the units, traditional means for assessing student performance (among other features) were challenged.

The underlying goal of instruction using MiC materials and based on the RME approach is to allow students to participate in the mathematization of reality by exploring aspects of several mathematical domains in real-world contexts, gradually shifting from reliance on informal reasoning, to creating "models of" specific problem situations, to creating "models for" mathematical reasoning and problem solving. In this process, teachers and students create instructional communities, with shared responsibility for learning and shared norms for mathematical argumentation and proof. Classroom assessment, in this perspective, should provide teachers with procedures to individually examine students' ability to integrate what they have learned and their understanding of mathematical concepts and procedures. The complete process is intended to allow students to come both to value and to understand mathematics as it is used in the world in which they live.

The studies described in this book show that making simple judgments about student work (i.e., marking an answer "correct" or "incorrect") fails to capture student understanding of the problem situation and the mathematical concepts involved. The RME approach as made operational in the MiC materials assumes that the teacher can document more than student scores on quizzes and tests. Because students are working on instructional activities that reflect actual mathematical practices, teachers can document individual student progress from informal to formal notions within and across mathematical domains. In doing so, they can both chart each student's progress and use the information to plan and modify instruction. They have the opportunity to make judgments based on observations of individual efforts and groupwork, notes from interviews of students, and so on. This shift in classroom culture also fosters student self-assessment as a particularly valued classroom norm.

The studies described here also verify the need for teacher professional development that focuses on assessment practices and suggest ways that such professional development could proceed. As schools work to change instruction in order to address the needs of individual students as well as the increasingly demanding educational needs of our work and professional worlds, they need to work to transform how student achievement is judged. As these studies show, new approaches to classroom assessment can be achieved, but they require strong teacher support and appropriate professional development.

PART II

TEACHING AND ASSESSMENT UNDER A REFORM CURRICULUM

The chapters in this part describe how teachers, as they taught units from *Mathematics in Context*, came to the realization that their assessment practices needed to change. As their students explored nonroutine problems, it became evident that conventional tests were not trustworthy indicators of mathematical performance.

In Chapter 2, "Instructional Innovation and Changing Assessments," by M. Elizabeth Graue and Stephanie Z. Smith, the authors report that, as a consequence of teaching MiC units, "not only their information gathering but also their evaluation of that information had changed. All the teachers described how they grappled with grading students' performance in a new way." In this story the importance of linking of assessment reform to changes in curricular materials and instructional practices is made evident.

Chapter 3, "Expanding Classroom Assessment Practice," by Mary C. Shafer, describes how the author found that as classroom instruction became more interactive, new possibilities opened for the teachers to learn about student thinking. This in turn led to a change in the teachers' pedagogy. However, the challenges faced in making such changes were significant.

In Chapter 4, "Practices in Transition: A Case Study of Classroom Assessment," by Marvin E. Smith, the author explains his finding that, when a teacher taught two classes, one using MiC materials and the other, traditional text, in both classes the teacher focused primarily on the *completion of tasks*, rather than on the *quality of the answers*, in assessing student performance. As a consequence, the MiC students engaged in very little communication about ways to produce higher-quality responses to learning tasks.

Chapter 2

Instructional Innovation and Changing Assessments

M. Elizabeth Graue
UNIVERSITY OF WISCONSIN—MADISON

Stephanie Z. Smith
BRIGHAM YOUNG UNIVERSITY

How do changes in mathematics instruction shape the kind of assessment practices that teachers use? This chapter examines the assessment beliefs and practices of four middle school mathematics teachers implementing *Mathematics in Context* (National Center for Research in Mathematical Sciences Education & Freudenthal Institute, 1997–1998) for the first time. Through observations of classroom interaction, teacher interviews, and analysis of instructional documents, we charted the beginnings of change in the types of assessment information that these teachers found valuable. Constraints on change in assessment included time available to develop, implement, and interpret alternative assessments, as well as parent and student beliefs about the meaning of "doing well in mathematics." But tightening the link between curriculum and assessment involves more than the development and implementation of excellent curricular materials—it also will require support from multiple audiences and broadening beliefs about the meaning of "doing and knowing mathematics."

Recent years have witnessed a struggle over the genesis of curriculum, instruction, and assessment practice in U.S. schools. Efforts to improve student achievement have brought forward innovations that attempt to link improvements in student performance to new forms of assessment, mandated curricula, and the imposition of external

Reprinted from *Journal of Mathematical Behavior*, *15*(2), M. E. Graue and S. Z. Smith, "Shaping Assessment Through Instructional Innovation," pp. 113–136; 1996, with permission from Elsevier.

standards. One of the most prominent reform strategies of the late 1980s and the 1990s was the use of assessment to leverage change in instructional practice. Researchers ranging from measurement experts to curriculum-content specialists explored the uses of assessment to change instructional practices. These discussions ranged from technical concerns about the reliability and validity of new forms of assessment to explorations of the social implications of the relations formed over new assessment practices. All of these efforts were based on the idea that assessment could be used to sharpen the focus of teachers by providing a target for their instruction.

On the instructional side of the reform coin, new materials and curricula have been developed to change the kinds of activities engaged in by students and their teachers. This has been a prominent focus of mathematics educators as they have worked to build consensus for appropriate practices in mathematics (National Council of Teachers of Mathematics, 1989, 1991, 1995). When teachers rethink their roles in the classroom and use new activities, interactions between teachers and students can change in significant ways. Questions that have not been pursued are: How would classroom practice differ if we linked changes in assessment to reform in curriculum and instruction rather than the other way around? What would assessment look like if its starting point were the instructional needs of teachers as they gathered information about students? How does the specific culture of the school shape the kinds of strategies chosen to generate information that will enrich instruction?

To search for possible answers to these questions, we assumed that assessment and instructional practices were not merely technical problems solved through learning appropriate strategies. Nor did we assume that they could be understood fully by examining the beliefs of individual teachers. Instead, teachers' practice should be situated within social relations that constitute its meaning. By exploring the meanings given to various aspects of teachers' work and how those meanings are generated in social, political, and cultural interaction, we can begin to understand how the complex connections among beliefs, knowledge, and pedagogy make only certain things possible.

DESCRIPTION OF THE STUDY

This study was carried out during the 1994–95 school year. To examine the interweaving of assessment and instruction, we explored the initial implementation of the MiC mathematics materials in a local middle school. We worked with a team of 4 sixth-grade teachers who were willing to collaborate with us. Anne Patterson, Tim Stanton, Dennis Teller, and Max Varso were all experienced middle school teachers. The first three had worked as a team for several years, and Mr. Varso joined the group during the year of our study, after a period of work as a school administrator. We observed instruction at least three times a week during the teaching of the MiC unit, Expressions and Formulas (Gravemeijer, Roodhardt, Wijers, Cole, & Burrill, 1998). Because the pairs of teachers sometimes team-taught, we frequently were able to observe two classrooms in one school visit. We had limited participation in the classrooms, taking notes from the back of the room. Along with observations, we interviewed teachers at two points during the unit, about a month into teaching and again about two-thirds of the way through the unit. The second interview coincided with the end of the first semester when teachers were involved in evaluation for report cards, an event that prompted much discussion of assessment issues and focused attention on the lurking responsibility of grading a unit quiz.

Setting

Harry S. Truman Middle School is in a primarily White, middle-class neighborhood in a midwestern city of 200,000 people. It serves approximately 500 students in grades 6–8, many of whom came from elementary schools that grouped students by perceived ability level for instruction in mathematics and reading. In contrast, these sixth-grade math classes were heterogeneously grouped, with instruction provided to all students by their homeroom teacher.

Curriculum

Expressions and Formulas, the MiC unit that these students engaged in during the period of our study, develops the algebraic concepts of formulas and order of operations by providing experience in a variety of contexts with informal formulas and arrow notations for representing changes. Through these experiences, students expand their understanding of numerical operations, formulas, and the conventional rules for the order of operations within expressions.

GENERATING INFORMATION ABOUT STUDENT LEARNING

We came to this project interested in teachers' assessment practices in the context of student learning. We told them that we thought of assessment in very broad terms, including virtually any teacher strategy to gather information about students. We also assumed that there were three basic ways that teachers could produce information about student learning: (1) by collecting student products that ranged from traditional worksheets, quizzes, and tests, to more recently suggested projects, investigations, and portfolios; (2) by asking their students questions in instructional situations ranging from classroom discussions to individual interviews; and (3) by simply observing activity as students conducted mathematical work. We also assumed that information was not collected but instead was generated by teachers, who set up particular situations that elicited student activity. From this perspective, information about student learning was as much a function of the assessment strategies chosen as it was related to student ability or achievement. The teachers were aware of our interest and engaged us in discussions about the challenges they faced during the unit.

Collecting Student Products

Student products range from end-of-unit tests to daily homework assignments. Teachers vary in the ways they use this information to develop understandings and evaluations about student learning. Ms. Patterson described how her colleagues had been forced to think about tests and quizzes in a new way as they began to work with new curriculum materials.

> It used to be that the majority of the tests were just computation of one kind or another. Because we have these new units with new focuses now, we have had to do a lot more questioning—whether they can explain something or tell us in detail how you go about doing something—as opposed to just doing it. Giving them multi-step problems that might involve various strategies, different ways in which they can go about solving it. So I think our tests have changed.

The idea of risk taking seemed generally to be a holdover from the one-right-answer mode that these teachers felt they were moving away from. In that model, student risk taking meant venturing an answer that could be wrong. The MiC units worked to value multiple strategies, opening up the possible range of acceptable answers in student work. Interestingly, the teachers used other materials along with the MiC units to develop mathematical competencies that were not so forgiving of student responses. These more closed-ended activities used for warm-ups and some homework constituted a kind of skill approach to mathematics, one that they had used for years. As a result, the students might have been getting mixed messages about what behaviors would help them be successful in the classroom and on open-ended activities and tasks.

Progressive Development of Quizzes. The changing of quizzes played out before our eyes as we worked in these classrooms. We illustrate that shift by comparing two quizzes—one given during the first week we were in the field and a second one developed as the teachers were evaluating students for report cards at the end of the first semester. The first quiz (see Figure 2.1) was given during a transitional period before the start of the unit, and it dealt with a common sixth-grade mathematics concept—rounding. Students were expected to demonstrate mastery of computational skills by obtaining correct answers rather than by solving problems or explaining strategies. There was no contextual support for student entry into these problems, and because only procedural knowledge was sought, no student reasoning was expected.

In contrast, consider the quiz developed by Mr. Stanton for the MiC unit, Expressions and Formulas (Gravemeijer, Roodhardt, et al., 1998).

Figure 2.1. Math quiz on rounding given before the start of the Expressions and Formulas unit.

1. Round to the nearest hundred.
   (a) 4,744
   (b) 975
   (c) 350
   (d) 40,417

2. Round to the nearest thousand.
   (a) 5,816
   (b) 27,384

3. Estimate the sums and differences. First round to the nearest hundred.
   (a) $475 + 312 =$
   (b) $780 + 820 =$
   (c) $913 - 475 =$
   (d) $2,725 - 499 =$

As he prepared to write the quiz, Mr. Stanton worried whether it represented the intentions of the unit's authors. He wanted to stay true to that spirit, particularly as he thought about an example of mismatch between unit philosophy and assessment that he had seen in another teacher's quiz on a previous unit. In an interview he stated:

> A person took a nontraditional unit and reduced it to our own "little old math teacher's" formula; that was, to make an objective test where you just memorized and regurgitated stuff. My point is that, when I make a quiz for this unit, I want to make sure that I don't fall into that same trap of emphasizing things that I think are basically trivial.

In this context of change, Mr. Stanton developed the second quiz (see Figure 2.2), which focused on a simplified, informal notion of formulas. Interpretation, representation, evaluation, and computation were key features. Unit goals represented by the quiz included using operation strings to describe a series of calculations, generalizing from a series of calculations to an informal formula, using a process of reverse operations to find the input for a given output, and understanding the importance of the order of operations. The quiz was a mixture of problems, some in context and some not, and included tasks focusing on more complex mathematical problem solving, communication, reasoning, and making connections. The problems varied in the levels of reasoning accommodated but were a significant move away from narrow questions solved by simple procedures and computation.

After teachers gave the quiz, we asked them to tell us how they thought it went. Three of the four were pleased with the results, particularly with the information they had gotten about student thinking. Mr. Teller, for example, told us, "They had to really show proof on quite a few of them, and you could sort of see by their work how they were thinking—certain steps that they were taking—which was easier than some of the assignments we were trying to give. And that helped me, too."

Issues of Problem Context. Whereas the format of the quiz provided teachers a window into student thinking that they had not had before, it also had (possibly unanticipated) implications. Mr. Stanton had taken seriously the notion of contexts as he developed the quiz. Each problem resided in a mini-story about one of the four team teachers. In its handwritten form, the problem was relatively long—three pages. In an interview, Mr. Varso stated:

Figure 2.2. Quiz developed for the Expressions and Formulas unit.

1. Mr. Varso has been named Donut Shop's "Customer of the Decade." His prize was his weight in donuts. If Mr. Varso weighs 70 kg and donuts cost $3.15 per kilogram, how much was his prize worth?

    (a) Write a formula using arrow language.

    (b) Solve the problem.

2. The formula for determining the height of a beech tree is—

    Age $\xrightarrow{\ 0.4\ }$ ___ $\xrightarrow{\ +1\ }$ Height

How old is a beech tree that is 85 meters high?

3. The formula for determining the saddle height of a bicycle is—

    Inseam $\xrightarrow{\ 1.08\ }$ Saddle Height

If Mr. Varso's inseam is 50 cm and Mr. Teller's saddle height is 80 cm, draw a picture showing Mr. Varso riding Mr. Teller's bike. Use math to prove that your drawing is accurate.

    Bike Picture $\longrightarrow$

    Proof:

4. Ms. Patterson flies to the Netherlands to buy a watch and some shoes. She buys 7 watches, one for each day of the week. Each watch costs 65 guilders. She also buys 7 pairs of shoes to go with her new watches. Each pair of shoes costs 95 guilders. Use the following formula to figure out how many American dollars Ms. Patterson spent. *Show your work.*

    Dollars $\xrightarrow{\ \times 1.65\ }$ Guilders

5. Mr. Stanton was thinking of a problem. (He does that often—his life is dull.) Please solve it for him-he is better at problems than he is at solutions.

    ? = $\xrightarrow{\ \times 2\ }$ ___ $\xrightarrow{\ +18\ }$ ___ $\xrightarrow{\ \div 6\ }$ ___ $\xrightarrow{\ -8\ }$ 16.5
    ? = ___

6. Make two more strings that give you the same output as the one below.

    In $\xrightarrow{\ \times 6\ }$ ___ $\xrightarrow{\ \div 3\ }$ ___ $\xrightarrow{\ \times 4\ }$ Out

Prove that your new strings give the same output.

There were too many words in the test. I mean, you had to read too much to get to the meat and potatoes, and some of the kids like Jared—that was too much of an effort for him. You know, given a formula, and just plug in the numbers—he can knock it out cold. They've got those formulas down. They really do. But hiding the numbers in a story problem, particularly as detailed as Tim's story problems were—that was an effort for some of them. You know how some kids will look at a story problem and just try to pick out the numbers and try to plunk them into the formula. So they didn't read it.

In addition to the issue of the amount of reading required, Mr. Varso felt that some students had difficulty finding their way into the contexts on the quiz. The students who did poorly on the quiz typically could not connect with the context. Less successful students did well when they were expected to find an answer to a problem stated in a formula, but they struggled if they had to define the format of the solution. I asked Mr. Varso how things went with the quiz, and he told me:

[A] few kids were real literal. Like, somebody would raise their hand during the quiz and say, "Well, why would Ms. Patterson go to The Netherlands to buy a watch?" And I'd say, "Well, it's just a problem." Then they couldn't get past that. . . . The bike problem though, me on Mr. Teller's bike, they could relate to that because they all have ridden bikes that were too big or too small for them. So nobody asked me about why I would ride Mr. Teller's bike. That seemed logical to them.

Although the other teachers felt that the quiz had gone well and that it provided an opportunity for them to know how their students were thinking, they all echoed pieces of Mr. Varso's concerns. Mr. Varso, in fact, brought up some very interesting points about the use of contexts in both teaching and assessment.

Situating mathematical content in real-life contexts that students could use to build understanding typically involves language-rich descriptions of situations that set the stage for problems. The teachers saw the contexts quite differently. For Mr. Stanton and Mr. Teller, the context provided a window to students' understanding. Mr. Varso viewed the context language as a barrier for certain students, and he was concerned about the nature of the contexts themselves.

Key to the idea of using contexts is the ability of students to access the context as a tool. If the context is so unfamiliar that they cannot relate to it, it actually can impede problem solution. The question that must be asked is, "Whose context does the problem represent?" Some of the contexts used in the quiz were closer to the students' experiences than were others. The question of using contexts is more complex than deciding who "knows" the material—it also involves providing activities that allow students to show what they know.

Issues of Time. In the past, teachers monitored student learning by collecting things that students did. These products took a variety of forms, from homework to student-generated problems. In particular, finding the time to really analyze what students were doing, was one issue that came up as these teachers began to rethink how they examined student work. Mr. Stanton felt that the volume of student work was more accessible and manageable when he used more computational, simple problem activities. He had not figured out how to gather information about students' learning in this new instructional format.

Interacting with Students in the Classroom

Mr. Teller's activity in the classroom paralleled Mr. Stanton's, but he found he could gather information more contemporaneously through classroom interactions. At one point, for example, the class had broken into small groups to work on problem sheets with tiles. As the students worked, Mr. Teller stopped to talk with Jessie and Adam, who were working as a pair in the back of the room. They asked some clarification questions, with Mr. Teller listening, pointing, and asking them questions. After Ms. Patterson and Mr. Teller realized that their access to information about student understanding lay in circulating about the room, he returned to watch Jessie and Adam, again asking and answering questions. He then moved to Jason and Michael, walking through clues with them, asking questions, and suggesting heuristics that might be helpful in their thought process. When they put their pencils down, he said with a smile, "I think you have pretty much gone through this in a thoughtful way. Are there any other clues you haven't tried?" More than just providing teacher guidance for students, Mr. Teller used these interactions as opportunities to gather information about student thinking and learning.

As Ms. Patterson circulated throughout the room, she also used her interactions with students as opportunities for assessment. As she stated in an interview:

The other thing, I think, would be to see how quickly they pick something up, given whatever help it is that I give them, and see if they're able to do one on their own after I explain it personally. The other thing, I think, is just whether, if you give specific directions to them and show them (as opposed to them looking at an overhead), and getting across a classroom—for some kids that makes a big difference. So it might be that they need more specific directions or something. When I assess what they're able to do, that if I give them direct directions, they're able to do something, as opposed to getting it in a classroom [whole-class] setting.

Issues in Student Participation. Teachers also can gather information about students through large-group discussions. An interesting dilemma came up in discussions with teachers and students related to the issue of discussion participation. These teachers found that the same students tended to volunteer answers and that they could not rely solely on evidence from these students. Ms. Patterson, for example, worried that she had more information about what she called her "high flyers" (simply because they participated more) and less about the less flamboyant students (who often kept their thoughts to themselves). Mr. Teller talked about how he tried to manage this dilemma.

There's probably a third who always have their hands up. You really have to watch that as a teacher. You can't always be calling on those kids, and I think the more experience you have as a teacher, you just don't do that. You say, "I'll give you one chance to answer something, kid, but not another one. It's going to have to be someone else in the room." So I try to rotate that a lot if I can.

Mr. Teller's students, however, had a different perspective. When we asked them how Mr. Teller knew what they were learning, we were barraged by comments about the problem of participation.

I don't think that [participation] really works because, like, if you're really bored out of your mind because you're really smart, and you're just sitting there, and you don't really want to participate at all.

He calls on people who never do participate, but when everyone else has their hands up, he always calls on them. When they don't have any idea, he still calls on them. He never calls on people that know it usually. If they have their hand up, he doesn't call them, like, hardly ever.

Ms. Patterson and Mr. Teller realized that their access to information was directly related to student participation, and they found that they could not leave that to chance. They tried to involve all students in class conversations by calling on the more reticent students, who needed additional support in their thinking. The very vocal students in these interviews (who were also the ones who were not being called on in class) realized that the teachers were managing the discussion, and they felt they were missing out. Realizing the value of their participation in their evaluations, they argued that they were jockeying for position for a ticket to talk. They were losing their advantage when the teacher intervened in what they seemed to view as a survival-of-the-fittest approach.

Student participation became a different kind of entity—not just an activity that students engaged in, but a source of assessment information. If equity in assessment and access to opportunities to show competence are connected (National Council of Teachers of Mathematics, 1995), differential participation becomes more serious than concerns about who has a chance to talk in class. Teachers will need to deal with the responsibility of setting up situations that allow students to show what they know in classroom discussions. They also will need to find ways to level the field so that no one gets left out.

Observing Student Work

Teachers have always learned about their students by watching them, but what teachers see is as bounded by the student activities as it is by student achievement. In an interview, Mr. Stanton described how the new *Mathematics in Context* approach to teaching mathematics expanded the kinds of information available about student learning.

> With the sort of more innovative approaches that we have with math now, linking with language and doing a lot of writing, there's more of an effort component that's possible to measure than there used to be. I can watch a kid in class here and see if he cooperates with other people, see if he's on task, whereas the traditional seatwork kind of stuff, the only thing you could tell if you gave a kid 50 division problems is whether you had the answers right. Here you see the kid operating in a greater variety of ways, and so it's easier to get some sort of feeling for what they're putting out.

All four of these teachers talked about ways in which they wanted to capitalize on their observations of students. Given, however, the pressure of time (which made organization of observation difficult), they relied on this data source primarily to further their knowledge of student effort and independence.

Teacher Note Taking. The more student-centered activities provided these teachers with a window into student work. Because students were engaged in group and individual problem solving as well as discussions, their process was open to more explicit examination by the teacher. Mr. Teller and Ms. Patterson came to recognize that these activities could allow information gathering on individual students. Mr. Teller described how he watched his students during instruction, making notes on their behavior.

> If somebody is making a particularly good comment or something, I sort of make a mental note of those sorts of things. Carol, the other day, she took about three risks in a row. We were talking about some of the homework, you know, and it was pretty tough stuff if I remember right . . . but she took a risk three times in a row of answering the question, and nobody else did. There were a lot of kids in the room that are a little better in math than she is, you know, but she just sort of thought, "I'm going to take a chance." She was on a roll that day, and I made a mental note of that, and then as soon as the math period was over, I jotted it down on some paper. I sort of tend to keep some anecdotal type of records like that, which helps me to remember things.

Mr. Teller valued students' risk taking as evidence that they were becoming independent mathematics thinkers—a disposition that he believed helped students to advance to more sophisticated understanding. As we noted earlier, this seemed to be a common holdover from traditional assessment, which undervalues multiple approaches to problem solving and focuses on problems with one right answer.

Recognizing Student Patterns. Mr. Teller's comment points to another issue related to teacher observations of student activity. His practice was to note patterns and breaks in student activity. These provided indications of student learning, with changes in activity marking transitions to more sophisticated understanding. He was using his background knowledge of the students' past behavior to interpret classroom interactions that might go unnoticed to the casual observer or within any single piece of assessment information.

Ms. Patterson also watched student patterns. In one instance when she and Mr. Stanton were team-teaching, she noticed that a student, George, was stuck on a problem. She sat and worked with him while the rest of the class worked through a set of problems. Ms. Patterson was able to point out where George had gone wrong and get him going with his classmates. When I asked her how she might use that information later, she said:

> It also helps me to keep watching him. And for other classes then, when I was teaching, I'd be watching to see if he gets stuck again. And I worry about it more. Not so much that he's going to screw up the arrow math, but I worry about his attitude. You know, if he's stuck like this continually, then he's going to get discouraged, and he doesn't want to deal with it at all. So the way I would assess that is to keep an eye on him, so that he is not sitting and feeling frustrated because he doesn't know where to go with that. I would worry about what it does to his attitude about math.

Ms. Patterson made a connection between George's autonomy in mathematics, his ability to get himself unstuck, and the excitement that would allow him to continue to progress in all areas of the curriculum.

INTERPRETING AND COMMUNICATING
ASSESSMENT INFORMATION

As these teachers explored a new approach to teaching mathematics, they found that not only their information gathering but also their evaluation of that information had changed. All the teachers described how they grappled with grading students' performance in a new way. We present some excerpts from the teachers' descriptions of grading, particularly as it relates to doing a report card at the end of a quarter. We begin with Mr. Teller, who was really struggling with alignment of the curriculum and evaluation.

> Especially with this new math unit, there's not so much—the old type of math, you know, where you used to have all the percentages that you could sort of add up and average out and everything. I found it really hard to grade this time. I'm still in the old mode of doing that sort of thing. And it's hard for me to slip over to evaluating in a different way now. I'm still struggling with that a lot. I

was looking at the report cards and I thought, "There's too many As here," you know? . . . I said, "Am I inflating my grades too much, or what's happening here?" Just too many high grades? Maybe that's okay, I don't know.

Mr. Teller was clear that his grading practices did not match the intent of the program, but he could not find a clear way to make a change. He relied on a modified system in which he gave points to various assignments and then weighed them in his mind to determine how they should form a grade. Mr. Stanton and Ms. Patterson found that they were looking at their students' learning very differently, and that translated into a major change in their grading. Mr. Stanton talked about grading quizzes and exams in this way.

> What I have had to do is sort of change my grading system. You know how all math teachers want to have numbers? I don't do that any more with those tests. I grade it like it was a history exam, so I'm more subjective, and I like that better, actually. I don't have to put a number. I don't have to put 40% on the top of it. It allows a lot of freedom that way if I have some kid that I know is struggling, I know doesn't handle it conceptually, but has done something right—I can give that kid a letter grade and not have to justify it on the terms of the percentage.

The image of Mr. Stanton shaking off the bonds of percentage grades is a powerful one that indicates how constrained he felt by his old grading practices. In particular, Mr. Stanton appreciated the way this process allowed him more latitude in describing the work of students who were working hard and gaining but were still not attaining perfect scores. He had come to realize that there was a difference between the score and the work—that the work was much more multidimensional and represented a learning process rather than a simple reaction to academic tasks. The fallibility of percentages had become clear to Mr. Stanton, and it allowed him to give up the reliance on numbers to a certain extent.

CONSTRAINTS TO CHANGE IN ASSESSMENT

Changes in assessment made in conjunction with changes in instructional practice did not occur without some constraints. A major bone of contention for these teachers was the struggle they waged against student and parental beliefs about the nature of mathematics and mathematics instruction.

Issues in Student Grouping

Some parents and students felt that the curriculum was not challenging enough for the most capable students. A number of students, for example, talked about their dislike of the heterogeneous grouping used for mathematics in their class.

> Having just one big group and then different groups . . . people who are more advanced still have to do the average stuff instead of just going on to the more challenging stuff. Because a lot of us like to work on more challenging stuff and just skip the average stuff, because we know that it's real easy for us and it's just not worth going through it.

This attitude could be linked to the differentiated instruction that they had experienced in their elementary schooling. Those who had been in the advanced groups lost their place in the hierarchy of ability groups and felt that heterogeneous grouping was detrimental to their education. Key to this attitude were their perceptions of the meaning of being a good student in mathematics. As Mr. Stanton noted in an interview:

> The problem of course, too, with math is that there's this notion that kids have of whether they're good in math or not. And if they are, they are supposed to get As. And if they aren't, they're not. So all of a sudden you take into account a kid's work habits and some of these other subjective things, and he's not doing so well, and then you give this kid a B, and the kid comes and says, "Wait, I'm the smartest math student in here." Well, whatever that means— you do well on a standardized test, I suppose. But you do run into that. Especially with sixth graders who come from elementary schools that have been ability grouped.
>
> One of the problems we've had here, really, is convincing kids that it was OK to be in a math class with everybody, and oftentimes what they'll do—they'll claim that your curriculum is too demeaning or the sixth-grade work course is boring. . . . But what I found is that if you take kids and pull them out of class and put them in a small group with three or four other kids whom they consider to be mathematically bright and give them the same things to do that

we do in here, then it's OK. Then the stuff is great. It's only if they're in this group and they've been used to this special treatment that they feel they're being somehow ill served.

Mr. Stanton noted that some students were unwilling to consider effort—the very thing that teachers used to boost the grades of students whom they thought were struggling—to be a component of good math performance. They felt that their math ability, as shown on tests given earlier and their elementary school placements in the high-ability group, was a ticket to an A.

The grouping issue was problematic because the teachers felt that parents and students thought that working in heterogeneous groups diminished the quality of the experience. In an interview, Mr. Varso stated that he was especially troubled by the idea of mixing students of different abilities during assessment activities.

> I feel real guilty if I take a brighter student who's catching on and pair him up with a kid whose head is somewhere else and then try to assess them. And they don't like that either. They sometimes never get past the fact that they're sitting next to so-and-so, and they don't want to be sitting next to so-and-so, and no matter what you say, they really don't want to be doing that. And so, I try to avoid that in the classroom. Those are problems I think I can control. You know, we've done it. You might have noticed, Doug and I do less grouping now than we did earlier in the year.

One way that Mr. Varso worked to solve this problem was to make grouping a student decision.

> If I ask them to do groupwork, that never ceases to fascinate me. I have stopped trying to say, "You three kids over here work together as a group." Now I just let them drift into groups. Remember, we did that? And they drifted into groups without really planning it, and I really liked how that worked.

Issues in Reporting Grades

In a context where parents and students were resisting teacher efforts to provide undifferentiated instruction, the teachers still had to translate the complexity and messiness of student work over the course of a quarter into a grade. These grades were accompanied on the report card by narrative statements chosen from a computer-generated list. That evaluation event, coupled with the pressure the teachers felt from the students and parents about the nature of mathematics and mathematics achievement, set limits on the degree to which teachers could completely transform their assessment practice. The idea of the report card lurked in the background as they looked over student learning and growth. In an interview, Mr. Stanton described how the act of doing report cards held him back and how those constraints might go away in a system that utilized portfolios or other forms of authentic assessment.

> I still feel a little bit uneasy about it, and I think there are a couple of reasons, but one is that I don't know where everybody is. But I also think part of it is sort of a traditional reliance that we have on tests. . . . And when I don't give them, I get nervous. I think part of it is—now we have to give grades this week, and if it were not for that report card, where I feel like I have to justify some sort of letter grade, I would not feel nearly as insecure about assessment. . . . We've given little quizzes and things, but I think if we're going to continue in this middle school to ask for letter grades on report cards, then what will probably happen—at least would happen with me—is that I would attempt to devise some sort of more formal means of assessing kids.

As he moved away from the quarterly grading pressure, the rebel in Mr. Stanton became more forceful. He could joke again that he did not put much importance on the link between the report card and his everyday instructional practice. In fact, he asserted that he was not willing to skimp on his instructional planning time for evaluation.

> To me, I don't even care that much because I don't think this report is what we're doing the math program for anyway. I mean, in terms of the number of priorities that I have, I will spend a lot more time and energy and thought preparing what's going to happen in class than I'm ever going to on evaluation. Evaluation is nice if you can get to it. And as you pointed out, it takes lots of forms. I mean, I think I evaluate kids continually by watching them and listening to them in class, looking at the things that they do. The report card—I don't even know who it's for. Who is it for? Is it for the parents? Oh, in one way it is, because they wish to be kept abreast of what their child's performance is. But in another way, teachers use it as a motivator, so in that sense it's not for the parents, it's for kids. How many times do you hear that? I've said it myself—you know—"You better get going. You're going to get a rotten grade."

DISCUSSION

We began the task of examining classroom assessment by examining the work of four experienced professionals who were interested in changing how they knew their students. Several themes that emerged from our observations and interviews with these teachers contribute to our thinking about instructional assessment. The nature and format of the curriculum can provide a context for change in assessment practice. The MiC curriculum set such a context for the teachers we studied, but it provided different kinds of stimulus for change for each teacher. Although all were using the same curriculum, implementation took on an individual flavor. Each teacher adopted both the curriculum materials and new assessment strategies in quite personal ways. This is a wonderful reminder that no curriculum package should be seen as the answer to changing life in classrooms—implementation is a subtle interaction among teacher belief and style, materials, and institutional culture. Curriculum materials can, however, be a step toward reform.

Although strategies for gathering contextualized information (e.g., observations, interviews, project work) were not yet fully developed or integrated into these teachers' work repertoires, they recognized that these sources of information about student growth were valuable. These teachers used observation, in particular, to provide information about student dispositions, but they were not comfortable using these more informal techniques to find out about content or process growth. One way to integrate these strategies into teachers' assessment techniques is to make them more formal, structuring them into the unit format and producing written documentation. Rather than providing a short quiz, these materials could remind teachers of the kinds of learning and thinking they should be looking for as students progress through unit activities. Information about informal assessment techniques such as observation should be included in preservice teacher education and inservice programs and with curriculum materials that guide instruction.

Constraints of various kinds limit teacher innovation in assessment, and the uneasy relationship between assessment and evaluation still exists. Formats for evaluation, particularly in the form of report cards, shape assessment practices in ways that do not always support alternative approaches for learning about student growth. The necessity of rating student performance using letter grades narrows the kinds of evidence that teachers find appropriate for supporting their evaluation judgments. The curriculum content and assessment communities could provide much support to teachers by exploring new ways to move from assessment information to interpretation to evaluative judgments. Scoring rubrics, whether they are holistic or analytic, are a step in that direction. Alternative evaluation techniques such as portfolios seem to provide a way to honor the complexity of student activity in this kind of mathematics curriculum, while generating a foundation for evaluation decisions.

Time constraints limit the kinds of strategies teachers can use to gather and interpret assessment information. Little time appears to be available within class periods for teachers to step away from the instructor role on a consistent basis to gather and document information on student learning. Without documentation of some kind, the status of observation information will remain tenuous as a decision-making tool. Given the lack of flexibility in daily schedules as well as the other demands on their professional lives, the time needed to reflect on and make sense of this very valuable but very messy kind of data is difficult for teachers to find.

Varying interpretations about the meaning of "doing and achieving in mathematics" provide obstacles for both the instructional implementation of new curricula and the development of appropriate assessment strategies. In the cases examined here, parents' experiences with elementary school mathematics were very different from those they had in the middle school math program. The teachers reported that they met with resistance that was rooted in this culture clash, particularly when they used broader criteria in their grading schemes. A shared vision of a reformed curriculum and some support for families who are making the transition between major school institutions, such as elementary, middle, and high schools, seem vital if curriculum and assessment reform are to succeed.

CONCLUSION

Thinking about assessment from an instructional perspective is a complex, rich, and confusing enterprise. Few categories superimposed on the subject remain discrete under scrutiny, and often an issue that appears to be related to assessment is actually about instruction. Should these difficulties be seen as liabilities? We would argue no, that examining assessment through the lens of instruction keeps us looking closely at the interactions and contexts in which learning occurs. Our challenge, then, is to help teachers develop strategies that make sense of their students' growth and learning—a process we view as primarily interpretive rather than objective.

Although new practices of assessment can develop over time in settings that motivate teachers to think about instructional activity in new ways, there is no inspirational switch or command from a central authority that will "turn on" the development of assessment reform within schools. Nor can we rely on new curricula alone to leverage innovative assessment strategies. Teachers' reconceptualization of assessment occurs in a social context and is shaped historically and culturally by actors within the classroom and in the community. Acknowledging these connections and using the resulting constraints as paths to reform can create a more contextualized, and perhaps more sustainable, approach to supporting teachers as they change their practice.

Chapter 3

Expanding Classroom Practices

Mary C. Shafer
NORTHERN ILLINOIS UNIVERSITY

Interaction in *Mathematics in Context* (MiC) classrooms is often complex, potentially promoting classroom assessment practices that deepen teachers' understanding of students' mathematical abilities and that affect classroom instruction. As MiC field-test teachers began to encourage students to express their thinking, they developed methods of assessment that became important elements of their pedagogy. This chapter features the results of three studies that describe teachers' assessment practices as they implemented MiC field-test units: emergent changes in assessment practice as teachers used MiC units for the first time; instructional decisions by a teacher who was familiar with MiC but was teaching a newly developed unit for the first time; and the development of models of students' thinking by a teacher who taught an MiC field-test unit for 2 consecutive years. These studies were based on three research questions: What was the nature of the newly developed assessment practices? In what ways did teachers capitalize on the information they were gathering about their students? What challenges did teachers face as they made changes in assessment practices? Collectively, these studies show that MiC did have an impact on teachers' attention to assessing the thinking of individual students and to refining their own understanding of the reasoning and mathematical abilities of students at a particular grade level with respect to particular mathematics content.

EMERGENT CHANGES IN ASSESSMENT PRACTICE

The first study of emerging assessment practices involved 15 fifth-grade teachers from five field-test sites across the country. During the spring semester of the first year of the MiC field test, interviews were conducted on the nature of the teachers' assessment practices as they taught MiC for the first time (Romberg & Shafer, 1995). These teachers re-evaluated their assessment practices and began to seek information beyond correct answers on quizzes and tests. They assessed students' understanding of mathematical content daily through various "on-the-spot" methods that emerged because of the increased classroom interaction generated by using MiC. The nature of classroom assessment for these teachers was dramatically different from assessment of student learning with conventional materials.

Focusing Assessment

As they gained experience teaching MiC, these teachers recognized the need for developing assessments that capitalized on the new types of information they were learning about their students through problem solving. At the same time, they found it difficult to decide which instructional goals in the MiC units were important to assess. In MiC, topics traditionally reserved for high school students are introduced to middle school students in real-world contexts, with emphasis on student reasoning rather than on procedures. These changes meant that teachers had not taught the content previously and were unfamiliar with the ways in which it was presented (Romberg, 1997). Also, the initial sections of each unit were often investigative in nature and designed to build on students' informal understanding of mathematics in order to develop a conceptual foundation for the mathematics presented in the units. Teachers wondered whether it was important to assess the seemingly exploratory activities. Furthermore, they experienced difficulty understanding the notion of mastery of concepts over time (rather than the goal of mastering mathematical content by the end of each chapter, as in conventional curricula). As one teacher explained:

> On a lot of these things, if not done explicitly in the fifth grade, it might be done explicitly in the sixth grade, or it might be sort of an accumulating thing. . . . I think people would have to look at it a little differently. You can't expect mastery. You're exposing the kids to this. I think sometimes we get hung up on expecting them to really, really master it. (Teacher 6, interview, April 7, 1994)

The new curriculum provided challenges in knowing which instructional goals to assess and when to assess them.

Assessing Individual Students

Teachers initially found it difficult to assess what individual students had learned during instruction. With MiC, teachers used less teacher-led presentation of a prescribed set of procedures; they no longer had pages of procedures to check students' mastery of particular skills. Rather, lessons often included a combination of whole-class discussion and small-group work, and students did not communicate their understanding of mathematical concepts well enough for teachers to gather the type of information they felt was necessary to assess student learning. As one teacher remarked:

> Because the daily activities were sometimes cooperative, individual, or in a large group, it was easier to find out where the students were that understood it than it was [to find out] where the students were borderline. . . . What did the borderline students know? Those who didn't get it—it was pretty obvious. Those who really did get it—it was pretty obvious. And then we have a large group in the middle who—we're saying we're not sure—we think they might [but] we don't think they do, so we try. (Teacher 5, interview, April 21, 1994)

As the year progressed, this teacher integrated reflective activities that encouraged students to "pull things together more often." For instance, he used writing prompts (e.g., What are you learning? How are you going to apply this? Where does this concept come in?). Many teachers in this study asked students to use notebooks as a means of organizing their work and to include written solution strategies and reflections. In some cases, worksheets or quizzes were stapled into notebooks. Used in this way, notebooks provided a way for teachers to monitor the work of individual students. During small-group work, some teachers assessed students' dispositions toward mathematics. They discerned students who could tackle problems on their own, those who were "becoming mathematical thinkers," those who were dependent on others, and so on.

Designing assessments for particular lessons was also challenging. Although the teachers used the few suggested assessment options listed in some field-test teacher guides, some teachers began to use section summaries for informal assessment. As one teacher stated, the section summaries "helped me, as well as it helped the kids, to really focus. What did we really cover in this section?" (Teacher 9, interview, March 30, 1994). Other teachers used quizzes on the content of a particular lesson or section of the unit. But time and collaboration with colleagues for preparing such assessments was difficult to find.

> Sometimes in the morning, we'd say, "Did you guys come up with anything to assess the kids on such and such?" And other times we'd sit down in a group and really come up with something. It just depended on what we had time for. (Teacher 6, interview, April 7, 1994)

Some teachers felt that end-of-unit assessments added another piece to their developing picture of students' mathematical understanding. Other teachers, however, expressed concern with end-of-unit assessment tasks that attempted to extend student learning: "Sometimes assessments actually tested more concepts than the kids had been introduced to, and so the kids kind of got hung up with the new material rather than being just tested over what they had covered" (Teacher 2, interview, March 28, 1994). This concern often led teachers to modify or totally replace assessments prepared by unit authors. In most cases, the teacher-constructed tests included matching, fill-in-the-blank, and short-answer questions that focused on vocabulary or specific procedures (e.g., constructing a bar graph for a given set of data), rather than on interpreting the data or allowing students to respond to new tasks that involved reasoning about and applying what they had learned.

Documenting Learning

Many teachers kept mental notes of the information they gathered about their students. They felt they could readily describe the progress of students in their classes, but time constraints prevented them from making written notations. Another perplexing issue was translating into grades the information they were gathering about their students. Teachers realized the difficulty of grading daily work and recording percent grades on each piece, as they previously had done with conventional curricula. Feeling uncomfortable with subjective grading, teachers began to use check marks in their grade books, checklists, or periodic written comments to indicate whether a student knew how to approach a particular problem, accomplished a task satisfactorily, or needed extra assistance. But summarizing such entries still involved the review of accumulated daily work.

Summary

Such issues as determining the important goals to assess, finding ways to help individual students reveal their mathematical understanding, and documenting assessment information were compellingly complex for teachers. Even so, teachers felt that classroom assessment would improve with time because students were learning how to discuss their work, and they were learning what they might expect from students.

INSTRUCTIONAL DECISIONS

The second study of expanding assessment practices focused on one teacher's specific ways of assessing students' thinking and the influence of the information gathered on instructional decisions (Shafer, 1995). During this study, Ms. Blakemore field-tested a newly developed eighth-grade geometry unit about similarity, Triangles and Patchwork (Roodhardt, Abels, et al., 1998). Data sources for this study included interviews prior to and after teaching the unit, classroom observations, and informal conversations with the teacher during groupwork and before or after observations.

In preparation for teaching the unit, Ms. Blakemore solved all the problems herself. This process allowed her to think about the specific problems that might cause difficulty for students, make preliminary decisions regarding effective instructional formats (e.g., whole-class discussion, small-group work, individual work), and plan for classroom assessment. To Ms. Blakemore, assessment was an ongoing process involving both informal and formal methods. She used the information she gathered during assessments to guide her instructional decisions, readily changing the format of instruction to assist students in their learning, whether it involved working with a single student, a small group of students, or the whole class.

Gathering Information

Ms. Blakemore focused her assessment on students' thinking and mathematical abilities. Classroom discussions, both whole-class and in small groups, provided ways for Ms. Blakemore to learn a variety of information about her students: "Sometimes I just know how well they've done—their facial expression when I'm standing in front of class talking about something, the kind of questions they ask. I try to get them to explain what they are doing, and I get an idea of what they know that way" (Blakemore, interview February 24, 1995). Ms. Blakemore did not limit herself to determining which students found correct answers, but looked for evidence of students' knowledge, reasoning, and communication. For example, she listed a set of questions that would guide her assessment.

- How do students decide which triangles they need in order to form a solution?
- How do students set up the problems? Are they using a variety of methods?
- Are they drawing the similar triangles, or do they use mental or written calculations?
- How do students prove that the triangles are similar?
- How does one student explain to another student how he or she did a problem?
- Can everyone in the small groups solve the problems, or are some students merely writing down others' work?
  (Blakemore, interviews, February 24, 1995, and April 7, 1995; observation, March 22, 1995)

In contrast to the numerical answers to exercises for finding missing lengths in similar triangles (generally found in conventional textbooks), this assessment evidence yielded multidimensional information about students' mathematical abilities: mathematical processes (e.g., decisions about the triangles to form, methods to use); knowledge of mathematics (e.g., criteria for proving similar triangles, determining the information to use in proving similarity); communication of mathematical ideas (e.g., articulation of reasoning, clarity of explanations); and dispositions (e.g., participating and contributing in groups). When reviewing students' written work, Ms. Blakemore considered their solution strategies as well as the accuracy of their answers.

Sometimes just by looking at what they are writing, I can see what they are thinking. Sometimes they are using the right process, but they just made some kind of mathematical error. Other times, they were assuming [that the triangles] were similar when they were not. And I could tell by what they have drawn. . . . I try to ask them to explain what they have done when I walk around the room: How did you get that answer? Why do you think it is right? (Blakemore, interview, April 7, 1995)

Informing Instruction

The types of information Ms. Blakemore gained from the assessment opportunities she created provided a rich foundation for making instructional decisions. She explained:

> I think assessment goes on all the time. Some is more formal than others. I think that assessment is the tool that I use to see how individual kids are doing, but it's also a tool to help me to decide then what I need to do—if I need to go back and teach something, or if I need to require this kid to come in during study hall, or no one's getting it . . . because they just didn't understand what I was saying. (Blakemore, interview, February 24, 1995)

Ms. Blakemore was prepared to take such action when the need arose.

> When I plan how I'm going to do lessons, I look at what I think might cause problems, and I decide what I'm going to do as a large group, or this they can work on in their small groups. And sometimes it doesn't work out that way. So I just kind of go with the flow—whatever they need. (Blakemore, interview, April 7, 1995)

Sometimes Ms. Blakemore moved the discussion of concepts from small-group to whole-class discussion: "Sometimes if I see they're not getting it when I walk around, or they're all making a common error, I'll go back to large-group instruction and point something out" (Blakemore, interview, April 7, 1995). At other times, if only one student or one group was confused, she provided individual assistance.

The instructional decisions Ms. Blakemore made in response to assessment information are illustrated in the following description of a lesson (observation, March 25, 1995) during which students investigated how similar triangles could be used to find the height of a tree, given the lengths of the shadows of a tree and a pole and the length of a pole (Roodhardt, Abels, et al., 1998, p. 28, No. 7a–c). In the unit, students were directed to draw a side view of the pole and its shadow, to complete the third side of the triangle (i.e., top of pole to tip of shadow), and to do the same for the tree. They were then asked to explain why the corresponding angles in the triangles were equal and, if the triangles were similar, to determine the height of the tree. At the beginning of the lesson, Ms. Blakemore reminded students of an activity during the prior school year in which they used shadows and a stick to find the height of a tree at the community environmental center. In doing so, she connected their experience with the unit problem. She briefly read through the problem and asked students to solve the problem in small groups. As she listened to the groups, she noticed that one group had started to calculate the height of the tree before proving that the triangles were similar.

Ms. B: How do you know that this angle [the right angle] and this [corresponding] angle in the other triangle are equal?

Thomas: The triangles are similar.

Ms. B: It hasn't told you that the triangles are similar. This whole problem is about proving that these triangles are similar or not similar. What do you need to know for the triangles to be similar?

Dana: It has something to do with the pole.

Ms. B: How do you know that?

Dana: The angles are equal because the lines are perpendicular to the ground.

Ms. B: Do you have enough information now to prove the triangles are similar?

Thomas: No, we only have two angles [one pair of corresponding angles].

Susie: Maybe something with the sun.

Ms. B: The sun forms the angles. Which angle is formed by the sun?

Thomas: This one.

Susie: They both are.

Ms. B: So those angles are equal. If we know those two pairs of angles are equal, then how do we find the third pair?

Susie: There are 180 degrees in a triangle, so if you know two angles, you can subtract them from 180 degrees.

In this situation, Ms. Blakemore redirected the group's attention from an assumption that the triangles were similar to proving similarity, and she guided them with assessment questions (e.g., How do you know those are right angles? If we know that two pairs of angles are equal, then how do we find the third pair?) and assessment questions (e.g., Do you have enough information to prove the triangles are similar? Which angle is formed by the sun?). The questions she posed allowed students to do the mathematical work in solving the problem. After listening to other groups, Ms. Blakemore addressed the whole class.

Through questioning during small-group and whole-class discussion, she had assessed whether students could prove that the angles made by the pole and the tree with the ground were right angles, determine why the two angles formed by the sun were equal, and reason that the third pair of angles were equal. Ms. Blakemore also encouraged students to use mathematical vocabulary. For example, a student said that the tree made "a straight up-and-down line" with the ground, to which she responded, "How can we say that in mathematical terms?" As the discussion progressed, she drew the triangles on the board, numbered the angles, recorded pairs of angles that were equal, and noted why they were equal. Also, instead of telling the students that the triangles were similar, she asked, "Now that you've proven that corresponding angles are equal, are these triangles similar?" After affirmative responses, she stated, "Now we can solve the problem. Because we proved that the triangles are similar, the sides are going to have the same ratio."

Throughout this interaction, Ms. Blakemore focused her questions on mathematical processes and procedures. She modeled the specific steps used in solving problems: the types of questions posed, the diagrams drawn and labeled, and the notes jotted down to support arguments that the two triangles were similar. Collectively, she assisted students in developing metacognitive tools for solving these problems by themselves.

Summary

When planning the unit, Ms. Blakemore determined ways to assess her students' knowledge, and as instruction unfolded, she used various informal methods to gather multidimensional information about her students' thinking with respect to similar triangles. Immediate instructional decisions included posing questions that enabled students to do the mathematical work; moving from small-group work to whole-class discussion to discuss a common difficulty; and jotting notes on the board to record the steps used and the arguments made for proving similar triangles. She used the information she gathered about her students to enhance instruction for the class.

MODELS OF STUDENT THINKING

The third study of expanding assessment practices was a case study of one middle school teacher's assessment of growth in student knowledge over time (Shafer, 1996). During this study, Mr. Michaels taught two grade 6 algebra units. The discussion in this chapter relates to the teaching of one of these units, Operations (Abels, Wijers, Burrill, Cole, & Simon, 1998), which focuses on operations with integers. Data sources for this study included interviews prior to and after Mr. Michaels taught the unit (the second year he taught this unit), classroom observations, and informal conversations with him during groupwork and before or after observations.

The Learning Environment

Mr. Michaels attempted to build a nonthreatening learning environment in which students explored mathematics. Each class period began with a warm-up activity that contained, for example, questions based on the previous lesson or a familiar problem changed in a way that made students think. The types of questions that Mr. Michaels regularly asked, provided many avenues for students to share their reasoning and to promote connections between the new ideas and previously learned concepts. After exploring subtraction of integers with the same sign, for example, Mr. Michaels posed the problem +2 – (–3) and asked, "Can you do that?" Later in that discussion, he inquired, "Can you make a rule for subtracting a negative?" (Michaels, field notes, November 13, 1995). On other occasions, he asked students whether they could use a different method to solve a particular problem. The final segment of whole-class discussion was the lesson introduction, which was used to familiarize students with the context of the lesson and to create discussion aimed at easing what he referred to as "sticking points" that students might encounter as they worked the problems in small groups. The greatest amount of class time was devoted to students working in small groups to complete several assigned unit problems. During small-group work, Mr. Michaels clearly expected active participation by all group members in thinking through and solving unit problems. Developing strategies used in solving the problems was deemed more important than simply providing answers.

Focusing Assessment

During his observations of small-group work, Mr. Michaels checked his students' understanding of the mathematical content. As he moved from group to group, he listened to their discussions, observed their approaches to problems, and looked for accurate solutions. Mr. Michaels encouraged students to rely on their own thinking by allowing them to struggle with problems. He felt that struggling was an indication of students' progress toward understanding the mathematics, but he intervened when he felt they needed his support. In this way, he opened opportunities to learn about students' reasoning, communication, and problem-solving abilities.

Groupwork was both worthwhile and problematic. It allowed students to accept more responsibility for learning the mathematics and gave Mr. Michaels the opportunity to observe and listen to students as they tackled problems, but his movement from group to group also limited what he learned about individual students. Mr. Michaels used quizzes and end-of-unit assessments to assess each student's understanding of the mathematical content. End-of-unit assessments, provided in teacher guides and often written to elicit student thinking, were "reasonably important," from Mr. Michaels's perspective, for learning about student thinking. These assessments furnished information about students' problem-solving abilities and whether students understood the content conceptually or needed extra help.

Benchmark Problems

To more effectively focus his observations and to learn more about his students' thinking, Mr. Michaels selected unit problems that he referred to as benchmark problems. When planning the lesson, he selected one or two benchmark problems, which incorporated several of the concepts underlying the preceding problems.

> If there are six problems in the group assignment, and if I look at Number 6, I'm pretty certain that if they can do that, they must have been able to do the rest of this, too. So I don't really have to look at all the rest of it carefully. I can just zero in on that one thing. If there's a problem, then we may have to go back and revisit something. (Michaels, interview, October 18, 1995)

Mr. Michaels remarked that this process enabled him to get "some sort of feeling for their thought processes."

When a benchmark problem was difficult for several groups, Mr. Michaels encouraged the students to think about the problem, but included a discussion of the problem in the warm-up or whole-class discussion in the next class period, as illustrated in the lesson described below. The mathematical model for integer multiplication, a tool to encourage conceptual understanding of the operation (processes involving chips with plus and minus signs on them), was introduced and used during whole-class discussion prior to groupwork. The problems completed during groupwork gave students opportunities to use the model on their own. Even after the elaborated introduction prior to groupwork, however, Mr. Michaels spent several minutes with each group to demonstrate the model for integer multiplication. In the problem (Abels, Wijers, et al., 1998, p. 43, No. 4c), students were asked to describe how they could show $^-3 \times {}^+4$ (with plus and minus chips) and then write the result.

Mr. M: I want to see your answers to 10a and 10b because everyone is getting those wrong. [For] 10a, zero is right. This is pretty good. You are close to getting everything right. The one thing they asked you to do, however, is to write the number sentence. So you should have $^-3 \times {}^+4$ = what?

Greg: Ah, $^+12$?

Susie: No, $^-12$.

Mr. M: Are you guessing?

Susie: Yes. . . .

Mr. M: Let's see if we can figure it out. [He proceeded to model the process.] What's left?

Greg: $^-9$.

Susie: $^-3$.

Mr. M: Count them: 1, 2, 3, 4, 5, 6, 7, 8, 9, 10, 11, 12.

Susie: $^-12$.

Mr. M: $^-3 \times {}^+4 = {}^-12$. It works, doesn't it? So that is the number sentence.

(Michaels, observation, November 26, 1995)

At the end of groupwork, Mr. Michaels commented:

> I tried, with the extra explanation this morning, to help them. When the material is conceptually difficult, even the better students shut down quickly. They don't think it through as much. I saw a lot of blank faces today. (Michaels, field notes, November 26, 1995)

Mr. Michaels began the next class period with a five-problem quiz in order to check each student's understanding of integer multiplication. Question 4 asked students to solve $^-3 \times {}^-2$, and Question 5 was, "Explain why the answer to #4 turns out the way it does. Use a drawing or diagram if necessary." These questions were variations of unit problems (Abels, Wijers, et al., 1998, p. 43, No. 11c). Some students found the correct answers to Question 4 but could not explain their work, as was the case with Loretta, who wrote, "I don't remember, but whenever you multiply two negative numbers, it always turns out positive" (Michaels, field notes, November 27, 1995). Mr. Michaels reviewed all questions in a whole-class discussion following the quiz. For Questions 4 and 5, he continued:

Mr. M: ⁻3 × ⁻2. This is the one I wanted you to explain. First of all, we need a prediction for what you think the answer is. Cameron?

Cameron: ⁻6.

Mr. M: How many people agree with him? [A few hands went up.] There must be people with a different answer. Bill?

Bill: ⁺6.

Mr. M: Now who thinks that they can explain this? [Pause] Greg? [Mr. Michaels drew the diagrams on the overhead projector as Greg confidently outlined the steps.]

Greg: And you end up with ⁺6.

Mr. M: He's exactly right, and it's a very good explanation. This problem says take away three groups of ⁻2. So in this diagram, we take away three groups of ⁻2 and get what? Cameron?

Cameron: ⁺6.

(Michaels, observation, November 28, 1995)

Through whole-class discussion and groupwork on one day, and the mini-quiz and quiz review on the following day, Mr. Michaels created a variety of ways to examine student thinking about integer multiplication. He experimented with a different lesson introduction, which placed increased emphasis on a conceptual model for integer multiplication. As the groupwork and whole-class discussion demonstrate, Greg's understanding of integer multiplication was developing: Initially, Greg was unsure how to use the conceptual model for integer multiplication, but on the following day, he clearly articulated the use of this model during whole-class discussion.

Based on his interactions with students while teaching this unit and on their work on written assessments, Mr. Michaels stated:

The whole idea of manipulating positive and negative numbers is definitely improved from the beginning of the unit. I don't have any question about that. I've had to revise my estimate upward of what kids can really understand and cope with. . . . I think the understanding was achieved, and it was real understanding. It wasn't just some sort of rote memorization. I think they really understood what they were doing, and I think there was some evidence of that on some of the [end-of-unit] assessments when some students used diagrams [of plus and minus chips]. . . . I saw that there were some problems that they would use the diagrams on, and other ones they didn't seem to need them. I didn't know whether they were just advancing before our eyes to more formal ways of doing things. I don't know why they did that, but I noticed that. (Michaels, interview, December 7, 1995)

Mr. Michaels's assessment practice and the MiC curriculum itself opened numerous opportunities for him to learn about students' thinking. Through observational assessment focused on benchmark problems, and in combination with other informal assessments, Mr. Michaels gathered multidimensional information about students' knowledge. As a result, he was developing an understanding of student thinking in relation to the particular mathematical content of the unit. In the case presented here, he became more focused on the development of students' algebraic knowledge and reasoning. The reasoning that students used with unit problems facilitated Mr. Michaels's understanding of students' thinking in algebra, and his understanding was continually revised based on new information gathered during classroom interaction.

Carpenter and Lehrer (1999) pointed out that when a teacher's pedagogy is focused on eliciting students' thinking, the information gathered can be used not only to provide appropriate instruction for each student, but to inform better models for understanding students' thinking. The information that Mr. Michaels gathered during assessment contributed to the development of models of sixth-grade students' thinking with respect to specific instructional units. These models of student thinking served as guidelines to monitor the progress of the class and to compare individual students' progress with that of peers. Each time Mr. Michaels taught a particular unit, he revised his models of student thinking with respect to specific unit content. This is significant for two reasons. First, this enabled him to anticipate "sticking points" in the lessons and to clarify aspects of lessons without compromising opportunities for students to reason and feel a sense of accomplishment in their work. Second, the models of student thinking in the domain provided a foundation on which to design problems that challenged students to reason at more complex levels or that provided opportunities for them to conjecture and test their ideas. Thus, his instructional and assessment practices enhanced opportunities for him to develop models of student thinking in specific mathematical domains such as algebra.

CONCLUSION

The studies presented in this chapter demonstrate that as classroom instruction became more interactive with MiC, new possibilities opened up for teachers to learn about student thinking, and assessment evolved into an important aspect of the teachers' pedagogy. Teachers explored effective ways for individual students to express their thinking and created situations in which they provided assistance without compromising the complexity of students' work. The changes in classroom interactions allowed teachers to enhance opportunities for instruction. Webb (1993) asserted that such changes are at the core of pedagogy that will enable students to use mathematics in more powerful ways.

> Unless there are fundamental changes in the daily interactions that take place between teachers and students, initiatives that would change educational goals, develop new curricula, and devise new methods of instruction will fall short of reaching the reform vision that all students should become mathematically powerful. Assessment is a critical link. (p. vii)

Although the teachers in these studies gained unprecedented information about students during enriched interaction, the challenges they faced were significant. The available information was valuable in informing instruction, but not every student necessarily received enough assessment consideration for the teacher to build instruction around the student's needs. Assessment also remained centered on goals for a single instructional unit rather than across a series of units over time. Yet the teachers were developing pedagogical content knowledge with respect to the MiC units, which included information about difficulties students might encounter as they learned new topics, typical sequences students might go through as they learned the topics, and potential ways of helping students overcome difficulties (Bransford, Brown, & Cocking, 1999). Over time, as teachers use MiC, their own understanding of the mathematics, their understanding of the ways in which the mathematics are presented in MiC units, and their developing pedagogical content knowledge related to the units will likely have a more significant impact on classroom assessment and instruction.

Chapter 4

Practices in Transition:
A Case Study of
Classroom Assessment

Marvin E. Smith
BRIGHAM YOUNG UNIVERSITY

This chapter summarizes a study (Smith, 2000) that examined transitions in classroom assessment practices made by Mrs. Taylor, an eighth-grade mathematics teacher, as she began teaching with *Mathematics in Context* (MiC; National Center for Research in Mathematical Sciences Education & Freudenthal Institute, 1997-1998). The study contrasted those practices with others she continued to use in a class she concurrently taught using a traditional textbook.

Mrs. Taylor began using the MiC curriculum materials to provide the learning activities for her prealgebra students, while she continued to use a traditional textbook with her algebra class. Although she espoused some of the cognitive and situative learning goals for students that were recommended by the National Council of Teachers of Mathematics (NCTM; 1989, 1991, 1995), she continued to use traditional, measurement-based assessment and evaluation practices with both of these groups of students. This produced some incoherence between her learning goals and her assessment practices. Although the learning tasks in the MiC materials required more conceptual knowledge and explanations of cognitive processes than the algebra textbook, Mrs. Taylor did not demonstrate a workable method for evaluating her students' performance of that kind of work. Consequently, she and her MiC students focused primarily on completion of the work and engaged in little communication about ways to produce higher-quality responses to learning tasks.

Mathematics educators have acknowledged significant shifts in the epistemology of mathematics and in the psychology of learning mathematics (Romberg, 1992). A shifted world view of mathematics education necessarily includes a shifted paradigm for assessment (Romberg, Zarinnia, & Collis, 1990). The dominant behavioral view of what it means to know mathematics consists of having mastered the valued behaviors and memorized the concepts that are tested in school as a collection of isolated facts, skills, and concepts. Similarly, a behavioral view for learning mathematics consists of reading a textbook, watching a teacher demonstrate and explain, and practicing simplified exercises until they have been mastered. Speed of basic computation and manipulation of abstract symbols are the valued behaviors. This view of knowledge is consistent with assessment and evaluation methods based on counting correct answers on teacher-made, textbook, and standardized tests, and calculating course grades on percentages of correct answers.

Documenting learning progress and achievement becomes more complex as students' mathematical activities involve more complex problem solving in diverse contexts. Short-answer, paper-and-pencil tests and quizzes can provide only part of the needed evidence of students' mathematical understandings and progress. To meet this challenge, more complex and diverse methods of assessment are required that can be more informative for students and teachers. Stenmark (1991) noted:

> New forms of assessment are not goals in and of themselves. The major rationale for diversifying mathematics assessment is the value that the diversification has as a tool for the improvement of our teaching and the students' mathematics learning. (p. 3)

To continue traditional testing, which focuses solely on correct answers to routine exercises for formal assessment and grading, while trying to implement a standards-based teaching model that attends to the thinking of individual students and the development of mathematical power, is incoherent and ignores the possibility of accumulating more meaningful information about the understandings of individual learners from classroom activities. As Romberg, Zarinnia, and Collis (1990) summarized:

A sufficiently detailed view of the process [of knowledge production] is essential. . . . If there is any lesson to be learned from the old paradigm, it is that parts of the process cannot be analyzed in isolation, and then aggregated, with the result regarded as an adequate indicator. (pp. 29–30)

Using more direct evidence of students' thinking and understanding from a wider variety of classroom activities for formal and informal assessment can provide important feedback to students during the learning process and can become the basis for documenting students' mathematical power in ways that support social-constructivist approaches to teaching.

One conjecture relevant to the study was that data-gathering opportunities during MiC learning activities could yield data that are substantially more complex and potentially more informative of students' thinking than the data that typically have been available from the testing of routinized skills following textbook-based, direct instruction of procedures. In this case, making sense of information available during MiC instruction envisions the use of alternative methods for accumulating data about individual students and groups of students, revised models for interpreting information about learning, and supportive ways of describing achievement and reporting progress. The use of reformed curriculum materials may serve to support changes in teaching practices, including assessment and evaluation. In classrooms that are using MiC, where students engage in problem-solving and sense-making activities that encourage reasoning and communication about mathematical concepts, teachers may have opportunities to do less direct instruction and more orchestrating of discourse; less testing and more assessment of students' thinking and understanding; and less counting of correct answers and more evaluating of the progress of students' mathematical power. The introduction of MiC materials does not ensure such changes; however, it supports the rethinking of assessment and evaluation practices that has been initiated through the NCTM standards in search of classroom practices that are coherent with the learning goals for students.

This case study reported in this chapter documented the efforts of one eighth-grade teacher dealing with the complexities and practicalities associated with classroom assessment during field trials of the MiC materials. Through comparisons between this teacher's textbook-based algebra class and one of her four prealgebra classes using the MiC materials, the study described differences in three aspects of her assessment practices: (1) setting goals for students, (2) monitoring students' progress, and (3) evaluating or grading students' achievement. The study then addressed the implications of these practices for providing additional information and suggestions about assessment in the MiC teacher guides.

The study posed an overall research question: What differences in classroom assessment practices were evident between one teacher's MiC-based, eighth-grade prealgebra classes and a textbook-based, eighth-grade algebra class she taught concurrently? More specifically, across these two classes:

- How did the teacher's goals for students differ?
- How did the teacher's practices for monitoring progress differ?
- How did the teacher's practices for evaluating or grading differ?

Answers to these questions were then used to reflect on the question: What recommendations should be made in the MiC teacher guides to encourage teachers to begin to assess and evaluate in ways that support the learning goals envisioned by the NCTM standards and the MiC materials?

To provide a framework for analysis of coherence between learning goals and assessment practices, the origin and history of various goals for learning, curriculum designs, instructional practices, and assessment methodologies can be categorized broadly according to their underlying theories about the nature of mathematics and how people learn. Educational psychology provides epistemological views (what it means to know) and theories of learning (how one comes to know) that can provide the foundation for educational beliefs and practices. Learning goals for students follow from beliefs about what it means to know mathematics and from processes by which students learn mathematics. To the extent that assessment seeks to provide information about what students know and can do, for comparison with educational goals, it is essential to provide foundational assumptions of what qualifies as knowing and doing. Greeno, Pearson, and Schoenfeld (1996) summarized four perspectives on knowing, learning, and assessing: differential, behaviorist, cognitive, and situative. These four perspectives on mathematics education include fundamentally different goals for learning, theories of learning, and recommended teaching practices so as to require fundamentally different assessment and evaluation practices to result in coherent classroom models. Realistic Mathematics Education (RME; Gravemeijer, 1994), which provided the foundation for the MiC curriculum, can be added as a fifth perspective from which to consider coherence between goals and practices. RME helps to reconcile some of the paradigmatic differences between the cognitive and situative perspectives.

Given these five perspectives, the choices of coherent assessment practices become methodological questions. The choices teachers make about assessment and evaluation practices come from their conceptions of (including knowledge, beliefs, and purposes for) schooling, knowing, learning, teaching, assessing, evaluating, and grading. These conceptions can exhibit features of differential, behaviorist, cognitive, situative, or RME perspectives. Methodologies for assessment and evaluation can then be matched to the purposes for these activities in ways that are consistent with these particular conceptions.

Taylor (1994) highlighted two general and incompatible models of assessment (the *measurement* model and the *standards* model) that emerged from fundamentally different assumptions about what should be assessed and how to best assess it. The measurement model continues to dominate assessment from differential, behavioral, and cognitive perspectives. The standards model provides a more coherent approach to assessment for the cognitive perspective and the only theoretically consistent approach for the situative and RME perspectives. In fact, examples of student work that represent the standards or criteria, referred to as *exemplars*, make statements of expectations concrete and tangible (Taylor, 1994). These standards for quality, criteria for expectations, and exemplars of student work are to be shared with students, teachers, and parents to promote a clear understanding of the educational goals and how they will be assessed.

The standards model requires professional judgment in the analysis of student performance by people who are knowledgeable in the discipline (Taylor, 1994). In mathematics, the knowledge required for analyzing student performance includes knowledge of the content domain, understanding of students' thinking, awareness of possible solution strategies, and developmentally appropriate expectations for performance quality. Use of professional judgment, after students have responded, allows assessments to be sensitive to the novelty and creativity with which students often perform when solving nonroutine problems. The "messiness" of authentic performance in realistic situations can be anticipated and appropriately considered during the judgment process.

STUDY DESIGN

The case study was summarized from data collected from 36 classroom observations and seven interviews conducted during a 7-week visit to Mrs. Taylor's junior high school in California. Mrs. Taylor was teaching a draft MiC unit entitled Reflections (Wijers, van Galen, Querelle, de Lange, Shew, & Brinker, 1994). The goals of this unit, as listed in the draft teacher guide, were as follows:

- To find and represent factors (and divisors) of a number.
- To recognize prime numbers as numbers with only two factors.
- To write composite numbers as a product of primes.
- To analyze multiplication and division algorithms.
- To explore the relationship between addition, multiplication, squaring, and their inverse operations.
- To explore different subsets of the set of real numbers. (p. iii)

The major mathematical content in the unit and a brief overview of the unit were provided on the cover of the draft teacher guide. Although the mathematical topics in the unit were familiar topics in the prealgebra curriculum, the suggested instructional approach was much different from the usual direct instruction approach supported by traditional textbooks. Solutions and samples of student work were provided in the draft teacher guide for each of the problems posed in the unit.

Instructions for teachers regarding assessment also were provided. These consisted of references to end-of-section summary questions and were found both in the introduction to the unit and in the hints and comments opposite some of the corresponding section summaries. A set of end-of-unit assessment activities consisted of five multipart problems with additional hints and comments for only two of the five questions.

Simultaneously, in Mrs. Taylor's algebra class, students were learning about rational expressions and systems of linear equations. Each of two chapters in the traditional text consisted of about 10 sections that contained definitions of key concepts, two to four examples of problem solutions, a small group of oral exercises, and a large group of written exercises. Some of these sections included challenge problems, an exploration activity, a self-quiz, supplemental information about the use of mathematics in careers or about mathematics history, or applications of the mathematics to computers. Each of these chapters concluded with a skills maintenance assignment, a chapter review, and a chapter test.

How Did Mrs. Taylor's Goals for Students Differ?

Mrs. Taylor's goals for learning varied both between her MiC and algebra classes and across the students in her MiC class. Her goals varied between classes on the basis of variations in the student populations and in the curriculum materials she and her colleagues had selected for use in those classes. Her goals for most students in MiC were very similar to those suggested in the NCTM (1989) curriculum standards for grades 5–8. However, her goals for algebra students were less consistent with those standards.

Mrs. Taylor's goals for students in both classes clearly reflected a philosophy of learning by doing. In the case of algebra, she intended students to learn particular behaviors (such as performing algebraic procedures) by observing direct instruction in those behaviors and practicing them during classwork and homework. In MiC, she expected students to achieve situative goals for learning (such as using language, tools, and symbols with understanding in solving problems) by conscientiously engaging in and completing the tasks in the MiC materials.

She differentiated her expectations for students among groups in her MiC class and between those students and the students in her algebra class. She indicated that she commonly discussed student performance in her classes with other teachers on the interdisciplinary team that worked with the same cohort of students. Consistent with differential trait theory, she frequently referred to her students as "A kids," "C kids," "special-ed kids," "normal kids," "bright kids," "lazy kids," and so on. She easily sorted students into "higher," "normal," and "special-ed" groups. There was more of this variation among the students in her MiC class than among students in her algebra class, so more of these labels were applied to students in her MiC class. Although these labels seem to have been based on prior performance rather than traits, and she seemed to hold open the possibility that these students could improve their performance, she clearly had varying expectations for students in these groups.

The student population in algebra was composed of what Mrs. Taylor called "the top 10%," making it a relatively homogeneous class in terms of work ethic, prior performance, socioeconomic status, and ethnicity. Consequently, her goals for these students matched the homogeneity of the class. That is, she had very similar expectations for all of her algebra students. She wanted them to behave themselves, do all of the assigned work, and learn how to do every one of the many procedures in the algebra textbook. Given the curriculum materials being used, most of her goals were related to the learning of procedures and were not particularly rich in terms of the various NCTM curriculum standards for grades 5–8 and 9–12.

She knew that new procedures would be introduced almost every day as students went from one section in the textbook to the next. She wanted students to keep up with her pace through the textbook; however, she also wanted each of them to have the flexibility she or he needed to be successful in learning to use all of those procedures on tests and quizzes. Given her own experience as a mathematics student, she thought that increased flexibility was one way to achieve the NCTM vision of success for all students. She also wanted her algebra students to learn to solve realistic open-ended problems, as called for in the NCTM standards. That type of problem was not provided in the algebra textbook, however, so she supplemented the textbook with some MiC activities and other problem-solving activities from a variety of sources. She also used MiC activities in her algebra class to build some understanding of important mathematical concepts; however, the injection of MiC activities along with procedure-oriented textbook chapters left these topics disconnected. Mrs. Taylor did not express a clear relationship between her goals for learning procedures and for learning to understand concepts and solve open-ended problems.

In contrast, Mrs. Taylor verbalized goals for MiC students that included much broader cognitive and situative goals (e.g., developing number sense, learning to solve many kinds of problems, learning to question things, being able to justify their thinking, becoming intelligent consumers, developing confidence). In many ways, these goals reflected a shift in favor of the NCTM standards and the stated goals of the MiC curriculum materials. In addition, her goals for MiC students included many more for social behavior (e.g., attendance, timeliness in completing work, self-discipline, neatness, working productively with others) than she expressed for her algebra students. She believed that improvement in achievement on such goals was related to improvement in achievement of mathematical learning goals.

The student population in MiC was much more heterogeneous than that in algebra and included a broader range of variation among students in work ethics, prior performance, socioeconomic status, and ethnic diversity. Mrs. Taylor's goals for students in her MiC class varied on the basis of these differences. Rather than hold similarly high expectations for all students, she adjusted her goals and expectations for each student on the basis of what she thought each could achieve.

How Did Mrs. Taylor's Practices for Monitoring Progress Differ?

In general, Mrs. Taylor used informal assessment to monitor students' progress. While she circulated among the students, she observed what they had written, asked them questions, and answered any questions they asked of her. In both classes, she monitored students' progress toward completion of the assigned work. Particularly in MiC, her initial interest in circulating around the room was to check on and encourage students in the process of settling down and engaging in the assigned work. She had to do more of this monitoring for management in MiC than in algebra, and she had particular students in MiC for whom she frequently provided this type of monitoring.

In both classes, Mrs. Taylor monitored students' progress toward completion of the assigned work; between the two classes, however, she monitored progress in different ways. This was due to differences in her goals for students' learning as well as the kind of work the curriculum materials asked students to do.

In the MiC class, where her goals included understanding and problem solving, she did some monitoring for understanding. To gather evidence about what students understood, she asked them questions related to what they were thinking. Some of these questions involved what students were learning from doing the assigned tasks, and some involved what students were thinking about while trying to complete the tasks. In MiC, she often would ask questions of students that would lead their thinking, rather than telling students what to do next.

For example, during one teaching episode from the Reflections unit, Mrs. Taylor asked questions of particular students to further their understanding of the mathematics.

Mrs. Taylor: Now, if I do 2 times 3, and I get 6, and I add 1 to it . . .
Cheryl: That's 7.
Mrs. Taylor: I need you to tell me if 2 goes into the new number.
Cheryl: No.
Mrs. Taylor: Why not, Cheryl?
Cheryl: It doesn't divide evenly.
Mrs. Taylor: It doesn't divide evenly. Juan, why?
Juan: 'Cause it's an odd number.
Mrs. Taylor: 'Cause what's an odd number?
Juan: 7's an odd number.
Mrs. Taylor: 7's an odd number. Ooooh! OK. So, I've got 2 times 3, and I'm adding on 1, and that gave me 7, and 7 is a prime number, and this new prime number I created, I may not divide by 2, or divide by 3, can I?
Several students: No!
Mrs. Taylor: Now make sure you understand that, because it's going to get a little more complex. That's your answer for [task] 10a.
Male Student: I'm not sure I understand. (Smith, 2000, pp. 129–130)

Mrs. Taylor then proceeded to explain again how multiplying 2 times 3 and adding 1 resulted in a number that was divisible by neither 2 nor 3, because doing so would always result in a remainder of 1. She then probed students for what they meant by their informal language, so that she could connect formal language and definitions to the concepts behind the informal language.

Mrs. Taylor: Why is this coming out to always be prime numbers, when you do this thing with a prime number multiplied times the next one and adding 1? Just because?"
Male Student: The 1 always messes it up.
Mrs. Taylor: The 1 always messes it up. Excellent reasoning. Now what does that mean, when the 1 always messes it up? What's really happening when that 1 messes it up?
Female Student: It makes it an odd number.
Mrs. Taylor: The 1 messes it up. This is a prime number, and it is not divisible by 2, 3, 5, 7, or 11. Right? (Smith, 2000, p. 130)

This monitoring of student understanding while teaching is also evident in the following exchange. After describing an attempt by one of her students in an earlier period to multiply all of the prime numbers between 2 and 47, she asked:

Mrs. Taylor: This is not a prime number. How do we know that?
Andy: It ends in a 0.
Mrs. Taylor: It ends in a 0. Dead give away. So, what would Euclid do now?
Andy: He'd add a 1.
Mrs. Taylor: He'd add a 1, and then what would happen?
Male Student: It's prime.
Mrs. Taylor: Juan, would you please tell me why you think it's prime? This is our answer. (pause) Cheryl, tell me why.
Cheryl: 'Cause it has a 1 on the end.
Mrs. Taylor: 'Cause it has a 1 on the end. But how do we know that it's prime?
Male Student: Because 1 can't be divided by anything but itself.
Mrs. Taylor: Was that what your logic was way back when we had these little itty bitty ones? The reason why this is prime is because 1 can't be divided by anything but itself?
Female Student: No.
Mrs. Taylor: What is the reasoning in why this is now a prime number?

Female Student: Because all those numbers can't divide into that
    number.
Mrs. Taylor: Let's call it this. This number can't be divided evenly by
    2, 3, 5, 7, dit, dit, dit, all the way to 47. Is that right?
Male Student: Yeah.
Mrs. Taylor: And that is the reason why you think it is a prime
    number? Because you are always going to have a remainder of
    1. . . . We added 1, and we really don't need to check it anymore.
    (Smith, 2000, p. 131)

In the MiC class, Mrs. Taylor was often in a teaching as questioning mode, and she did much less telling in her MiC class than in her
algebra class. When MiC students asked questions, they were often of
the type, "What does this question mean?" These elicited other questions from Mrs. Taylor to probe what students understood about the
tasks and relevant concepts. She would then ask additional questions
to help build understanding by connecting new ideas to what students
already understood. She characterized her MiC students' thinking processes as much less organized and much less logical than her own. These
differences created a genuine interest and provided a real incentive for
her to ask students questions to find out what and how they were thinking. Because this was her first experience teaching with these MiC units,
however, she had no previous experience with students' thinking about
these particular tasks to provide a frame of reference for interpreting
the quality of that thinking. Consequently, she continued to compare
her students' thinking with her own.

Mrs. Taylor indicated she was aware that she monitored students'
progress somewhat differently in her algebra class. She attributed some
of these differences to variations in the students; others she attributed
to the curriculum materials and variations in her teaching practices.
In algebra, where her goals for students emphasized learning procedures, she often was able to infer the procedures students used by looking at their written work. Only when she could not interpret their
processes from what they had written, did she ask students to explain
their work. In algebra, Mrs. Taylor often taught by telling, which seldom provoked verbal exchanges that would provide evidence of student understanding. When students asked questions, they were often
"How do I do this?" kinds of questions that elicited a telling response.
Mrs. Taylor often answered those questions by telling students what
to do and how to do it, sometimes including demonstrations with her
explanations.

How Did Mrs. Taylor's Practices for Evaluating and Grading Differ?

In general, Mrs. Taylor used formal assessment to provide scores for evaluation and grading, and there were very few differences between how she determined grades in MiC and in algebra. For formal assessment and grading, she followed the measurement model with which she was very experienced. She used the same grading software and essentially the same categories and weights for assignments in both classes. She graded quizzes and tests on the basis of correct answers, and assigned points to homework on the basis of completion.

In MiC, Mrs. Taylor read packets of completed assignments to get a sense of how well students understood the mathematical concepts in the unit, as evidenced by their explanations. In contrast, in algebra, she looked over packets of completed assignments to get a sense of how well students were able to do the procedures in the textbook. In both cases, homework was not graded based on the quality of the work.

In algebra, where most exercises were meant to result in a correct answer, it was reasonable to have students check their answers on homework to provide nongraded feedback on the accuracy of the procedures they had practiced. By making homework part of students' course grades, Mrs. Taylor provided incentive to complete the homework without grading answers for accuracy during what was primarily a learning mode.

In MiC, however, students needed to receive personal feedback on the quality of their thinking, conceptual understanding, and problem-solving strategies evidenced by their written classwork and homework. Mrs. Taylor read through this work to inform her instructional decisions but provided little feedback to students on the quality of their work. When she did provide feedback, it was through general comments or questions such as, "How?" "Explain," or "Lousy." These comments typically were provided several days after the work originally had been completed, generally after each section of the unit.

This was reasonable given that it was Mrs. Taylor's first time teaching the Reflections unit and the draft teacher guide was much less complete than it would be in the final published version. The draft teacher guide for Reflections provided examples of expected student responses to the tasks but provided no guidance for how to give students feedback on the quality of their thinking, understanding, and written work.

Formal assessment differed between the two classes primarily in the nature of the tasks and the nature of the support provided by Mrs. Taylor during those assessment episodes. In the case of algebra, Mrs. Taylor's formal assessment emphasized procedures for algebraic manipulation, consistent with the behavioral tasks in the curriculum materials and her emphasis during instruction. The primary purposes of these assessments, which were to (1) determine how many algebraic manipulations could be performed correctly in the production of correct answers, and (2) record the number of correct answers and the number of possible answers into the grading program to produce a grade for the course.

In the MiC class, her formal assessment practices were less consistent with the learning activities in the curriculum materials and the thinking and understanding students may have developed during instruction. Although the formal assessment tasks typically were taken from the MiC units, they were scored on the basis of correct answers, which provided little feedback to her or her students on the quality of the thinking and explanations. By marking students' responses as either good enough to receive credit or not good enough to receive credit, Mrs. Taylor provided students only minimal guidance about their developing understanding of the concepts and problem-solving contexts emphasized in the unit. This feedback signaled to students only that they could go back and redo their work if they wanted to try to improve their grades.

The support Mrs. Taylor provided during formal assessment varied across the two classes. In algebra, where her formal assessments asked students to recall procedures and use them to manipulate algebraic expressions, she wanted students to work on their own at the beginning. She did not provide direct assistance until she was assured that students could not be successful without it. Although few of the problems in algebra were set in realistic contexts that needed to be explained, she commented often on the mathematical contexts of the problems to help students understand what was expected of them on the assessment tasks.

In MiC, Mrs. Taylor often said quite a lot about the context of the assessment problems to help students understand what was expected on the assessment and to make sure that students had entry points for their thinking. When students commented to her that they didn't understand the problem or they didn't know what to do, she often responded with questions that guided students' thinking in directions similar to her own thinking. At other times, she responded with ideas or processes students might try to help their solutions along. When it came to the "explain" part of the problems, she wanted students to provide explanations in their own words about what they were thinking, so she provided only suggestions for the beginning of explanations when students seemed not to know where to start on their own.

CONCLUSIONS

Compared with her algebra class, Mrs. Taylor's use of the MiC curriculum materials in her prealgebra classes represented major differences in curriculum and instruction. It also was accompanied by some important differences in her assessment and evaluation practices across the classes. Other changes that would have been consistent with and supportive of these differences did not occur.

In both of these classes, she continued to reflect differential perspectives of students' abilities that reinforced the differences in how these students were (1) selected for enrollment in algebra or prealgebra, and (2) stratified in Mrs. Taylor's mind into groups of varying abilities within her prealgebra classes. Mrs. Taylor had yet to develop a workable strategy for completely abandoning her differential perspectives and dealing equitably with students with various needs.

Mrs. Taylor's assessment and evaluation/grading practices varied in degrees of coherence internally with her purposes and externally with the curriculum and instruction she used in these classes. Her assessment practices did not manifest the kind of transitions that Graue and Smith (1996) reported in their study of 4 sixth-grade teachers (see Chapter 2).

In algebra, her assessment, evaluation, and grading practices formed a system that was reasonably coherent both internally (between forms of evidence and purposes of grading and motivating students) and externally (between assessment practices and goals for student learning, curriculum materials used, and instructional practices). Her grading system used percentages of possible points based on (1) completion of assignments and (2) numbers of correct answers on assessment tasks. This was consistent with her goals of motivating students to complete assignments by focusing on the practice of procedures taught through direct instruction in order to be successful on assessment tasks that required those same procedures to produce correct answers.

In contrast, Mrs. Taylor's assessment, evaluation, and grading practices in MiC represented a less coherent system, both internally and externally. She used essentially the same grading system based on percentages of possible points. Similarly, these points came from (1) completion of assignments and (2) numbers of correct or acceptable answers on assessment tasks. However, tasks on classwork assignments, homework assignments, and assessments required more conceptual knowledge and explanations of cognitive processes in MiC than in algebra. This often resulted in a broader range of acceptable answers than was typical in algebra, and she did not have a very workable method for providing specific feedback to students in this broader context.

Although Mrs. Taylor's instruction was fairly coherent with her expanded goals for MiC students and with the more cognitively complex tasks in the MiC curriculum materials, her evaluation and grading system was not very coherent with the curriculum and instruction in MiC. Her evaluation and grading system provided little information about the quality of students' responses on the more cognitively complex classwork, homework, and assessment tasks found in the MiC materials. Her assessment system provided some motivation for students to complete the MiC classwork and homework tasks, but it provided little feedback that would move students toward producing higher-quality responses to those tasks. The resulting focus emphasized completion of the assigned MiC tasks, with little attention paid to the quality of responses. She expressed some confidence that if her MiC students completed the assigned tasks, they would learn what she wanted them to learn. However, her practice ignored (1) the expectation that the quality of participation in socially organized practices affects the quality of knowledge produced through that participation, and (2) the importance of goal-related feedback in motivating students to achieve learning goals.

Mrs. Taylor used a quality scale (see Table 4.1) for open-ended problems. This scale was posted above the chalkboard on the left wall of her classroom, where it was constantly visible to students. For scoring open-ended problems, Mrs. Taylor realized that she needed a scale that went beyond correct or not correct. She communicated the scoring rubric to students before they completed the task, and used the rubric for scoring students' completed work. She was comfortable with this process in that particular context, where the open-ended nature of the problems made wide variations in students' responses possible. In that context, she used the four-point scale to communicate her judgments about the quality of students' written responses to the open-ended problems.

Mrs. Taylor used this scale, however, only for the open-ended problems she used occasionally to supplement the curriculum in both MiC

Table 4.1. Four-point rubric for scoring open-ended problems.

Points	Description
4	Fully accomplishes the purpose of the task. Shows full grasp of the central idea(s). Recorded work communicates thinking clearly, using some combination of written, symbolic, or visual means.
3	Substantially accomplishes the purpose of the task. Shows essential grasp of the central mathematical idea(s). In large part, the recorded work communicates the student s thinking.
2	Partially accomplishes the purpose of the task. Shows partial but limited grasp of the central mathematical idea(s). Recorded work may be incomplete, misdirected, or not clearly presented.
1	Little or no progress toward the purpose of the task. Shows little or no grasp of the central mathematical idea(s). Recorded work is barely (if at all) comprehensible.

and algebra. She did not refer to this scale in any of the feedback she provided to students about their work from the MiC units, which would have been a reasonable thing to do. Apparently, she had not made the connection that the four levels in the rubric for open-ended problems could be used to provide students with feedback on their thinking, communicating, and performance, and to encourage all students to work toward higher levels of quality. This quality issue arises only when goals for learning are expanded (beyond an exclusive focus on those behaviors for which a measurement model of assessment will suffice) to include complex cognitive and situative performance goals that re-quire a standards model of assessment. In one way, this four-point scale could represent an absolute quality scale, as evidenced by the descrip-tions for each of the four levels. In another way, it could be viewed as corresponding to letter grades from D to A, which also could be viewed as absolute levels of quality with given descriptors such as "excellent."

Mrs. Taylor's computation of letter grades from percentages of aggregated points, however, clearly represented achievement relative to the maximum number of points possible, rather than absolute levels of quality. When she recorded the scores from the open-ended rubric into her grading program as the number of points earned out of the number of possible points, any absolute quality meaning that could be attributed to the four-point scale changed to the relative meaning of percentages in her grading program. Scores that could have been used in a standards model of assessment thus were forced into a measurement model for purposes of aggregation, evaluation, and reporting. By calculating grades for her MiC classes based on points for completion of the work without adjustment for variations in quality, she provided motivation for students to complete the work without attending to its quality. As Curwin (1976) suggested, good evaluation methods provide feedback to students about specifically where they have done well, where they need improvement, and how to modify their performance in those areas needing improvement. Mrs. Taylor's evaluation system in MiC failed to provide that information to students.

Another conclusion from this study is that the measurement-style grading system provides a formidable obstacle for acceptance of other perspectives on gathering and using assessment evidence for other purposes identified in the NCTM (1995) assessment standards. Stephen Covey's (1989) admonition to *begin with the end in mind* is a two-edged sword. On the one hand, it is essential to mathematics reform that teachers begin with new goals and standards. On the other hand, traditional grading systems, standardized tests, or our expectations of the next mathematics course for which we are trying to prepare our students can constrain our classroom assessment practices.

EPILOGUE

Based on these experiences gathering the data for this study and discussing assessment issues with many other teachers who had been using the MiC materials, a recommendation to the MiC staff was made that the teacher guides provide an explicit link between assessment opportunities and unit learning goals. Consequently, a table for organizing and relating corresponding unit goals and unit assessment opportunities was designed, with some accompanying explanation, to assist teachers using the MiC materials in their planning for assessment. Similar materials were then prepared by the authors of the MiC units and included in the teacher guide for each MiC unit.

Table 4.2 shows the content of the goals and assessment table in the final published version of the teacher guide for *Reflections on Number* (Wijers et al., 1998). The goals in the table are divided into three categories: (1) conceptual and procedural knowledge; (2) reasoning, communicating, thinking, and making connections; and (3) modeling, nonroutine problem solving, critically analyzing, and generalizing. These categories used familiar language from the NCTM curriculum

Table 4.2. Goals and assessment for *Reflections*.

Goal		Ongoing Assessment Opportunities	End-of-Unit Assessment Opportunities
Conceptual and Procedural Knowledge	1. find the factors and multiples of a number (including prime factors)	Section A, p. 24, #30, #31	Multiples in Columns, p. 131 Primes in Columns, p. 132 Factor Trees, p. 133 Crack the Code, p. 135
	2. write composite numbers as products of prime numbers	Section B, p. 42, #21	Factor Trees, p. 133 Crack the Code, p. 135
	3. find a product or quotient of two- and three-digit numbers	Section C, p. 52, #7, p. 72, #27	Packing Crates, p. 136
Reasoning, Communicating, Thinking, and Making Connections	4. understand that division by zero is undefined	Section C, p. 72, #25	
	5. understand how multiplication and division algorithms work	Section C, p. 54, #9, p. 58, #11a	Packing Crates, p. 136
	6. understand the relationship between operations (addition, multiplication, and squaring) and their inverse operations (subtraction, division, and taking the square root)	Section D, p. 80, #8, p. 82, #9	Division Game, p. 134
Modeling, Nonroutine Problem Solving, Critically Analyzing, and Generalizing	7. develop number sense by operating on numbers in a convenient way	Section C, p. 52, #7	Division Game, p. 134 Packing Crates, p. 136
	8. begin to understand the structure of the real number system, including rational and irrational numbers	Section D, p. 80, #8, p. 82, #10; Section E, p. 100, #23–25	

standards (1989) to describe aspects of learning from the RME model in ways that were intended to be useful for teachers while planning and interpreting MiC assessment activities.

The ongoing assessment opportunities identify specific tasks in the unit (by section, page number, and task number) that correspond to the particular unit goal and could be used to provide evidence of progress toward that goal. The end-of-unit assessment opportunities identify by name and page number those assessment tasks provided in the teacher guide that correspond to the particular unit goal and could be used to provide evidence of attainment of that goal.

Recommendations in the teacher guides about scoring and analyzing students' responses on assessment tasks included the following:

> Students may respond to assessment questions with various levels of mathematical sophistication and elaboration. Each student's response should be considered for the mathematics that it shows, and not judged on whether or not it includes an expected response. Responses to some of the assessment questions may be viewed as either correct or incorrect, but many answers will need flexible judgment by the teacher. Descriptive judgments related to specific goals and partial credit often provides more helpful feedback than percentage scores. . . . Openly communicate your expectations to all students, and report achievement and progress for each student relative to those expectations. When scoring students' responses try to think about how they are progressing toward the goals of the unit and the strand. (Wijers et al., 1998, p. xviii)

Additional recommendations were given for using student portfolios, student self-evaluation, and summary discussions to form a complete picture of student progress and achievement during MiC units. All of these recommendations, of course, were prepared for the published version of the MiC materials, after Mrs. Taylor's initial experience teaching with MiC documented by this study. Although the MiC teacher guides did not suggest alternative systems for producing course grades that could be coherent with both the unit goals and the suggested sources of assessment evidence, some suggestions for alternative approaches to grading were made in the NCTM assessment standards (1995).

These suggestions in the MiC teacher guides have turned out to be consistent with recent recommendations by Wiggins and McTighe (1998) about the value of *backwards* curriculum design that begins with clearly describing learning goals and identifying acceptable evidence from assessments that will be used to determine the achievement of those learning goals. This concept is a logical application to curriculum design of Covey's (1989) suggestion to *begin with the end in mind*. Wiggins and McTighe (1998) stated that "all assessment logically begins with a clear, apt, and worthy achievement target" (p. 123). They explained that developing these achievement targets involves taking broad goals (such as those found in the NCTM standards) and making more precise statements of expected outcomes of particular learning experiences that can be assessed.

These results suggested that further development is needed along the lines of Taylor's (1994) "standards model" of assessment to produce a system of assessing and grading that is coherent with the goals of MiC units and is a practical replacement for measurement-based practices. Additional research is needed to (1) assess the usefulness of directly linking unit goals with assessment opportunities as now included in the MiC teacher guides; (2) determine workable performance standards and absolute quality scales needed to score MiC assessment tasks and relate the quality of student performance to standards for key goals; (3) determine practical methods for aggregating scores across assessment tasks and reporting students' progress in terms of standards of quality in key learning areas; and (4) assess the impact of professional development activities that could have helped Mrs. Taylor deal with issues of assessing and grading in ways more coherent with the goals of the MiC materials and a standards-based assessment model.

PART III

THE DESIGN OF NEW
ASSESSMENT TASKS

Most teachers using a reform curriculum see the need for changes in their assessment practices, but find making such changes hard to accomplish. Furthermore, if such changes in assessment are not made, goals are not met. In particular, as teachers taught MiC units they realized that they needed new test items (assessment tasks) that would yield information about student strategies, thought processes, and so on). Creating such tasks and interpreting student responses to them have proven to be difficult. Teachers need assistance to accomplish this work.

In Chapter 5, Developing Assessment Problems on Percentage, Marja van den Heuvel-Panhuizen points out the problems teachers encountered in using information derived from such tasks, noting in particular that because tasks were designed to elicit a variety of student strategies and responses, teachers had a hard time making reasonable judgments about student performances.

Chapter 6, Analysis of an End-of-Unit Test, by Monica Wijers, describes the results of a test, used by three teachers in their first year of implementing the MiC curriculum. The test showed that students in their classes were able to do all kinds of different problems related to area, developed a broad understanding of the concept of area, and demonstrated growth in their understanding and their use of informal, preformal, and formal strategies. However, there were differences between the students in the different classes. The differences, although subtle, were possibly due to different teacher emphasis and classroom culture. Having new tasks is necessary but not sufficient if reform goals are to be met.

In Chapter 7, The Design of Open–Open Assessment Tasks, by Els Feijs and Jan de Lange, the authors point out that the creation and use of "open–open" tasks proved to be very complex. They note, for example, that differences in visual presentation of a diagram or use of language could cause significant differences in student response, sometimes even determining whether students engaged in the task or problem. The authors argue that teachers need to become at least passive experts in classroom assessment tasks so they can adequately judge the quality of the tasks they select, adapt, and create. Such expertise should include understanding the role of the problem context, judging whether the task format fits the goal of the assessment, judging the appropriate level of formality (i.e., informal, preformal, formal), and determining the level of mathematical thinking involved in the solution of an assessment problem.

Chapter 8, Investigations as Thought-Revealing Assessment Problems, by Martin van Reeuwijk and Monica Wijers, discusses student work in relationship to and the role of "investigations" in revealing student thinking. An example illustrates the features of investigations and the difficulties in designing, administering, and scoring such tasks. In particular, the authors demonstrate that students need to learn how to solve such complex problems by designing a plan, trying different strategies, and being aware of varied expectations for the problems. Teachers too need to learn how to supervise such tasks and how to judge the quality of different products by students.

The focus in each these four brief stories is on both the characterization of assessment tasks and how to judge the variety of student responses to such tasks. As a consequence of having and using such tasks, teachers saw the need to become more knowledgeable about them and about judgment procedures.

Chapter 5

Developing Assessment Problems on Percentage

Marja van den Heuvel-Panhuizen
FREUDENTHAL INSTITUTE, UNIVERSITY OF UTRECHT

This chapter focuses on the development and construction of problems used for assessment. As discussed in Chapters 2, 3, and 4, recognizing the need for change is the first step in the change process but is not enough. Assessment tasks, like teaching materials, do not appear out of the blue. We need to have a clear vision of what kind of assessment is needed and how to achieve assessment that reflects the reform approach of teaching and learning mathematics. The project reported here was designed to document the development of a set of assessment problems by the authors of the Per Sense unit (van den Heuvel-Panhuizen, Streefland, Meyer, Middleton, & Browne, 1997) in *Mathematics in Context* (National Center for Research in Mathematical Sciences Education & Freudenthal Institute, 1997–1998).

The story in this chapter involves the use of a set of guidelines based on the realistic mathematics education (RME) instructional philosophy and its iterative developmental approach to create a set of assessment problems. The insight derived from this study is that good assessment tasks can be created but their validity must be judged in terms of how students respond to the tasks. A task's face validity as judged by developers or teachers is not sufficient.

THE MIC UNIT: PER SENSE

This unit was designed to help fifth-grade students make sense of percentage. The unit starts with exploring students' informal knowledge.

The approach to percentage starts with estimations and the connection with easy fractions and ratios. The percentage or fraction bar (which later becomes a double number line) and the ratio table are introduced to support student thinking, estimating, or calculating. The problem situations, or contexts, used in this unit were chosen in such a way that the students eventually see the need for standard procedures to work on percentage problems.

Contexts

The content in the Per Sense unit was developed from three general problem situations. The first section includes a set of problems in the context of parking. The students are asked to compare parking lots with respect to their fullness. "Occupation" or percentage-full meters, which students fill in, introduce the concept of percentage. In the beginning, the comparison of the fullness of parking lots can be made using common fractions. Later on, the percentage bar is used to make estimates of the percentages. The ratio table is used for determining whether parking lots are equally occupied.

The second context deals with attendance at stadium games. In this context, the students have to work with larger numbers and are confronted with situations in which an estimate will not always do. The notion of 1% is introduced in the context of a (very small) number of supporters who attended a certain game. Students are not told how to calculate 1% but discover that a certain number is approximately the one-hundredth part of the total number of people attending. The approximation of 1% can be helpful in estimating and calculating all kinds of percentages, or the numbers that refer to a percentage. Later this strategy for using an easily recognized percentage is extended.

The last context concerns determining tips and is used to deepen what was learned in the earlier parts of the unit. This context offers the students more experience using percentages in real-life situations. Connected to this context are the three main tools the students have encountered: the percentage bar, the ratio table, and the use of reference percentages.

Assessment Activities

The Per Sense unit contains several kinds of assessment activities. Since teaching should be built on and linked with students' informal knowledge, an initial assessment is provided at the beginning of the unit to evoke students' informal knowledge of percentage. It consists of a series of little stories that have something to do with percentage in daily-life situations. The stories are discussed in class, and the teacher assesses what the students bring to the unit. Like the initial assessment, the assessment activities during the unit do not differ essentially from ordinary teaching activities. A series of optional tasks and problems, scattered throughout the unit, offers the teacher an opportunity to observe how students cope with key aspects of percentage. The end-of-section assessments, which can be taken from the summary activities that conclude each section, offer both the teacher and the students an opportunity to reflect on what was learned in the section. The final assessment for the unit has the broader goal of gathering information about the students' strategies. It focuses on whether the students understand the use of the relevant tools, procedures, and concepts, and whether they can spontaneously apply what they have learned to solve new, nonroutine problems.

DESIGNING ASSESSMENT

Designing assessment takes into consideration a number of factors. The following section discusses example tasks for both the initial assessment and the end-of-unit test that were field-tested for the Per Sense unit. Before developing tasks, an initial question must be answered: What needs to be assessed? The MiC Per Sense unit tries to cover key concepts, develop key abilities about percentage, and meet computational goals as well as higher-order goals concerning the understanding and use of percentage. In this unit, percentage is treated as a relation between two numbers or magnitudes expressed by a ratio. Students need to show awareness that percentages are always related to something and that two percentages cannot be compared without taking into account what they refer to. They need to be aware that if, for example, the total amount of something changes but the "part" in question remains the same size, then the percentage represented by that part changes. Students also need to be aware that a percentage remains the same if the ratio between the part and the whole remains the same, even if the total amount changes. Asking students to work through such situations instead of merely giving definitions for students to memorize encourages the deepening of their insight into the concept of percentage. Assessing students through problems that are set in contexts that focus on these aspects of understanding is valuable but difficult. Computations involving percentages (e.g., expressing a fraction as a percentage, computing the part of a whole when the percentage is given) are widely accessible and easy to score, but more valuable is the ability to use percentages in more complex situations (e.g., when different parts of different wholes have to be compared in terms of percentages, such as 27 g of sugar in 12 oz of beverage vs. 15 oz of sugar in 5 oz of beverage):

Together with answering the question about what needs to be assessed, decisions must be made about how this mathematical content should be assessed. In line with the principles of RME, the following guidelines were used for developing assessment problems on percentage:

- The problems should reflect situations that are familiar to the students and in which they can meet the mathematical content in a natural, self-explanatory way. The context should make the problems accessible to the students.
- The problems should engage and be meaningful to the students; something has to be solved that is important to the students and they should be offered possibilities for "breaking into" the problem.
- If the purpose of the assessment is to collect information to inform instruction, the use of open tasks should be considered. Such tasks generally provide more—and more useful—information. In an open task, students use their own words, create their own notations, and often arrive at different "correct" solutions through a variety of strategies. Problems that provide some latitude are more informative for the teacher.

A more extensive description of the RME consequences for assessment can be found in van den Heuvel-Panhuizen (1996).

These guidelines, along with the need for clear wording and avoidance of a confusing presentation, were kept in mind during the development of problems for the final assessment of the Per Sense unit. In this respect, development research involves testing ideas that are tenable but must be tested to gain insight into what will work and why.

The following example illustrates how to assess students' informal knowledge. Teaching percentage does not "start" when the term *percentage* is mentioned for the first time in a classroom. The concept has its roots in all the "so-many-out-of-so-many" scenarios dealt with in everyday situations. In the Per Sense unit, because instruction builds on the informal knowledge of the students, the teaching of percentage should start with assessing what students already know about percentage. A series of little stories, to be discussed in class, was developed to assess informal knowledge. One of the stories was about the results of an exam: "A 50% score is needed to pass the exam. John missed 14 problems. What do you think, can we congratulate John or not?" The feedback from the field test of this problem was positive. Both U.S. and Dutch classes were observed, and positive experiences concerning the stories were found. This problem did well for several reasons: (1) the context was familiar to the students, (2) the wording was clear and simple, (3) the numbers were chosen in such a way that neither thresholds nor confusion was built in to make the problem unnecessarily difficult, and (4) the problem intrigued the students. Students were offered the opportunity to manipulate the data to produce a desired outcome: In a way, John's failure or success was in their hands.

The results of these problems provided very useful information for guiding further teaching. In a small group of eight Dutch fifth-grade students, for example, only one student was not able to understand the relative character of percentage. This student answered: "No, if you have 14 mistakes then you have only one point and that is not good." Two students were aware of the relative character of "50 percent of _____": "Actually, we do not know [if John passed the test, i.e., got 50% of the items right] because we do not know how many items the test had." Five students, however, were quite able to deal with both the absolute and the relative data in the problem. One student noted: "50% = one-half. First you have to know how many items John made. At least 50% of the items must be answered right. If there are more than 28 items or exactly 28 then he succeeded, because you have to do 2 × 14."

THE FINAL ASSESSMENT FOR THE PER SENSE UNIT

The final assessment developed for the Per Sense unit consisted of a student booklet and a short teacher guide. The test contained 10 problems, some with more than one question. Table 5.1 gives a concise overview of the problems and their mathematical content. Each problem occupied an entire page so that the students had space to work on their solutions. The teacher guide contained an overview of the problems, some general information about the purpose of the assessment, and the criteria important in grading and gathering information for further instruction. The guide also contained a list of all the goals (with related problems) covered by the test as well as guidelines for analyzing students' responses.

The Per Sense unit was pilot-tested in two regular grade 7 classes (39 students total) from two U.S. schools. The teachers of the two classes

Table 5.1. Mathematical content of the problems on the per sense test.

Problem	Mathematical Content
Earthquake Damage	a. $\frac{4}{5}$ part of an amount equals ___%. b. 200 out of 8,000 is ___%.
Black Currant Jam	a. Same ratio implies same %. b. 60% of 450 g is ___; 60% of 225 g is ___ .
Camp Sites Information	a. 36 out of 200 is ___%. b. Free spaces 30, occupied 80%, the total number of spaces is ___.
Best Buy	Comparison of 40% discount and 25% discount.
Ann's Length Curve	Choosing a point of reference; from 50 to 75, is ___% growth.
Out on Loan	Comparison of 2,813 out of 6,997 and 3,122 out of 8,876.
Gulf Mail	Comparison of 100,000 pounds in 9 days and 335,604 in 15 days.
Sneakers	Choosing a list price; calculating the 40% discount price.
Binoculars	a. The 25% discount price is $96; The list price is ___. b. Checking the previous answer.
The Twax Bar	An extension of 25% with no change in price means a discount of ___%.

administered the test. There was no time limit, students worked individually to complete the test, and both the teachers and the author analyzed the results. We have chosen to examine three tasks and the responses to those tasks to illustrate both the variety of tasks and the analysis of responses. An analysis of these problems and the further development of assessment tasks for this unit can be found in van den Heuvel-Panhuizen (1995).

The "Best Buy" Problem

The "Best Buy" problem, situated in the familiar context of a sale (see Figure 5.1), assessed whether students understood that percentages are always related to something and cannot be compared without

Figure 5.1. "Best Buy" problem from Per Sense unit final assessment.

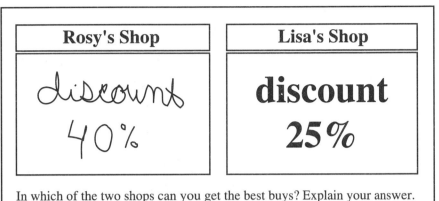

| **Rosy's Shop** | **Lisa's Shop** |

discount 40%   discount 25%

In which of the two shops can you get the best buys? Explain your answer.

first taking into account what they refer to. Students were told that two shops are having a sale. The first shop is offering a discount of 25%; the other, a discount of 40%. The shops' window posters suggest that the wares that the shops sell are not of the same quality. This cue is given to alert the students to consider what the percentages refer to.

The analysis of the responses (see Table 5.2) showed that at least half of the students (20 out of 39) understood that they could not compare percentages without taking into account what these percentages referred to. The majority of this group solved the problem by explicitly indicating that the answer depended on the list price. Three students did this indirectly by taking as an example an item that had the same list price in both shops, then doing the calculations. Roughly half of the students compared the two percentages as absolutes. Two other students proceeded in the same way but came to the wrong conclusion. This raised the issue of evaluation of such responses. Although the correct answer was not given, clearly these students knew that a percentage was related to something. These responses were not assessed as "correct close reading" or "carrying out tasks precisely," but they were still considered to be (and valued as) reasonable responses.

The responses not only show different levels of understanding but also provide a global view of the learning path. This can be very helpful for planning further instruction. Different levels in class also can be exploited in instruction in a very concrete way: Having different students discuss what they understand in their own language is often far more convincing and engaging than a discussion guided primarily

Table 5.2. Student responses to the Best Buys problem.

	Response categories	Students (N = 39)	Examples
Correct answer (46%)	Taking into account the original price	15	• "It depends on the original price of the objects they are selling." • "Both, I mean how much does the items cost, nobody knows." • "Lisa's because if you buy something that s already been used, you will have to fix it up or . . . ."
	Taking the same price as an example	3	• "Rosy's, if something at both stores was $30.75. At Rosy's, it would be $12.33, at Lisa s it would be $28.95."
Reasonable response (5%)	Taking the same price as an example; wrong conclusion	2	• "Lisa's, because, for example, a shirt cost $50, 40% = $20 and 25% = $12.50, with Lisa's deal you re paying less."
Incorrect answer (46%)	Comparing the percentages absolutely	18	• "Rosy's, 40% is better than 25%." • "Rosy's, because it is closer to one hundred percent, so there would be more off."
No answer (3%)	No answer	1	

by the adult talk of the teacher. When students discuss what they know, they often learn from one another even when they need to learn different things.

Clearly, the students who compared the two percentages must learn that percentages cannot be treated as absolute numbers. A first step might be to present them with another "best buys" problem in which the discount in each store is the same. Students who gave a reasonable response but ended up with the wrong conclusion would need to learn to check their reasoning by making sure that their outcome was in line with an expected outcome. Students who took as an example an item with the same price in both stores could be prompted to explain their reasoning in a more general way. Even the students who explained their reasoning more generally could be asked to describe a scenario in which a given item would be cheaper in the 25% discount shop than in the 40% discount shop.

Apart from the evidence gathered that can be used to inform further instruction, the analysis of the students' work also yields indications for improvement of the problem; for example: What is the degree of certainty that this problem offers valid information about the level of students' understanding? Do the students who simply compared percentages really lack understanding of the relativity of percentages? To address the second question, the problem could be extended with an additional question such as, "Is there any possibility that your best buy could be at Lisa's? If yes, give an example." Because the function of such a question, in this case, is to identify those students who understand the relativity of percentages but who still need extra help in expressing it, this question is called a "safety net question" (van den Heuvel-Panhuizen, 1996).

The "Black Currant Jam" Problem

In daily life, percentages often are used to describe the composition of different substances. In this case, percentages do not refer to a change that is happening or that has occurred but describe a fixed situation: the part of a substance that consists of this or of that. Because the composition of packaged foodstuffs is not hidden, this context was chosen to assess whether students understood that a percentage remains the same as long as the ratios of the mixture remain the same, even when the absolute amounts or numbers of the mixture change. The "Black Currant Jam" problem (see Figure 5.2) is about a jam that contains 60% fruit. The jam is sold in large and small jars, and the first part of the assessment focused on whether the students were aware that the size of the jar did not influence the percentage of fruit in the jam. In other words, was their understanding strong enough to withstand a visual distractor? The same context was used also in the second part of the problem to assess whether the students could compute a part of a whole when the percentage was given: "How many grams of fruit are in 450 grams of jam?"

Only 10% of the students (4 out of 39) recognized that the percentage of fruit was the same in the two jars (see Table 5.3); one student also guessed the correct answer. With respect to the second question, about 40% of the students (16 out of 39) gave a reasonable answer (9 of these gave the correct answer; see Table 5.4). In contrast, 22 students (56%) did computations that made no sense. It seems as if these students were trying to recall and reuse a computational procedure.

All the students needed more experience expressing a "so-many-out-of-so-many" situation by means of a percentage, perhaps by offering

Figure 5.2. "Black Currant Jam" problem from the Per Sense unit final assessment.

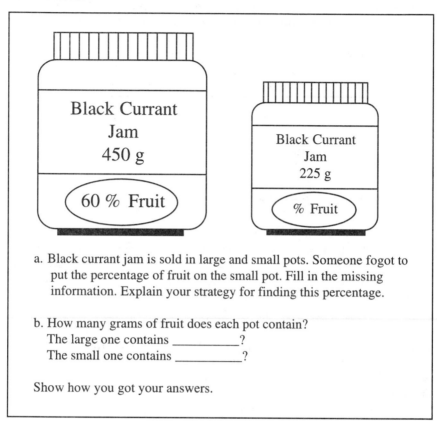

a. Black currant jam is sold in large and small pots. Someone fogot to put the percentage of fruit on the small pot. Fill in the missing information. Explain your strategy for finding this percentage.

b. How many grams of fruit does each pot contain?
   The large one contains _____ ?
   The small one contains _____ ?

Show how you got your answers.

them problems in which they could investigate consequences of all kinds of changes. The students who got stuck in senseless calculating needed to acquaint themselves with the informal strategies of their classmates. That most of the students thought that the percentage of fruit was not the same in the two jars does not necessarily mean that they had no insight at all into the ratio aspect of percentage. It might also be the case that their understanding was still unstable and that they could not yet withstand the visual distraction of the problem presentation. To check whether the latter is the case, this problem could be improved by a safety net question: "Let's take a look at the taste of

Table 5.3. Student responses to the "Black Currant Jam" problem, Part A.

	Response categories	Students (N = 39)	Examples
Correct answer (13%) [a]	Explanation indicates insight into "same ratio, same percentage"	4	• "They are the same, except one is at a smaller scale, both pots contain $\frac{6}{10}$ of fruits." • "Big got 60%, little got 60%."
	No reasonable explanation	1	• "Guessed."
Incorrect answer (85%)	"Halving g, halving %" (Answer = 30%)	25	• "You look at the bigger bottle and its half g, so you take half of the %." • "225 is $\frac{1}{2}$ of 450, so 30% is $\frac{1}{2}$ of 60%." • "450 devide [sic] by 2 is 225, so you divide 60 by 2 and you get 30."
	Other or no explanation (3) (Answer = 30%)	5	• $450 \div 60 = 7.5$ and $225 \div 7.5 = 30$
	Other strategies (Multiple answers)	3	• 25%: "Both divided by 9, got my percent." • 22%: "First subtracted the grams to get the difference ($450 - 225 = 245$), then 22 by 10, and put a decimal, is 22%."
No answer (2%)	No answer	1	

[a] Correct answer = 60%

the jam in the two jars. Will they taste the same or not? Explain why you think so."

The "Twax Bar" Problem

The third problem to be discussed here is the "Twax Bar" problem. It is about a candy bar that was made 25% larger but was sold at the same price as the original bar. Students were asked to compute the discount in price inherent in the new size (see Figure 5.3).

Table 5.4. Student responses to the "Black Currant Jam" problem, Part B.

	Response categories	Students (N = 39)	Examples
Correct answer (23%) [a]	Based on a standard strategy	5	• $450 \times .60 = 270.00$ • " $\frac{\%}{450} = \frac{60}{100}$; $\frac{270}{450} = \frac{60}{100}$ "
	Based on an informal strategy	1	• "10% of 450 is 45; 45×6 ["from 60%"] = 270."
	No information about strategy	3	
Reasonable response (18%)	Based on a standard strategy (Answer = 275)	2	• $450 \times 0.60 = 275.00$
	Based on an informal strategy (Multiple answers)	4	• 263: Bar, approximated 60% by repeated halving. • 200: " $450 \div 2 = 225$ and you have to take a little more away to make 60%."
	No information about strategy (Answer = 250)	1	
Incorrect answer (56%)	Not able to work with percentages, or no information about strategy (1) (Answer = 450 g)	12	• "It says so on the bottle." • Bar divided in parts of 15%. $450 \div 225 = 2$; " $\frac{1}{2}$ of 60% is 30%."
	Not able to work with percentages, or no information about strategy (3) (Multiple answers)	10	• 390: $450 - 60 = 390$ • 7.5: $60 \div 450 = 7.5$ • 13.3 or 13: " $\frac{60}{450} \times \frac{?}{100}$ "
No answer (3%)	No answer	1	

[a] Correct answer = 270 g

Figure 5.3. "Twax Bar" problem from the Per Sense unit final assessment.

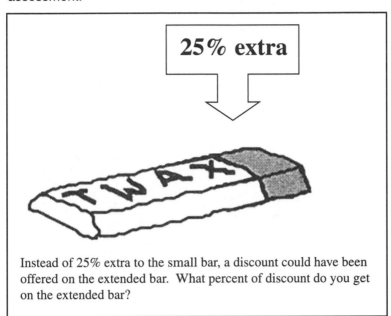

25% extra

Instead of 25% extra to the small bar, a discount could have been offered on the extended bar. What percent of discount do you get on the extended bar?

Although only about 20% of the students (7 out of 39) succeeded in solving this difficult problem (see Table 5.5), more often than not, the answers that these students gave contained excellent explanations (see, for example, the explanation marked by footnote b in Table 5.5). Recognizing the quality of the answers, however, requires not being distracted by the students' clumsy wording. The 28 incorrect responses (72%) varied greatly, but the most common misbelief was that the percentage stayed the same.

Interestingly, some students really used the picture to solve the problem. One did some additional drawing (see Figure 5.4a); others drew a bar or a number line to find the discount. In this case, the students' worksheets contained a nice example of the ways this kind of assessment might suggest instructional ideas. On one sheet, the teacher, while grading, used the same strategy as one of her students (shown in Figure 5.4a) to explain the problem to another student who gave the wrong answer (see Figure 5.4b). The bold handwriting in this figure is the teacher's. Whether the teacher adopted a student's particularly apt

Table 5.5. Student responses to the "Twax Bar" problem.

	Response categories	Students (N = 39)	Examples
Correct answer (18%) [a]	Taking into account the change in the amount of reference	7	• Marks and words in the picture. • Number line, 4 parts and 1 part, each "25"; at the end "total" and "each 20%." • Without the 25% extra, each part (bar) is divided into 4th. But if you have $\frac{1}{4}$ more, it becomes so that each part into 5ths. So if you divide 100 by 5, you get 20. So 20% is the discount." [b]
Incorrect answer (72%)	No taking into account the change in the amount of reference, or no strategy described (Answer = 25%)	14	• "Because 25% extra is like 25% discount." • 100 + 25 = 125 and 125 − 25 = 100 • "I guessed."
	No understanding of the problem (Answer = 125%)	2	• "100% = the total candy bar + your 25% = 125%, which equals the total of the new candy bar."
	Other strategies (Multiple answers)	12	• 15%: "added." • 15%: Bar, 5 parts, 25-25-25-25-15. • 75%: "100 × .75 = 75%" • 1/4: "Divide it into groups of that size and see how big it fits in."
No answer (10%)	No answer	4	• Twax was changed to Twix. • "Don t understand instructions."

[a] Correct answer = 20%

[b] An excellent explanation

visual strategy or simply happened on it herself is not clear because there is no way to determine the order of grading. We do note, however, that she used this "new" explanation on only some of the papers, which would seem to suggest a change in her marking.

Among the students who were unable to solve the problem, there were at least three who did not understand the question and others who did not understand what the problem was about, possibly due to the wording of the problem and its presentation. One possible way to

Figure 5.4. "Twax Bar" problem. (a) One student's notation on picture. (b) Teacher's explanation to a different student.

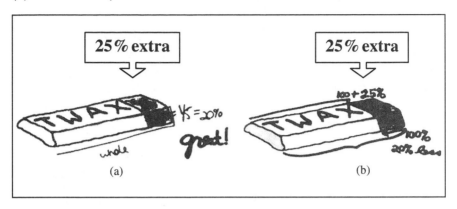

rework the problem would be to use two advertisements: one in which a four-part bar is extended by 25%, and another in which a discount is given to a five-part bar. Whether this actually would be an improvement would need to be investigated.

DISCUSSION OF PRACTICAL ASSESSMENT ISSUES

In this section, we discuss general findings from our work in developing this assessment and from the responses of the students and teachers involved.

Simple Marking Fails

Offering rich problems to students can result in rich answers. But simply marking students' responses to these problems will not work, and breaking down student responses and giving them credit for good work in a rich problem is a hard job. A "correct" response can take many forms, and students can give reasonable answers that, strictly speaking, do not fit within narrow criteria of correctness. Grading such answers as incorrect, however, also does injustice to the richness of response. An emphasis on reasonableness of strategy and response does more justice to the students' own way of thinking: The assessment not only becomes more fair but also allows teachers and students to make better sense of their work and to better identify what needs improving.

Furthermore, a new, unexpected interpretation could be elicited by the problem and "discovered" while analyzing students' work.

The Cutoff Point

One difficulty in applying the criterion of reasonableness is that the cutoff point often is not easily determined. What matters is the message conveyed by the student's response. Sometimes an incorrect answer shows that a student has insight; sometimes question marks must be put to a correct answer. When the teacher analyzes students' work, specific difficulties of the students also might be taken into account in determining the "reasonableness" of the response and might result in different cutoff points.

Overall, the three problems analyzed in this chapter turned out to be suitable to document the achievements of these students. The tables show that the problems revealed different levels of understanding and ability. Because the problems disclosed the students' reasoning, strategies, calculations, and estimations, they also provided good information for making decisions about further instruction. In addition, as illustrated by the "Twax Bar" problem, these problems at times yielded good teaching material. Finally, results of the field test also suggested how the problems could be improved.

The findings reported here were derived from a written test. Although judgments about students must involve much more than test scores, written tests can provide valuable information, depending on the problems used. Different kinds of problems will evoke different results. The richer and more open the problems, the more students' responses reveal their level of understanding and skills. Responses to such problems are often more difficult to interpret than are responses to closed and bare problems, but student responses to a few powerful problems can reveal more than answers to a large number of easy-to-grade problems.

FINAL REMARKS

What started as an apparently concrete and straightforward job—to develop a series of problems for the final assessment of the Per Sense unit—became a complex, iterative process, resulting in a multilevel series of problems designed to assess a specific domain. Yet the output included more than just concrete materials: Arising out of this process were theoretical ideas, new insights, and new concrete possibilities about assessment that we had not specifically looked for. This is a characteristic feature of developmental research.

The guiding principle for this assessment project was the idea that the new approach to teaching mathematics requires assessment problems that (1) reveal what students are able to do, and (2) offer stepping stones for further teaching. Most important, the problems need to be open so that they can be solved in different ways and on different levels. To meet these requirements, we developed open problems that would be meaningful to the students and were set in contexts that gave support for solving them. Evidence suggests that all these aspects are important if we are to offer students the opportunity to show what they are able to do.

Chapter 6

Analysis of an End-of-Unit Test

Monica Wijers
FREUDENTHAL INSTITUTE,
UNIVERSITY OF UTRECHT

This chapter reports on the ways students performed on an end-of-unit test in classes taught by three teachers who implemented *Mathematics in Context* (MiC; National Center for Research in Mathematical Sciences Education & Freudenthal Institute, 1997–1998). The project started in August 1997 with a group of teachers in two middle schools in Providence, Rhode Island. During the summer, teachers of the participating schools were prepared to implement MiC in their classes.

The story in this chapter extends the insights about the development of end-of-unit tests discussed in Chapter 5, examining the variation in instruction and assessment of student progress while teachers were teaching an MiC unit for the first time. Although the teacher guide for each MiC unit contains suggestions for assessing student progress during instruction and tasks for an end-of-unit test, teachers may create their own tasks rather than following those suggestions. Student performance on end-of-unit assessment tasks can reflect differences in the teachers' patterns of instruction.

The teachers involved started with Reallotment (Gravemeijer, Pligge, & Clarke, 1998), the MiC unit on area and related topics. This unit was chosen because area is a topic that is familiar to all teachers, must be dealt with by all students, and requires no specific prerequisite knowledge.

THE REALLOTMENT UNIT

The concept of area is a difficult topic in middle school mathematics (de Moor, 1999; Freudenthal, 1984). The approach to area in the Reallotment MiC unit is different from the traditional approach (de Moor, 1999). The main difference involves the way the *concept* of area is developed gradually over the course of the unit and is supported by informal strategies for finding areas. The major characteristics of this unit are:

- The concept is not limited to simple shapes but is broadened to irregular shapes and three-dimensional forms right from the start.
- Shapes are qualitatively compared and ordered according to their area, without calculating the areas.
- Area is represented by other quantities that seem more "concrete" to students (e.g., cost, the amount of cookie dough, weight, paint).
- Shapes are constructed and reconstructed by students (e.g., in the context of "tessellations," as shown in Figure 6.1).
- Preformal strategies for finding area get attention; the central strategy in this unit is reshaping. This is done on different levels.
- Gradually, strategies that are more formal are discovered and introduced; the formulas for the areas of rectangles, parallelograms, and triangles are derived from the reshaping strategy.
- A connection is made to other topics from geometry, such as tessellations.

TEACHING THE UNIT: DIFFERENCES BETWEEN CLASSES

Teachers sometimes felt insecure teaching the unit because it was the first one from the new curriculum, and they were unfamiliar with the different instructional sequence. In addition, students were unfamiliar with the different type of problems and needed to be guided in what was expected of them. Thus, new classroom norms and culture needed to be established.

Two of the teachers, Ms. Aberson and Ms. Baker, both experienced teachers who worked closely together, already taught in accordance with the goals and philosophy of the reformed curriculum. They specifically paid a great deal of attention to the informal strategies that

Figure 6.1. Tessellation activity. From "Reallotment" (p. 8) by K. Gravemeijer, M. A. Pligge, & B. Clarke, 1998, in National Center for Research in Mathematical Sciences Education & Freudenthal Institute (Eds.), (1997–1998), *Mathematics in Context*, Chicago: Encyclopædia Britannica. Copyright © 1998 Encyclopædia Britannica. Reprinted with permission.

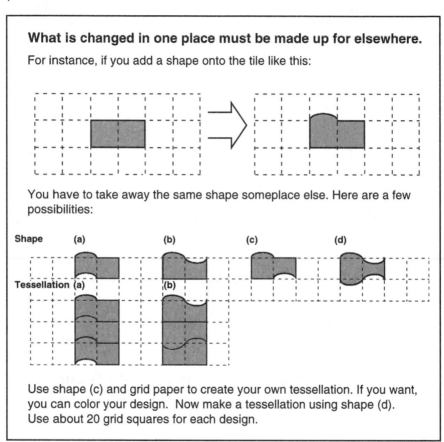

What is changed in one place must be made up for elsewhere.

For instance, if you add a shape onto the tile like this:

You have to take away the same shape someplace else. Here are a few possibilities:

Use shape (c) and grid paper to create your own tessellation. If you want, you can color your design. Now make a tessellation using shape (d). Use about 20 grid squares for each design.

students used. Strategies were demonstrated by students in front of Ms. Aberson's class and discussed in whole-class discussions. Both teachers also stressed the need for (written) explanations and for students to show the work.

The third teacher, Mr. Collins, a new permanent substitute, had problems managing his classes. Students in his classes worked individually and, occasionally, in small groups. Little attention was paid to whole-class discussions of strategies or explanations. Mr. Collins, more than either Ms. Aberson or Ms. Baker, tended to teach in front of the class, without interaction, and he focused more on the use of formulas. His teaching in terms of style as well as content could be described as more traditional.

In all classes, the unit took more time than the intended 4–5 weeks, which had a negative effect on the motivation of teachers and students. Therefore, during the teaching of the unit, the researchers developed a "shortcut"—a route through only the core content of the unit. By following this shortcut, teachers could finish the unit in less time but still teach the core of the unit.

ASSESSING STUDENT PERFORMANCE IN THE UNIT

During the teaching–learning process, all three teachers used different techniques and instruments to assess what students had learned so far. Homework, specific problems from the unit, performance in class discussions, information from observations, quizzes, and a project task were used for this purpose in most classes. Both Ms. Aberson and Ms. Baker chose one particular problem from the unit and made it into a test to give students an opportunity to practice writing good explanations (van Reeuwijk & Wijers, 2002). They also both used a project task ("the carpet problem") to assess "higher goals" such as mathematical reasoning and communicating (see Chapter 8). Furthermore, often they informally assessed their students' performance during class discussions.

Mr. Collins had a more traditional way of assessing his students during the teaching of the unit. He often gave small quizzes, for which he used problems from the unit as well as self-made problems. He made less use of informal assessment instruments such as checking homework and observing students' performance in class discussions. This is, of course, consistent with his more traditional style of teaching and less developed class management skills.

Even though the teachers used a variety of informal classroom assessment procedures, they were displeased with what they learned about their students' understanding of area. After the core content of the unit was finished, the general impression that remained with all teachers was that a lot of students seemed to still be using mainly very informal strategies for finding area. Students favored strategies such as counting squares or cutting and moving little pieces—even in situations where more formal strategies could easily have been used and in situations where informal strategies would not give reliable answers.

The teachers were interested in knowing what students actually had learned; which strategy or strategies they could use, whether they had developed a broad understanding of the concept of area, and whether indeed they had moved from an informal to a more formal level of understanding. The unit provides suggestions for end-of-unit assessment; however, the teachers felt that they were not yet able to use these problems to design an appropriate test. They felt that the approach toward area in the unit was too new to them to be able to capture the essentials of it in a test. Therefore, they asked the researchers to design a new end-of-unit test. The teachers were willing to formulate criteria, review the first draft, and design supplementary problems if needed.

DESIGN OF THE TEST

The philosophy and principles underlying the MiC curriculum were used as a reference when designing the test. Seven open problems were created or selected (six by the researchers and one by the teachers). After review, the teachers felt that the test met their expectations. One of them remarked: "I like this test because it is very much like the unit. Since it is our first test, I prefer it like this." Suggestions for the scoring of the test were included in the draft designed by the researchers. Sometimes only a short answer was expected, but for most problems, students were expected to show their work. The test focused not only on basic skills, but also on higher-order skills, process goals, and conceptual knowledge. Furthermore, students were allowed to choose the strategies for answering most of the problems. The maximum total number of points for the whole test was 30, and each score could be converted into a percentage. A score of 55% or more was "pass." Scoring points were divided over the problems in such a way that students who had only basic knowledge and skills would have a score of around 55%. A "good" student would score between 90 and 100%. A class mean of around 60% was considered a satisfactory result. The end-of-unit test was administered in six classes of the three teachers involved in the study. To make statements about the scores related to the teaching style and classroom norms of each teacher, the results of one representative class for each of the three teachers were examined. All students were allowed to work on the assessment for one class period. Based on the comments of the teachers and the fact that most students completed the test in this one class period, the length of the test was deemed appropriate. First, one of the researchers scored the student work, and then the teacher for the class checked it. Table 6.1 shows the summarized results.

The results of the three classes are quite close. In all three classes, the class means were around 60% and the range of the scores was approximately the same. The number of students who passed—that is, whose score was 17 points or above (over 55%)—is a little lower in the class taught by Mr. Collins. Histograms of the scores (Figure 6.2) show different patterns in the scores for the three classes. The distribution of the scores for Mr. Collins's class has two (relatively low) peaks: one for scores between 12 and 17, and the other for scores between 21 and 27, so there is a dip around the mean. This may indicate that in this class students either do well or do not do so well on the test: There are no mediocre students. The other two classes show a more normal distribution, with most scores around the center. This difference in the distribution is likely related to differences in teaching styles or classroom cultures.

To determine whether students developed a broad understanding of the concept of area, an examination of the students' work on each question is given in Tables 6.2 and 6.3. The partial scores on each problem give a more detailed picture of the differences in the results among the three classes. The problems on the test, the expectations about students' possible answers, and a summary of the results are presented in the following sections.

Problem 1. Urba and Cursa

Problem 1 on the end-of-unit test (Figure 6.3) asks students to compare informally the areas of irregular shapes. The prompt, "Explain your

Table 6.1. Summary of results on the end-of-unit test.

	Teacher and class (number of students)					
	Ms. Aberson Grade 7, period 4 (26 students)		Ms. Baker Grade 8, period 3 (23 students)		Mr. Collins Grade 7, period 3 (26 students)	
	No.	%	No.	%	No.	%
Class mean (points)	19	63	19	63	18	60
Range (points)	4–29	13–97	4–29	13–97	4–30	13–100
Passing rate (students)	18	69	16	70	14	54

Figure 6.2. Histograms of student scores on end-of-unit test.

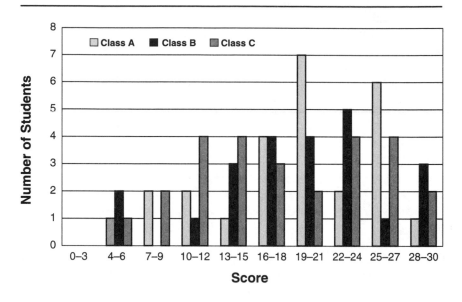

Figure 6.3. End-of-unit test Problem 1—Urba and Cursa.

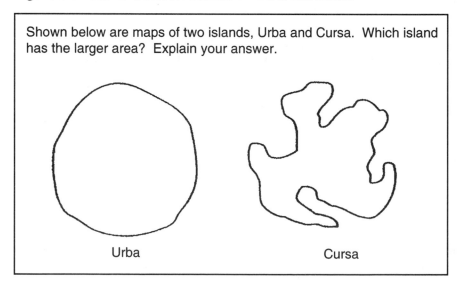

Shown below are maps of two islands, Urba and Cursa. Which island has the larger area? Explain your answer.

Urba   Cursa

Table 6.2. Mean scores on the end-of-unit test, by problem number and class.

Problem	Possible score	Class teacher		
		Ms. Aberson	Ms. Baker	Mr. Collins
1	3	2.3 (78%)	1.1 (36%)	2.2 (74%)
2a	2	1.6 (79%)	1.5 (74%)	2.0 (100%)
2b	3	1.7 (58%)	1.4 (46%)	1.5 (50%)
3a3c	4	2.7 (67%)	3.0 (75%)	2.7 (66%)
3d	1	0.7 (73%)	0.9 (91%)	0.7 (73%)
3e	2	1.3 (63%)	1.7 (85%)	1.5 (77%)
4 (area)	1	0.4 (42%)	0.5 (48%)	0.4 (38%)
Method 1	2	1.7 (87%)	1.9 (93%)	1.2 (60%)
Method 2	2	0.8 (38%)	1.2 (59%)	0.7 (37%)
5a	1	0.6 (58%)	0.7 (74%)	0.7 (73%)
5b	2	0.7 (37%)	0.6 (28%)	0.4 (21%)
6a	2	1.5 (73%)	1.5 (74%)	1.6 (81%)
6b	2	1.3 (63%)	1.2 (59%)	1.2 (58%)
7	3	1.4 (47%)	1.8 (61%)	1.3 (41%)

answer," was added to guarantee that students would write more than just the name of the larger island; it also helps teachers evaluate the extent to which students know the meaning of area. This problem was chosen as the first problem in the test for a number of reasons. It is the most "informal" problem in the sense that no calculations need to be made, and it focuses on the "topic" of the test, namely, area. Although we expected that most students would be able to do the problem, we also expected that some students might confuse area and perimeter. Asking students to explain their answers was intended to reveal this kind of confusion.

The scores in Table 6.2 show that students in Ms. Baker's class did not do well on this problem. Examining the students' work revealed that the low scores were the result of many students comparing the perimeters of the islands instead of the areas. One student, for example, wrote: "Urba I know this because I measured it with a string and Urba

Table 6.3. Strategies used and further analysis of student performance on end-of-unit test.

	Class teacher		
	Ms. Aberson	Ms. Baker	Mr. Collins
Problems 1 and 2	Strategies: Counting squares and reshaping.	Use of formula; unclear strategy for 2b.	Calculation is explanation (implicit use of formula).
Problem 3	A lot of explanations for a…c	Good; some explanations.	Few explanations.
Problem 4			
• 2 correct methods	8 (30%)	10 (43%)	5 (19%)
• 1.5 correct methods	3 (11%)	5 (22%)	3 (11%)
• 1 correct method	10 (38%)	6 (26%)	4 (15%)
• Described at least 1 method correctly	21 (79%)	21 (91%)	12 (45%)
• Less than 1 correct method	3 (12%)	2 (9%)	—
• No good method or did not try	2 (7%)	—	5 (19%)
Problem 5			
• 100% scores	7 (27%)	5 (22%)	4 (15%)
Problem 6	Some students drew rectangles for 6a.	Some students drew rectangles for 6a.	Some students drew rectangles for 6a.
• 100% scores	12 (46%)	10 (43%)	13 (50%)
Problem 7			
• 100% scores	7 (27%)	11 (48%)	7 (27%)

fit more string than Cursa." The illustration showed the perimeter for Urba accentuated.

Ms. Baker was the only teacher who completed the last two lessons in the unit, which were on perimeter. In retrospect, when Ms. Baker's students started the test, "perimeter" may have been on their minds more than it was for students from the other classes. Although the scores for the classes taught by Ms. Aberson and Mr. Collins do not differ, the most popular strategies in each class differed. Students in Ms. Aberson's class often compared the areas by "putting the islands on top of each other." One student, for example, wrote: "Urba because if you put Cursa inside of Urba you can see the spaces from Urba" (see Figure 6.4). Students in the class taught by Mr. Collins drew grids and compared the areas by comparing the number of units in each island (see Figure 6.5).

Problem 2. Find the Area

Problem 2 (Figure 6.6) deals with finding the area of a rectangle (a) and of a parallelogram (b) with the same base and height. Measurements are given in centimeters, and no grid is presented. The shapes are relatively simple; the main goal of this problem is not to test whether students can calculate the area of (complex) shapes but to find out whether students are able to relate the shapes explicitly or implicitly by using the same formula. Work must be shown; this is indicated by the phrase, "explain how you found your answer." Of course, different strategies can be used to calculate the areas.

Noteworthy is the 100% score on Problem 2a—finding the area of the rectangle—by students in Mr. Collins's class. The other classes scored a mean of only around 75%. Also, there was a difference in the strategies used by students in the classes of Ms. Aberson and Mr. Collins. Students from Ms. Aberson's class used informal strategies such as drawing a grid and counting the units, often combined with a calculation. Students of Mr. Collins, on the other hand, most often wrote only the

Figure 6.4. Response to Problem 1—Urba and Cursa (Aberson class).

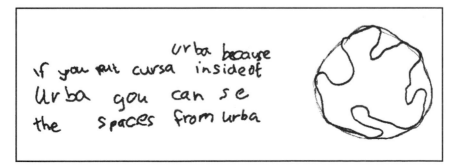

Figure 6.5. Response to Problem 1—Urba and Cursa (Collins class).

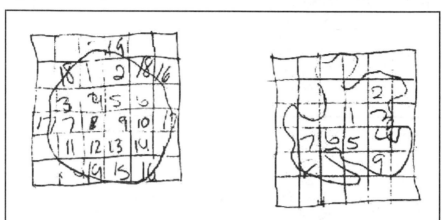

calculation 3 × 5 = 15. They implicitly made use of the formula, *area = length × width*. This difference in the choice of strategies was undoubt-edly due to the differences in classroom culture: In Ms. Aberson's class, much attention was paid to informal strategies and explanations in-volving these strategies, whereas in the class taught by Mr. Collins, the emphasis was more on the use of the formula. In Ms. Baker's class, a

Figure 6.6. End-of-unit test Problem 2—find the area.

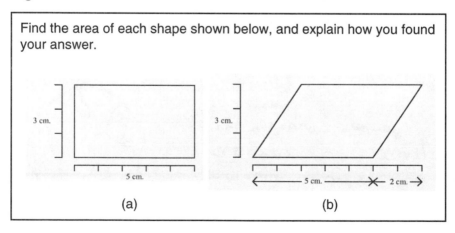

mix of the use of informal strategies and the explicit use of the formula was found.

Problem 3. Prices of Shaded Pieces

In (b) through (d) of Figure 6.7, the area of the shaded parts of the rectangle (representing priced pieces of wood) must be related to the area of the rectangle itself. The price of $18.00 for the rectangular piece of

Figure 6.7. End-of-unit test Problem 3—prices of shaded pieces.

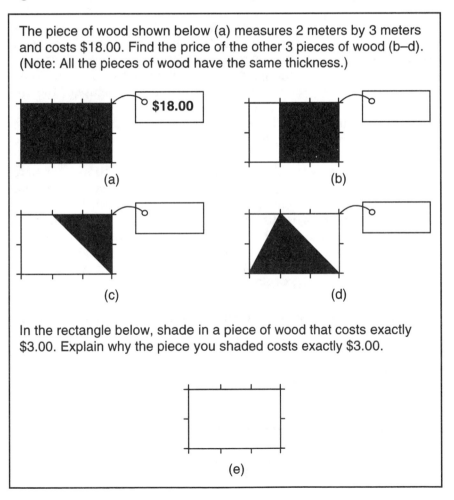

wood is used as an intermediate measure. As in Problem 2, using relations between the shapes is a powerful strategy. Part (e) of Figure 6.7 was added to the original version of the problem and serves two purposes.

1. It is a production or construction problem, where students must construct a piece of wood that costs exactly $3.00.
2. It asks for a justification of what they did.

Part (e) gives students the opportunity to show what they can do rather than what they cannot do. The explanation for (e) gives information about the strategies students used for (e), but it also may reveal students' level of understanding of the problem and their strategies for (b) through (d).

The highest scores for Problem 3 were for Ms. Baker's class. It is not obvious, however, why the scores for this class were higher. Almost all students in Ms. Aberson's class wrote explanations or showed their work for (b) through (d), even though this was not explicitly asked for. Some of the students wrote elaborate explanations and made use of the answers they already had found (see student work in Figure 6.8).

It can be assumed that this was already an established aspect of the classroom culture. This is very different from what students did in the class taught by Mr. Collins, where almost no work was shown for (b) through (d). When we analyzed student work on question (e), where students had to shade in a piece that costs exactly $3, we noticed that students in all classes came up with different shapes. In the explanations provided for (e), this difference in shape can be traced to the strategy the student used to find the correct part. If one whole square unit is shaded, the explanation refers to the whole rectangle consisting of 6 of these squares costing $18. For example: "There are 6 units. The whole rectangle is worth $18.00. $18.00/6 units = $3.00 for each unit. That's why it cost $3.00."

Another common solution is that a student shades half of a strip, as in Figure 6.9. For this shading, different explanations are given. For example, the following explanation by one student is a very nice one and shows a good understanding of fractions: "It cost exactly $3.00 because it is half of 1/3, and half of 1/3 will cost $6.00. Each 1/3 cost $6.00."

Problem 4. Two Methods for Finding Area

In Problem 4 (Figure 6.10), the area of a triangle on a grid should be found in two ways, and both methods should be described. The

Figure 6.8. Response to Problem 3—prices of shades pieces (Aberson class).

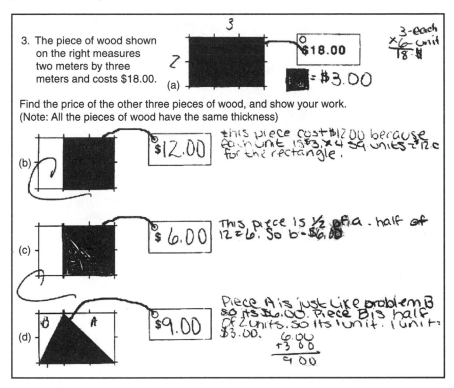

Figure 6.9. Response to Problem 3—prices of shaded pieces (Collins class).

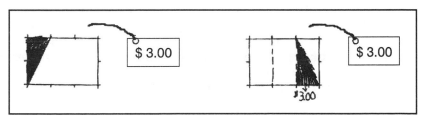

Figure 6.10. End-of-unit test Problem 4—two methods for finding area.

Below, you see a triangle drawn on a grid. Use two different ways to find the area of this triangle in square units, and explain each method you used. You can use drawings if you want to.

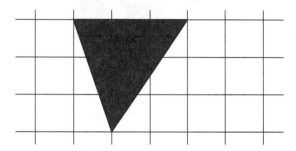

First method:

Second method:

purpose of this problem was to find out whether students actually know more than one strategy for finding area and whether they are able to communicate these strategies. The sentence, "You can use drawings if you want to," was added to clarify that the students' explanations need not be written. The problem can be characterized as a "reflective problem"; students must actively reflect on what exactly they are doing when finding an area.

The scores on this problem were lowest for Mr. Collins's class, in which only 19% of the students were able to describe two methods correctly, and 55% could not even describe one correct method. This may have been the result of less attention in this class having been paid to different methods for finding area and to giving explanations. The scores of the other two classes were satisfactory. Also note that in the classes of Ms. Aberson and Ms. Baker, 80 to 90% of the students could describe at least one correct method for finding the area, but only around 50% actually could find the correct area. This may be due to the wording of the problem. The emphasis is on describing the methods, and some students simply seem to have forgotten to write down the area.

Problem 5. Photo Frame

Jenny has a photo of her dog. She is making a frame to put the photo in. For the frame, she needs glass and a strip of wood for the edges. The photo is 10 inches long and 5 inches wide.

(a) How much glass does Jenny need for the frame? Show your work.
(b) How many inches of wooden strip does Jenny need? Show your work.

This problem was added because the teachers felt that the test needed to include a problem that combined area and perimeter. One of the teachers provided the idea for this problem. Students must be able to recognize the amount of glass as an area and the amount of wooden strip as a perimeter. No drawing was provided, so students must do this purely based on the measurements given, although of course they can make their own drawing to structure the problem. The context of the photo frame can function in two ways: as an artificial context or as a realistic one. The wording of the problem does not provide any help to decide which interpretation is meant. If students see the context as an artificial one, they will give mathematically correct answers such as, "You need 30 inches of wooden strip and 50 square inches of glass." If, on the other hand, students see the problem as real, they might answer, "You need two strips of 5 inches and two strips of 10 inches and a piece of glass 5 (10 inches," or, if students see it as even more real, "You need 2 strips of 6 inches and two of 11 inches in order to make the corners fit."

Because the wording was unclear, answers corresponding to either interpretation were seen as correct. As expected, some students answered this as a purely mathematical problem ("50 sq. inches of glass"), and some as a real-world problem ("glass of 10 by 5 inches"). Although the real-world answers were not common, a few students actually were so involved in the context that they dealt with the extra wood needed to get the corners right (see Figure 6.11).

Figure 6.11. Response to Problem 5—photo frame.

How much glass does Jenny need for the frame?
Show your work.

she needs $10\frac{1}{2}$ inches long and she needs $5\frac{1}{2}$ inches wide

How many inches of wooden strip does Jenny need?
Show your work.

She needs 11 inches long for both ends have a extra half and she need 6 inches wide for both end have extra half

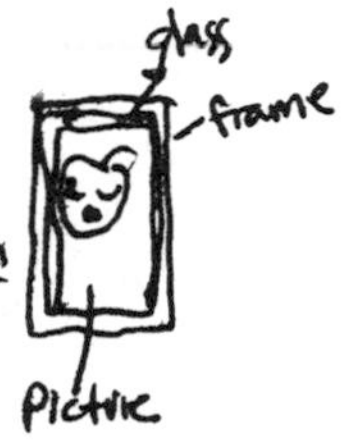

Most students who were able to solve this problem either were familiar with it as a common kind of problem in mathematics (as Mr. Collins explained), or automatically (because of the mathematics classroom setting) turned it into an area and perimeter problem. Scores on this problem are about the same for all classes. The scores on the perimeter question (5b) were lower than those on the area question. This is understandable because perimeter got much less attention than area during instruction. In Ms. Baker's class, however, even though more attention was paid to perimeter than in the other two classes, students did not perform better on this task.

Problem 6. Creating Shapes with a Given Area

(1) On the grid, draw a parallelogram with an area of 8 square units.
(2) On the grid, draw a triangle with an area of 8 square units.

Students must, on a grid, create a triangle and a parallelogram with a given area. This is an own-production problem. Having students create the two shapes gives insight into students' level of understanding of the concept of area. Implicitly, it can give extra information on the strategies that students have available for finding area. It also reveals whether students know shapes by name.

About half of all students could draw both a parallelogram and a triangle with the given area. This is a very satisfactory percentage, considering that no such problems were in the unit. Furthermore, this problem requires students to be able to think on a more abstract level about area. Constructing an area is different from finding (counting or calculating) it. Some strategies are not reversible: An area can be found by moving little pieces and putting them together to get whole units, but a shape with a given area cannot be constructed by reversing this strategy.

As expected, most students were able to successfully complete this production problem. In each of the classes, around 15% of the students drew a rectangle where a parallelogram was asked for. Either these students were clever and simply drew the simplest parallelogram, which is indeed a rectangle, or they didn't know how to draw the required parallelogram and instead drew a rectangle. Maybe they were thinking: Producing an incorrect answer is always better than producing nothing at all. In some of the students' work, a "trial and improve" strategy can be recognized from the redrawing of a shape too small or too large, where old lines are still visible, or from the counting numbers that have been put into the square units (see Figure 6.12).

Some students clearly showed how they used a rectangle as the starting figure and turned this into a parallelogram (or a triangle) by cutting off and moving a triangular part, or turned it into a triangle by cutting it in half (see Figure 6.13). Most often, however, only the resulting shapes are seen. The shapes that occur most are a rectangular

Figure 6.12. Response to Problem 6—creating shapes with a given area.

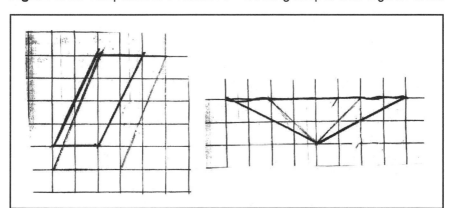

Figure 6.13. Response to Problem 6—creating shapes with a given area.

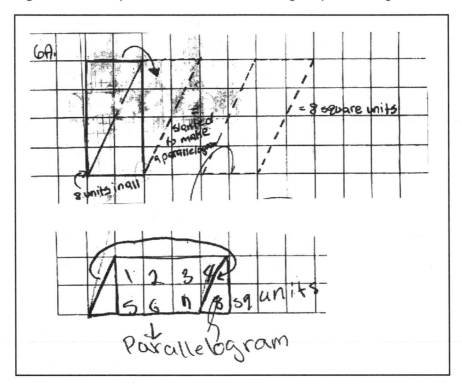

triangle, half of a 4 × 4 square, and a parallelogram with *base* 4 and *height* 2.

Problem 7. Tessellation

Problem 7 (Figure 6.14) was chosen to be the final problem because it is a "playful" problem. In this problem, we felt that students would have the opportunity to deal with area in a different context. No specific knowledge of the making of tessellations is needed. Students can apply certain strategies for finding area in a new situation where the grid is only partly visible. For instance, the structure of the tessellation can be used.

Ms. Baker's class had the highest scores on this tessellation problem. A possible reason for this is that students in her class had made

Figure 6.14. End-of-unit test Problem 7—tessellation.

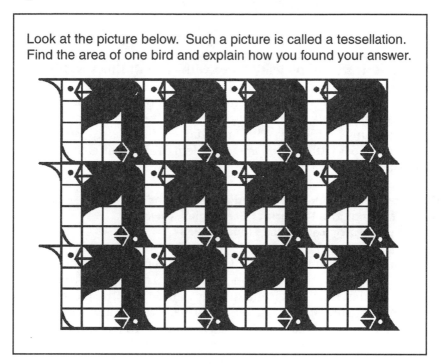

some tessellations before the unit started. No connection between tessellations and area was made, however. Scores in the other two classes did not differ.

CONCLUSIONS

The four research questions that underlie this study can now be answered.

Question 1: Did the Test Work as Intended?

From the results on the end-of-unit test, one can conclude that the test worked as intended. Scores were satisfactory, and students in general could do all kinds of problems related to area. Only Problem 5, added by the teachers, provided ambiguous results.

Question 2: Have Students Developed a Thorough, Broad Understanding of the Concept of Area?

Most students developed a broad understanding of the concept of area: broader than often results from teaching that is more traditional, where students tend to identify area with "length times width." This clearly was not the case here. In Problem 1, for instance, the area of irregular shapes was not a problem for the majority of students. If students had known area only as *length × width*, they could not have successfully done Problem 1. The fact that students also were able to construct shapes with a given area (Problem 6) also points to this broad understanding of the concept.

Question 3: Did Students Indeed Grow Beyond Using Informal and Preformal Strategies Toward More Formal Strategies for Finding Area?

A number of students knew at least two methods for finding area, as can be seen from the results on Problem 4. The method that almost all students described first is the strategy of moving little pieces around to make whole units. This is a very informal strategy and it is not very reliable for the particular shape in this problem. On the other hand, if this had been their only available strategy, students could not have done Problem 6b, constructing a triangle with an area of 8 square units. To be able to do this problem, students must know at least that the area of a triangle is half the area of a rectangle. The (implicit) use of a formula in Problem 2 also seems likely. Especially in the class of Mr. Collins, many students implicitly used the formula on this problem. It seems likely—when taking into account the teaching of the unit—that this is because the teacher used a more traditional style of teaching combined with a strong emphasis on formulas. Problem 2a has characteristics of a traditional area problem. Especially if the results of this class are combined for Problems 2 and 4, we see that not many students described the formula as a method for solving Problem 4. It is therefore unlikely that these students actually moved from informal to formal strategies for all area problems.

Many students in the classes of Ms. Aberson and Ms. Baker multiplied 3 by 5 to solve Problem 2a, which points to their knowledge of the formula. A number of students, however, combined this written explanation with the drawing of a grid and numbering (or counting of) all squares from 1 to 15, which seems to be a very low-level, informal strategy. It can be assumed that this was caused by the prompt asking for an explanation. Many students in Ms. Aberson's and Ms. Baker's classes got confused by the request for an explanation, didn't value "3 × 5 = 15" as a good enough explanation, and therefore added the grid and the numbers later in order to make sure they could give an explanation.

Question 4: Can We Relate Differences in Students' Work and Scores to the Observed Differences in Teaching Style and Classroom Culture?

Students in Ms. Aberson's class showed their work for almost all problems even if they were not explicitly asked to do so. Students in Ms. Baker's class also showed their work, although not as often, and students in the class taught by Mr. Collins almost never showed their work. This result can be explained by the different classroom cultures and the different teaching styles. If a teacher puts a lot of emphasis on giving explanations and showing the work, and puts this in practice by having students share their work, students are likely to follow the same practice on a test even if no prompts are added: It has become part of the classroom culture. Ms. Aberson and Ms. Baker both taught the unit in this style, whereas Mr. Collins used a more traditional style of teaching in front of the classroom, with less input from students. Students in Ms. Aberson's class may have shown their work more than students in Ms. Baker's class because Ms. Aberson explicitly reviewed the unit lesson before the test and explicitly pointed out once more the importance of students always showing the work. Differences in teaching style and classroom culture may have caused small differences on assessment tasks. Such differences are often subtle, however, and do not necessarily lead to differences in overall scores. Closely analyzing student work on particular problems can bring differences to the surface.

Chapter 7

The Design of Open–Open Assessment Tasks

Els Feijs

Jan de Lange

FREUDENTHAL INSTITUTE, UNIVERSITY OF UTRECHT

In Chapters 5 and 6, many of the assessment task formats were open–open tasks. De Lange (1995) argues that this format offers great opportunities for assessing and promoting student understanding. The term *open–open* refers to a task that is open for both processes used and solutions found. In other words, the answer can still be a number, a graph, or a formula, but the process of obtaining the result can involve a range of strategies. These may be higher-order student constructions that differ in their representation of informal, preformal, and formal mathematical ideas. This task format offers students multiple avenues to a problem solution, allows greater connections to be made within and between content strands, and furthermore allows for a greater range of student ideas to be exchanged. However, as shown in the previous two chapters, designing open–open problems is a demanding task. Subtle differences in visual presentation of a diagram or use of language can cause significant differences in student responses. Sometimes these differences can result in students engaging or not engaging in the problem.

The examples in this chapter are open–open tasks that have been designed by teachers and curriculum developers and that illustrate how a task can be altered to potentially yield a greater range of student strategies. Data for this study were gathered through classroom observation, teacher and student interviews, and teachers' analysis of student work. The classrooms were in middle schools with teachers using *Mathematics in Context* (MiC; National Center for Research in Mathematical Sciences Education & Freudenthal Institute, 1997–1998).

Our work with teachers shows that it is necessary to have teachers be at least passive experts when it comes to classroom assessment tasks so they can adequately judge the quality of the tasks they select, adapt, and create. Passive assessment expertise for teachers should include: (1) understanding the role of the problem context, (2) judging whether the task format fits the goal of the assessment, (3) judging the appropriate level of formality (i.e., informal, preformal, or formal), and (4) judging the level of mathematical thinking involved in the solution of an assessment problem.

PASSIVE ASSESSMENT EXPERTISE

To illustrate the importance of "passive assessment expertise," the first example focuses on the alignment of the test with the goals of the unit. An experienced teacher used the Looking at an Angle unit (Feijs, de Lange, van Reeuwijk, Spence, & Brendefur, 1998). The unit included 15 goals for students:

1. Understand the concepts of vision line, vision angle, and blind spot.
2. Understand the concept of steepness.
3. Understand the concept of glide ratio, or tangent.
4. Construct vision lines and blind spots in two- and three-dimensional representations.
5. Measure blind spots (or shadows).
6. Measure angles.
7. Understand the difference between shadows caused by a nearby light source and shadows caused by the sun.
8. Make scale drawings of situations involving steepness.
9. Understand the ratio between an object and its shadow caused by the sun for different times of the day and the year.
10. Make relative comparisons involving steepness problems.
11. Understand the relationship among steepness, angle, and height-to-distance ratio.
12. Choose appropriate views (top, side, or front) to draw situations involving steepness.

13. Understand the correspondences between contexts involving steepness that can be represented by a right triangle.
14. Use ratios to solve problems involving steepness.
15. Solve problems involving tangents.

To determine the kind of end-of-unit test a teacher would develop for this unit, the initial design was left completely to the teacher. The test as designed by the teacher (Figure 7.1) was then given to the stu-

Figure 7.1. The teacher's test.

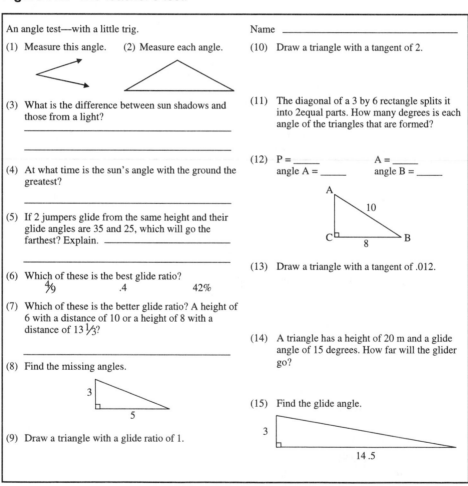

dents. The students' test results were, according to the teacher, surprisingly good. He was satisfied that the experimental unit had "taught" the students much *relevant* mathematics (in the sense of outcomes that are considered relevant from the more traditional point of view). Later, the test was presented to other teachers who also had taught the unit and who had participated in professionalization activities in order to be more successful in teaching the unit. These teachers found that the test (1) did not represent the content of the intended learning goals (i.e., vision lines and other important mathematical concepts were not addressed); (2) was not balanced in relation to the three intended levels of mathematical competencies (most problems require only Level 1 reasoning); and (3) did not present any problems in context.

From these experiences, a number of important lessons relevant to classroom assessment practices were learned. First, the teachers' interpretation of the goals of the curriculum unit can be quite different from the designers' intended learning goals. Second, the results of discussions with the other teachers indicate that teachers can reach at least the level of passive expertise. They may not be able to design and construct excellent assessment tasks themselves, but they are in a position to comment on and judge an existing problem on the basis of quality criteria. This also demonstrates the importance of professional development for teachers in the area of classroom assessment. It is both necessary and useful to provide teachers with such professional development activities.

DEGREES OF OPENNESS

Once a designer has a clear overview of the goals of the unit, there are still many choices to be made while designing an end-of-unit test—choices that are seldom easy. The more difficult decisions are related to the distribution of problems over the three levels and, in relation to this, the degree of openness of the problems in the test. To clarify such difficulties, we present another end-of-unit test that better fits the goals of the same experimental unit, Looking at an Angle. Three tasks within one context are presented in Figure 7.2. The relevant mathematical concepts are addressed at different levels by the various tasks. The context is one that is not only close to the contexts featured in the unit but is also close enough to the students for them to become engaged. The three tasks were included in the end-of-unit test when the unit was published.

Figure 7.2. Context tasks for Looking at an Angle test.

This is the map of the area they are in:

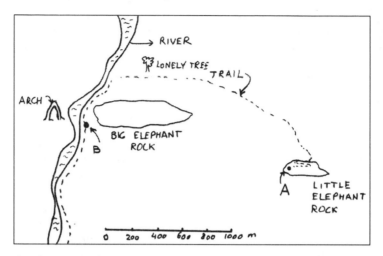

They have just climbed Little Elephant Rock. Theresia is at Point A to make a hang glider flight. But she will start the flight only when Jorge has descended the rock and has arrived at Point B. Jorge will hike, following the trail. Theresia follow Jorge with her eyes, from where she is sitting at Point A. After a while, near Lonely Tree, Jorge disappears behind Big Elephant Rock. Theresia waits and waits but Jorge seems to stay out of sight forever. He has been in the "blind area" for half an hour now.

1. Draw the blind area behind the rock.

2. How long is the part of the trail in that blind area? (Make an estimate using the scale line.)

Under normal circumstances, a person can walk about 2 or 3 kilometers per hour on a fairly easy trail.

3. Is there reason for Theresia to be worried?

Before the final test was published, however, another version of it was considered and tried out with teachers. The only task in the second version of the test was, "Is there a reason for Theresia to be worried?" It may look like a minor difference, but the goals assessed using this task in the first version (with two preceding tasks) differ considerably from the goals assessed by this stand-alone task. The difference became very clear when two groups of teachers worked on the two different versions of the test. The teachers responded to the tasks, and in their discussions that followed made it clear that the "long" version "led" the students to a solution for Theresia. The initial two tasks were not surprising to the students, making this a nice problem in three steps, with each of the steps involving only Level 1 reasoning. A student who starts immediately with Theresia's concern, however, has to mathematize the problem, and the best strategy to use may not be immediately clear. Omitting the initial two tasks therefore creates a problem that involves at least Level 2 reasoning.

This example shows the delicacy involved in designing open–open tasks. What constitutes a good test depends on many factors and requires much creativity. It is unreasonable to expect teachers to design their own tests. Our experience indicates that teachers can become passive experts, but becoming active experts is quite another matter. In summary, it is possible and necessary for teachers to become at least passive assessment experts. Components of passive assessment expertise are:

- the ability to align the goals of classroom assessment with those of the curriculum, and
- an understanding of the consequences of different degrees of openness among assessment problems.

THE CHALLENGES OF DESIGNING OPEN–OPEN ASSESSMENT TASKS

In the past, designing an end-of-unit test was not a major challenge for a teacher: Look at the exercises in the textbook; choose some simple, intermediate, and difficult problems; change the coefficients or signs, and there you go. Those rules are no longer valid in real-world-oriented, context-rich mathematics instruction that builds on students' present knowledge and follows a path from informal to formal mathematical concepts. However, it is not always obvious for teachers or for students that the rules have changed.

In a recent study in a U.S. inner-city school, a teacher designed an assessment task to go with the MiC unit, Expressions and Formulas (Gravemeijer, Roodhardt, Wijers, Cole, & Burrill, 1998). The teacher concentrated on the final, more formal questions, making the assumption that the information provided in the assessment could be rather scant and that pictures could be left out because the students would recognize the problem from similar problems in the unit. The results of the assessment problem were disastrous. A number of the lower achievers in the class did not even try to start solving the problem and only the very best were able to solve it successfully. A classroom discussion afterward revealed the weaker students' difficulties with the assessment: They did not try to understand the problem because it was too abstract and complex. Regrettably, the teacher made a small error in the layout as it was presented to the students, so that the illustration followed the text instead of being inserted into the text. Although the error substantially reduced the value of the assessment results, it shows how students are trained for tests. The moment they see an open space, many students start writing down answers—even before any questions have been asked. Figure 7.3 provides an example of student work to illustrate this phenomenon. It may come as no surprise that some of the students' work led to the teachers' reaction: "I don't understand your work." That is exactly what these students must have thought when they looked at the problem.

Following the disappointing experience described above, the teacher, together with the designers of the curriculum, redesigned the assessment problem. The new problem can be characterized as follows: It consists of a single, rather simple question in plain English, supported and illustrated appropriately for those students who are more visually oriented or have problems with the English language. Many students were successful in tackling the new version of the problem, and all students at least tried to solve it. Also helpful was that the picture provided was similar to pictures that students had seen before in the unit.

Although the assessment problem consisted of only one very straightforward question, students' solutions were not so straightforward. Students who solved the problem demonstrated at least four distinct strategies. The most informal solution was based on a drawing (Figure 7.4), a second strategy was of a very arithmetic nature (Figure 7.5), and finally students used two strategies that qualify as prealgebra: using arrow language (Figure 7.6) and using the tree rep-

Figure 7.3. Student work showing confusion.

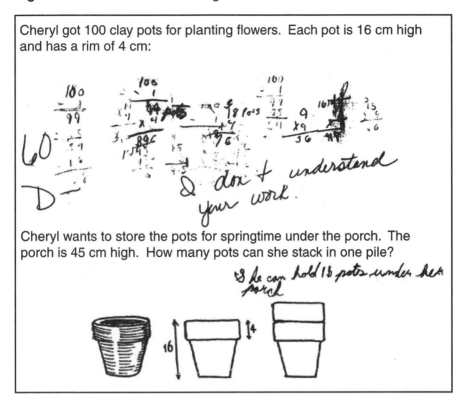

Cheryl got 100 clay pots for planting flowers. Each pot is 16 cm high and has a rim of 4 cm:

I don't understand your work.

Cheryl wants to store the pots for springtime under the porch. The porch is 45 cm high. How many pots can she stack in one pile?

She can hold 15 pots under her porch

resentation (Figure 7.7). Designers, teachers, and students alike considered this to be an excellent task. All students engaged in the problem, and its openness resulted in a variety of successful strategies. These strategies gave rise to very valuable feedback to the students, which in turn supported and enriched their learning process.

Reflecting on the design process, the strong points of open—open tasks are the simple language, visual support, straightforward questions, and the possibility of solving either by "common sense" or by formal mathematical procedures. Additionally, the interesting prealgebra solutions gave rise to a new learning experience, which illustrates how assessment can be a part of the learning process. In summary, if teachers are to be passive assessment experts, they need the ability to judge the elements of a good test: accessibility, understandability, fair use of representations, and openness to a variety of strategies.

Figure 7.4. Student work based on the drawing.

I already Know that one whole cup is 16 cm. and the Rims are 4. So I used 1 whole cup and I kept Stacking and each time, I stack I add 4cm. To 16cm (whole cup) I kept ~~stacking~~ and adding until I hit the number closes to 45cm

Answer: So Cheryl can probably stack 8 pot without going over 45 cm.

Great!

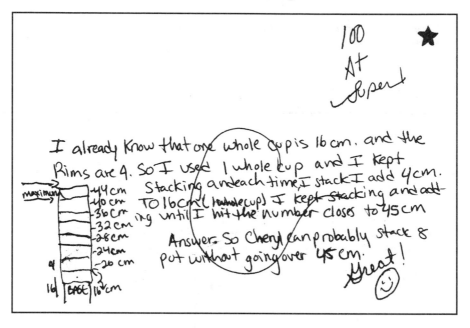

Figure 7.5. Student's arithmetic strategy.

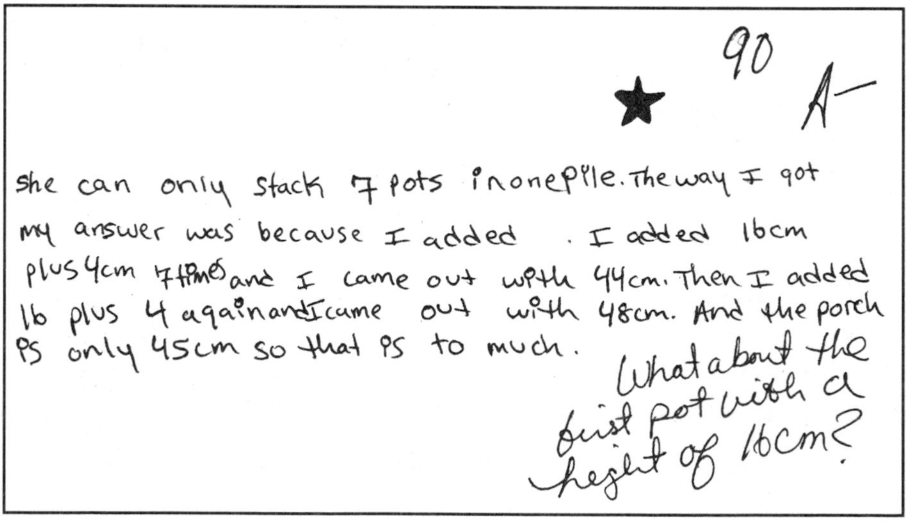

she can only stack 7 pots in one pile. The way I got my answer was because I added . I added 16cm plus 4cm 7 times and I came out with 44cm. Then I added 16 plus 4 again and I came out with 48cm. And the porch is only 45cm so that is to much.

What about the first pot with a height of 16cm?

Figure 7.6. Student's use of arrow language.

SIMPLE BUT COMPLEX ASSESSMENT

When designing an end-of-unit assessment task or test, the "rules" are:

1. Goals are made operational at all levels.
2. The use of context is balanced.
3. The test starts with easy "entry" problems.
4. Different modes of representation are used.
5. The mix of formal and informal is adequate.
6. The test offers opportunities for different solution strategies.
7. A fair amount of the mathematical content of the unit is covered.

In addition to an end-of-unit test, most teachers will use shorter, 10- to 20-minute quizzes covering a specific part of the unit or a specific content area. Such quizzes can address different levels. A teacher could, for example, design a task that "just" shows whether the students reproduce the mathematical content at the same level as it was presented in the unit, in which case the assessment problems will resemble those from the unit. However, it is valid to use test items that are somewhat more complex and give students the opportunity to show that they understand a certain mathematical concept, in which case

Figure 7.7. Student's use of tree representation.

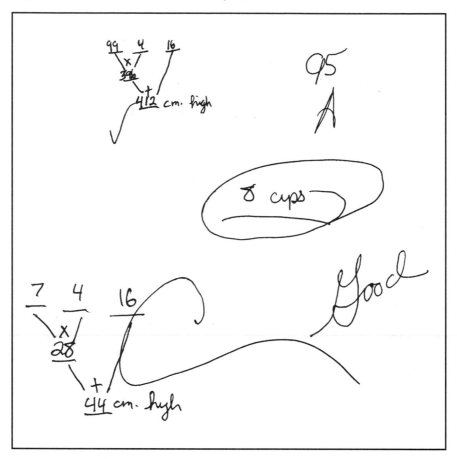

the assessment problem goes well beyond the problems in the unit but can be done by students who really understand the ideas.

An example of a more complex test was designed for and in consultation with a teacher at an inner-city middle school. The students had worked through the MiC number unit, More or Less (Keijzer, van den Heuvel-Panhuizen, et al., 1998), which deals with a variety of percent problems. The aim of the test was to see how well students understood percents and whether they were able to use percents in a somewhat more complex setting. The designers wanted the test to be realistic and simple. Two advertisements resulted from the design process. The first ad (Figure 7.8) was for a store called "Runaway" and promised a $30 discount on shoes, a $9 discount on T-shirts, and a $10 discount on sweaters. The second ad (Figure 7.9) was for a competitor, "Finishfirst," and showed blanks for two discounts: an overall percentage discount and a dollar discount on the purchase of three items.

Students were asked to answer the following question:

Complete the ad for the Finishfirst store by filling in a percentage that makes Finishfirst a better place to shop for one pair of shoes,

Figure 7.8. "Runaway" ad.

Figure 7.9. "Finishfirst" ad.

a sweater, and a T-shirt. However, do not give more discount than necessary to beat Runaway.

Although most, if not all, students clearly understood the question, they were not all equally successful in finding a solution. The teacher got a clear insight into the way that students worked with percents, however, even if they did not find the correct answer. For instance, the teacher could see how students dealt with the following problems: "What percentage of $89.95 is $59.95?" or "How much discount is $30 off of $89.95?" One student first computed 30% of $89.95, which is $27. Then he subtracted $27 from $89.95 to get $62.95. This came close, so he subtracted $2.70 (3% off), which resulted in $60.25. Next he subtracted 90¢ (1%) to get $59.35, which was close enough for him to conclude that the discount altogether amounted to 34%.

Another student made a table of percentage discounts from 33% to 38% and the resulting price with each discount, then concluded that the discount should be 34%. The student's notation was mathematically incorrect, but his conclusion was correct and so was his reasoning. Another student reasoned that 30% off is $27 and 35% off is $31.50, which is close enough.

It was also interesting to see whether and how the students solved the "big" problem. One successful student did not need much time: The regular price was $139.85 and the sale price was $90.85, so the customer would save $49. A 30% discount is $42 and a 35% discount is $49. So 140 × .35 = $49.00 and 140 × .40 = $56.00. Therefore, Finishfirst should give a 40% discount. It is interesting to see that the majority of successful students gave 40% as their answer instead of 36%, really taking the context into account. An example of student work on this problem is shown in Figure 7.10.

Figure 7.10. Student's solution of the "big" problem.

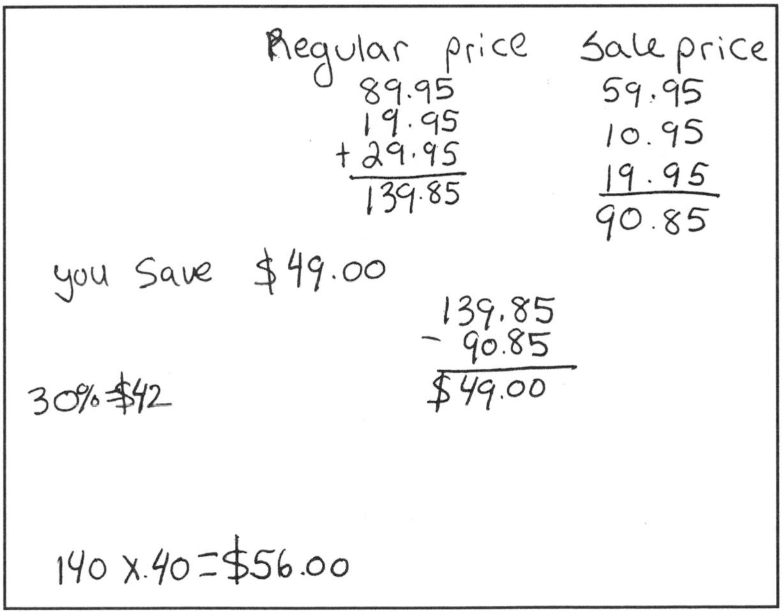

Reflecting on this test, both teachers and designers decided that it was very valuable. Solving an assessment problem that goes beyond the problems that were presented in the unit is worthwhile for the students. For teachers it becomes possible to measure whether students understand the subject, and students are offered an opportunity to demonstrate real problem solving. Such an assessment problem does not need to look complex and complicated. Simplicity and accessibility may very well be accomplished.

FINAL REMARKS

Open–open assessment problems offer a wide range of opportunities to get insight into students' performance. Although this is only one of many formats necessary to get a "full" picture of students' progress in learning for understanding, it is one that is close to teachers' and students' experience and therefore is very useful in building passive assessment expertise. However, these examples show how difficult, complex, delicate, and demanding the design and the understanding of the qualities of open–open assessment problems actually are. It is necessary to document problems and progress with respect to classroom assessment, as quality assessment is essential in order to achieve fairness to both students and the curriculum. The examples in this chapter show that assessment can provide excellent insight into students' progress.

Chapter 8

Investigations as Thought-Revealing Assessment Problems

Martin van Reeuwijk

Monica Wijers

FREUDENTHAL INSTITUTE, UNIVERSITY OF UTRECHT

In reformed mathematics education, complex cognitive skills like reasoning, mathematizing, generalizing, designing an appropriate plan to solve problems, reporting on the solving process, and communicating the findings are becoming important to the curriculum. To help students develop these complex skills, teachers need problems that demand the use of these skills, and there is an even larger need for problems that can be used to assess complex cognitive skills.

Larger problems in which students naturally act as professional problem solvers are called "investigations." The study of investigations reported in this chapter builds on *Framework for Classroom Assessment in Mathematics* (de Lange, 1999). Investigations were designed to deal with complex problems that involve mathematics from several content strands and to get insight into the thinking and understanding of students. We argue that investigations as assessment instruments can reveal student thinking and understanding, but only when similar kinds of activities are part of instruction as well (van Reeuwijk, 1995).

RESEARCH ON ASSESSMENT PRACTICES PROJECT

This project addressed a major research question, "How do teachers' assessment practices change when they are using reformed curricula?"

and a related subquestion, "How can the thinking processes of students be assessed?" In this chapter, we will discuss some of the findings related to this subquestion. The study was carried out with five middle school mathematics teachers at two inner-city middle schools in Providence, Rhode Island; these teachers were observed and supported over a period of 2 years. The teachers used the *Mathematics in Context* (MiC) curriculum (National Center for Research in Mathematical Sciences Education & Freudenthal Institute, 1997–1998). The first year of the study was also the first year of the implementation of the MiC curriculum at the two schools. The purpose of the study was to get insight into the teachers' assessment practices and document changes in these practices when a transition from conventional to reformed mathematics curriculum was made.

To facilitate the assessment of complex cognitive skills (related to Level 2 and Level 3 goals as described in the *Framework* by Jan de Lange), we identified problems from each unit of instruction that could be used as investigations: thought-revealing problems that would provide insight into students' competencies with respect to the complex cognitive skills. When we could not identify appropriate problems in a unit, we "borrowed" problems from other sources and edited them to match the content that was to be assessed.

At the beginning of the study, students working on investigations did not know what to do or what was expected from them. The problems were too open; much guidance was needed to help the students, and they asked for structure. It also appeared as if not every potential thought-revealing problem in an instructional unit was suited for use as an investigation. Also, teachers were not used to dealing with investigations for assessment purposes and therefore did not know what to look for, how the goals of a unit should be operationalized in an investigation, or how to recognize the level of abstraction on which their students were operating.

THE FLOOR-COVERING PROBLEM

"Floor Covering" (Figure 8.1) is a problem from the MiC unit, Reallotment (Gravemeijer, Pligge, & Clarke, 1998), an introductory unit on measurement and area in the MiC geometry strand. In the teacher guide, comments on this problem are presented as well as a sample student response. These indicate that students have to make decisions about how much of each covering must be purchased and that students must consider the costs as well. Different possible strategies are

A lobby of a new hotel is 14 yards long and 6 yards wide. It needs some type of floor covering.

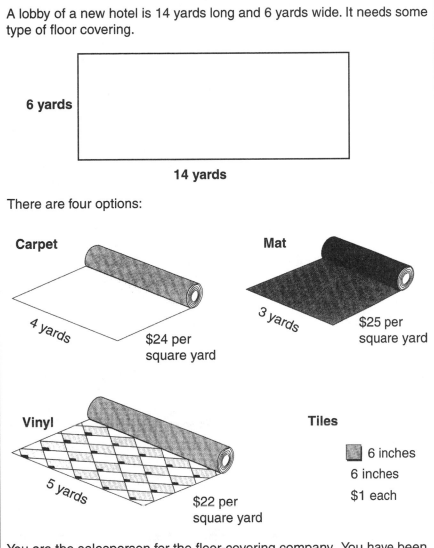

There are four options:

You are the salesperson for the floor-covering company. You have been asked by the hotel manager to present the total cost of each option along with your recommendation and your reasons for it. Write a report that explains your choice for the best floor covering for the hotel lobby.

described in the teacher guide, and illustrations of possible coverings are incorporated as well. These provide teachers with more insight into the problem and the possible student solutions. It is clear, for example, that patching is necessary for some types of covering and that students need to take into account the costs of any leftover floor covering.

Students and teachers started with this unit at the beginning of the school year. This problem illustrates the potential of, as well as the features and difficulties involved with using, investigations as assessments. In one of the classes, after the problem was presented, the students—in small groups—were left on their own; no additional information was given nor was an introductory class discussion enacted.

It was difficult for the students to engage in this problem. The context of the situation was too distant from their reality, and students were not used to investigation problems. "What do we have to do?" and "How do I have to start?" were questions raised by most students. The students were left on their own for a while. Some students started to manipulate the numbers. The area of the floor was calculated, and multiplications and divisions without clear explanations appeared on the students' papers (Figure 8.2).

The students had difficulties visualizing the situation and could not think of a way to use carpet from a roll that was only 4 yards wide to cover a floor with dimensions of 6 × 14 yards. The teacher decided to provide more information and suggestions on how to start the problem. On grid paper, she drew the floor to be 6 × 14 squares. Then, from another piece of grid paper, she cut one long strip four squares wide and rolled it up like a roll of carpet. She asked how much she would have to cut off this roll to cover the floor. The first suggestion was to cut a strip 14 yards long. After a discussion of how to cover the rest, one student suggested she cut four pieces, each 2 yards long, and put them on the remaining space that measured 2 × 14 yards. This filled the remaining area with only 2 square yards wasted. Another student came up with the idea of cutting pieces 6 yards long. Four 6 × 4 pieces would cover the floor, leaving a small strip of 2 × 6 yards as waste.

The ideas of the two students were discussed in class. The class agreed that the same strategy could be used for the vinyl and mat sections of the problem. Tiles were easier because six tiles in a row equal 1 yard. The problem was reduced to finding ways to cover the 6 × 14 floor with the four coverings. Most students could handle this simplified task, and started to cut and paste. The concrete material really helped. Some students needed the physical roll of covering and a pair of scissors for all options, while others moved to a more abstract level and made drawings of the floors.

Figure 8.2. Examples of student work on the floor-covering problem, starting calculations.

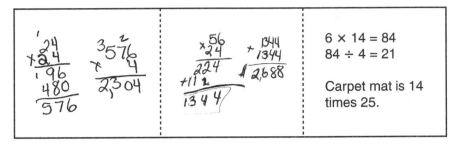

For each of the four coverings, Kim made drawings of the floor (Figure 8.3) and used the cut-and-paste strategy to find pieces that would cover the floor. She then calculated the costs by multiplying the number of square yards she had used of each covering by the price per square yard. Her work gives insight into the strategies she used. She cut pieces 14 yards long, which resulted in quite a bit of waste for the carpet (a strip 2 × 14 yards) and even more waste for the vinyl (a strip

Figure 8.3. Examples of Kim's work on the floor-covering problem, all four coverings.

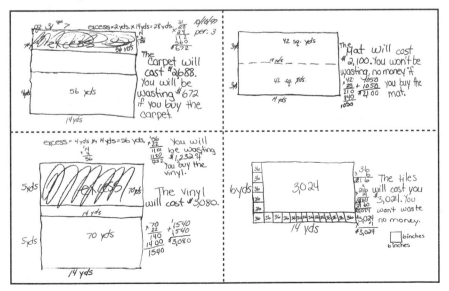

4 × 14 yards). Although she apparently did not think of other ways to cut and paste the coverings, she explained clearly what she had done. For each situation, she wrote a sentence and a conclusion that included the total cost for that covering. The drawings she made together with her calculations give a good picture of what she did. Kim was a typical student in the way she calculated the costs. She communicated her findings more clearly than most of the other students, and the quality of her sketches was higher.

After the floor had been covered, the next step was to find out the total cost. While it was possible to cut pieces of carpet (4 yards wide) and mat (3 yards wide) without any waste, using vinyl (5 yards wide) would result in waste. For the tile option, inches would have to be converted into yards. Because of these complications, finding the total cost for each material was not simply a matter of multiplying 84 (the area of the floor in square yards) by the price per square yard.

Although the calculations themselves were relatively easy, there were several to perform, and students had to organize their work to keep track of the results. Many students got so deep into the calculations that they lost contact with the overall problem. Although the purpose of the calculations was no longer clear, that did not hinder the students. The calculations themselves were sufficiently challenging and kept them busy. When the students had to organize the work, more than half of them became frustrated and gave up. They needed guidance to see the point of all the calculations. The teacher helped the students develop a chart to neatly put the results in. The students copied the chart and used it to record the findings for the four coverings and to compare and decide which of the four coverings was the best deal. The teacher's intervention helped get the students back on track toward solving the original problem.

The presentation of the problem and the calculations all happened in one class period. From the experiences in this class, it was learned that a more thorough introduction and more guidance was needed. Other teachers were informed about these experiences. Now they knew what they might expect. They introduced the problem with a brief class discussion and had the model of the carpet roll ready when they started.

As Kim's work (Figure 8.3) illustrates, there are several ways to cut and paste the coverings. Liesbeth was also a typical student, like Kim. Figure 8.4 shows Liesbeth's work for carpet and vinyl. She used drawings on grid paper to represent the floor. On the left is the floor and on the right is the piece of covering she used to cover the floor. Unlike Kim, Liesbeth looked for the solution in which she could use as few yards of material as possible. She wanted to minimize waste. From a

Figure 8.4. Examples of Liesbeth's work on the floor-covering problem, carpet and vinyl.

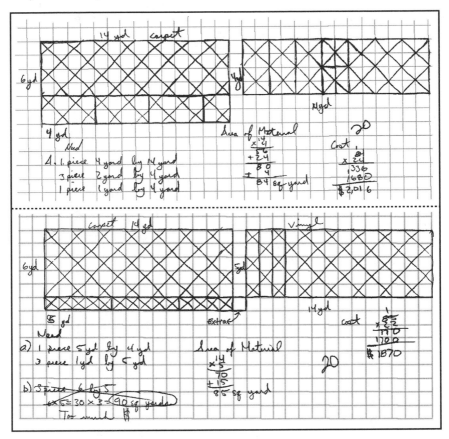

mathematical point of view, her results are "better" than Kim's, but Liesbeth was less organized, and it is harder to follow her scribbles and her strategies for finding the costs for each situation.

The drawings, sketches, and calculations show the various strategies the students used to cover the floor and to find the costs of each covering. A careful analysis of the student work shows that there was more involved than just finding prices. Students had to demonstrate an understanding of area measures, visualize the problem (although not really necessary, it did help), and write a conclusion for each of the four situations. All of these aspects gave insight into students' understanding and thinking.

SCORING AND GRADING

Finding the costs for each of the coverings was only part of the problem. Students were asked to write a report that explained the choice for the best floor covering. To help her students, one of the teachers wrote down guidelines for the report and shared them with her students.

GRADING SYSTEM FOR INDIVIDUAL REPORTS AND GROUP PROJECT

20 points for the group portion (5 points for each floor covering).
10 points for choosing a floor covering for your report.
20 points for the cost done correctly and written in your report.
20 points for listing the correct sizes of the pieces you needed to purchase.
20 points for explaining why you chose that floor covering over others.
10 points for explaining how much waste you had to purchase.
Total Possible Points: 100

Each student had to hand in a report using the group results from the first class period (covering the floor with each of the four options). The grading system helped the students quite a bit. Now they knew what they were expected to do and what their report should include. During the second class period, the students worked on the investigation, using the grading system as a checklist, and they could do much more on their own. The teacher walked through the classroom and helped individual students but did not need to have a whole-class discussion because everybody understood what to do. At the end of the second class period, students were given a homework assignment: to write the report using the grading system as a checklist. Two days later, students handed in their reports, and the teacher graded their work.

Kim's report by itself does not give much insight into what she did: "If I were the salesperson, I would advise you to buy the mat. Because it's cheaper and it fits better so you're not wasting any money." Using only the report to judge her work would be unfair. Liesbeth's report was similar to Kim's. Giselle's and Justin's reports explain quite clearly what strategy they used. The reports don't give insight into what they actually did, but they do give a nice, clear solution to the problem. Giselle wrote, "I pick vinyl. I bought the prices by multiplying five times seventeen. It cost $1,870. It wasted 1 sq. yard-unit. I bought it because it might look nice when you put in and more easier to put and nice on kitchen floor." Justin wrote:

> I think that the carpet is the best one to buy. First of all, the carpet is the least expensive one to buy. One other reason is because it [is] comfortable to walk on. It only costs $2,016. It is because I got a 4×14 piece, then I got a 4×4 piece and cut it through the middle horizontally. Which gave me two 4×2's, then I got a 4×3 piece and cut it through the bottom line, which gave me a 4×2 and a 4×1. Then I took the 4×1 and cut it in half horizontally. When I finished, I had no scraps left over.

Most of the reports are like those written by Giselle and Justin: a couple of paragraphs in which the student explains his or her choice of floor covering and gives the cost. Giselle based her choice on what "might look nice" and be "easier to put." These are two valid arguments, but they are not related to the mathematics. Her conclusion is not based on vinyl being the cheapest option. Justin also used an effective argument for his choice, which he described as "easier to walk on," but he also explained his calculations. Although the cost is incorrect, he tried his best to make a point. He explained clearly how to cut the carpet and cover the floor without waste. For Justin, "no waste" was more important than "cheapest." Justin's report was one of the better ones in the class. For Kim, it is unfair to base an opinion on the report alone. Giselle's and Justin's reports look nice, but for a final picture of their work, the calculations also should be taken into account. The teacher had given the students guidelines, so the quality of their work can be based on the criteria in the guidelines.

REFLECTIONS ON THE PROBLEM

The floor-covering problem is complex. Students must demonstrate different kinds of skills: basic standard algorithms as well as complex cognitive skills such as reasoning and generalizing. The first time this problem was presented, students initially had difficulty in taking ownership of it. Although the context seems transparent, it is quite different from that of students' daily activity. Students also were not used to such an extensive problem, and that may have been an important factor in their initial difficulties. Students also were not used to making sketches or using concrete materials. Instead, they focused on the numbers and the calculations. Later in the school year, after students had done more investigations, these engagement problems disappeared. The reports that students wrote at the end of the year and the way they organized their work were of higher quality.

Students were asked to write a brief report, but such "products" do not guarantee that the thinking processes of the students will be elucidated. It is not easy to grasp students' thinking processes. The report by itself, with a simple conclusion in the form of advice to the hotel manager, is not enough to get a good picture of students' thinking. The guidelines presented by the teacher helped communicate what was expected.

Finding open problems with clearly stated expectations is not a trivial task. The reports produced by the students included not only the mathematical arguments they used to decide which floor covering would be best. Students presented other effective arguments such as "easiness," "looks nice," and "more fun"—arguments that often are used to make real decisions. Finally, this problem involves a lot of computation. Students gave most of their attention to the calculations and eventually lost the connection with the overall question, "Which covering is the best choice?"

FEATURES OF INVESTIGATIONS

Not every problem is suited to being used as an investigation. The floor-covering problem illustrates that one needs to carefully think over the task that students are expected to do. From this and other studies (e.g., Kemme & Wijers, 1996), a list of crucial features of good investigation tasks has been developed.

- An investigation should fit the curriculum. This means that the problem should be functional and fit a long-term learning process. For example, "area" in the floor-covering problem is a topic in the regular curriculum for these students. A good investigation is integrated into "regular" mathematics instruction. An investigation will not contribute much to the learning of mathematics when it is very different from the regular mathematics curriculum.
- The problem should provide students the opportunity to use the mathematics they have learned as well as the opportunity to develop new mathematics and mathematical thinking. In the floor-covering problem, students have to demonstrate their understanding of area, and they are given an opportunity to come up with new strategies for covering the floor.

Related to the previous point is the feature that the problem should be open enough to allow for more than one approach; this allows students to operate on a comfortable level of abstraction. An example of such an open problem is shown in Figure 8.5. This is a problem from the MiC unit, Ups and Downs (Abels, de Jong, et al., 1998). Students have to match tables, graphs, and reports on sunflower growth and create the missing elements. Although this problem may not have all the characteristics of an investigation, the open-endedness and the different approaches on different levels of abstraction are very clear. One rather concrete approach to handling the problem is to start with the written reports, sketch a graph for each, and look for graphs with the same "shape." In another approach, students may start with the tables and look for matching graphs, and if these are not available, create the graphs from the table. The reports are the last items to match in this somewhat more abstract approach.

To create the opportunity to have students demonstrate a variety of skills, an investigation might have two components: (1) solving a problem and (2) designing (or constructing) a "product." This second component appeals to students' creativity and can make the problem more realistic. Writing a report to a (business) organization, writing an article for a (fictitious) journal, or designing a model of the problem situation are examples of product design.

The following is an example of an investigation with such a product. This is a problem from the MiC unit, Tracking Graphs (de Jong, Querelle, Meyer, & Simon, 1998). A graph of the race of three runners, A, B, and C, is presented (see Figure 8.6); the product students have to deliver is an article for the school paper that includes all of the important facts about this race. To be able to write the article, students need to interpret the graph in terms of the context. For instance, a student cannot write in an article, "Graphs A and B intersect at (12, 2600)." Although from a mathematical point of view, this is a correct statement, in terms of the race this has no meaning. For the article they should translate this into the context of the race and write, for instance, "At 12 minutes into the race runner B overtook runner A, whose speed was dropping badly." Because the product is specified, students need to do more and different mathematical activities.

Another feature of investigations is that the initiative to solve the problem should be with the students. Students should be encouraged to come up with their own problem-solving strategies. To make it interesting to students, the investigation needs to be authentic—or realistic—and challenging. In this context, realistic means "real to the students." The problem does not necessarily need to be embedded in a

Figure 8.5. Sunflowers. From "Ups and Downs" (p. 13) by M. Abels, J. A. de Jong, M. R. Meyer, J. A. Shew, G. Burrill, & A. N. Simon, 1998, in National Center for Research in Mathematical Sciences Education & Freudenthal Institute (Eds.), (1997–1998), *Mathematics in Context*. Chicago: Encyclopædia Britannica. Copyright © 1997 by Encyclopædia Britannica. Reprinted with permission.

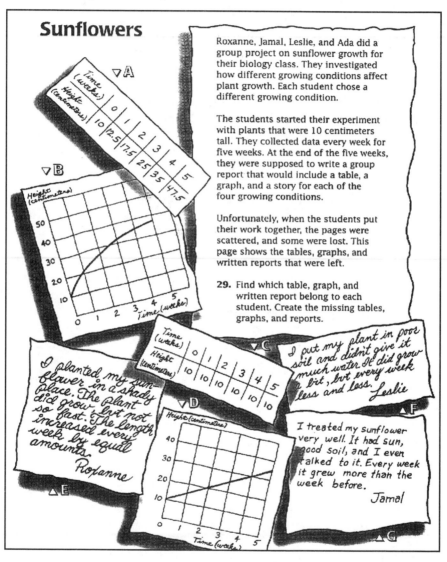

Figure 8.6. Graph of a race. From "Tracking Graphs" (p. 8) by J. A. de Jong, N. Querelle, M. R. Meyer, & A. N. Simon, 1998, in National Center for Research in Mathematical Sciences Education & Freudenthal Institute (Eds.), (1997–1998), *Mathematics in Context*, Chicago: Encyclopædia Britannica. Copyright © 1997 by Encyclopædia Britannica.

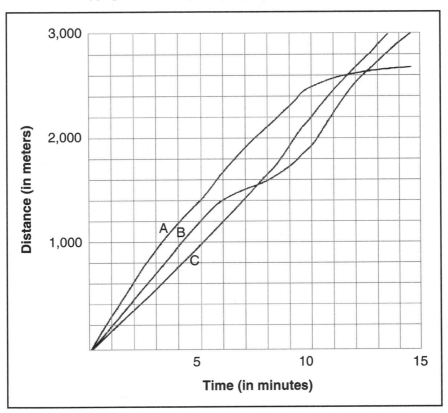

real-world context—mathematics itself also can be the context—but the problem situation needs to make sense to the students.

Often investigations can best be done in groups. This allows students to learn from one another by discussing the options, using convincing arguments for or against choices that are to be made, and splitting up the work that is to be carried out. In the floor-covering problem, students worked in groups but each individual had to hand in a report.

It must be clear to the students what they are expected to do. In the example of the race, students had to hand in answers to the entry questions and an article for a newspaper. The product (e.g., a report, a presentation, a letter to somebody, advice) that students hand in as the result of their investigation should include a solution to the problem, insight into the process by which the solution was found, and a conclusion. This implies that the criteria that are used to evaluate the product need to be specified and to be clear to the students.

Students should organize their work and come up with a format for the product themselves. In order to be able to judge the quality of the product, guidelines are needed. Teachers need these guidelines so that they can judge the quality, and students need guidelines so that they know what is expected from them. A good investigation takes this into account. In the floor-covering problem, students are asked to play a role in the problem. For example, "You are the manager of a company, and you have to write a letter to your staff explaining the decisions that the company has to make."

REFLECTIONS ON INVESTIGATIONS

During instruction, students need to learn how to solve investigation problems. In the beginning of the learning sequence, the problem can be formulated as less open, and more direction may be needed (e.g., providing hints and suggestions on how to design a plan to solve the problem). This helps students develop strategies for solving larger problems. When students have become familiar with investigations and have developed ways to approach and solve the problems, less guidance may be needed.

Investigations are good means for getting insight into students' thinking, but even relatively simple ones like the floor-covering problem are time-consuming to administer. The distinction between instruction and assessment is not so clear with respect to investigations. Students can learn a lot through investigations, and a teacher does not need to grade and score all of the investigations that the students work on. A good investigation—because of its features—is not easy to design. As mentioned before, most reformed math curricula integrate investigations, but the mathematics addressed in the investigation are not always clearly stated. For each investigation, therefore, a teacher needs to ask, "What mathematics are addressed?" and "What do I expect from my students?" in order to clarify the goals of the investigation.

Based on our experiences, investigations clearly can play an important role in documenting students' thinking. Especially promising is the potential for finding out what level of reasoning the students are using. The investigations and their products described in this chapter show the potential of investigations, what they might look like, and how they can be used. To gain more insight into the exact characteristics of a good investigation, more research is needed and investigations need to be designed and tried out with a wider variety (in both age and ability) of students. To document growth over time, investigations need to be administered with the same students over a longer period. Then we will be able to tell how students develop problem-solving skills and higher-order thinking skills. Finally, a discussion of investigations would be incomplete without mentioning perhaps their most important feature, especially for students: "Investigations can be fun!"

PART IV

EMBEDDING ASSESSMENT IN INSTRUCTIONAL PRACTICE

In this part, four stories are presented involving the problems of embedding standards-based formative assessments in instruction. These problems also were identified during the development and implementation of the MiC materials.

In Chapter 9, Making Instructional Decisions: Assessment to Inform the Teacher, Martin van Reeuwijk discusses his finding that because the MiC materials are to be used flexibly, teachers needed to plan with a possible path in mind, but be willing to modify the plan as needed based on both informal and formal assessments.

Chapter 10, Enriching Assessment Opportunities Through Classroom Discourse, by David C. Webb, documents that the teachers' primary goal was to facilitate students' successful completion of a unit of instruction, with success gauged by students' responses to verbal questions, engagement in daily lessons, and completion of individual seatwork or homework. Tests and quizzes then were used to confirm information gathered through these indicators. Although teachers used evidence gained through assessments to calibrate test grades and inform reports of student progress, they were more inclined to devote considerable time to the investigation of classroom assessment when they understood its potential for improving student learning.

In Chapter 11, Collaborative Partnership: Staff Development That Works, by Ann Frederickson and Michael Ford, Frederickson, a sixth-grade teacher, reflects on her experiences and the need for a professional development program that focuses on classroom assessment. She contends that this is critical if the reform goals are to be met.

Similarly, in Chapter 12, Retracing a Path to Assessing for Understanding, by Teresa Her and David C. Webb, Her reflects on her development as a consequence of using the MiC materials and being involved in a research project. She sees the process of learning she went through as a potential model for practical pedagogical change.

Overall, these stories show how the common distinction between instruction and assessment is problematic when teaching a reform curriculum. Furthermore, these studies make the need for an ongoing professional development program on classroom assessment apparent.

Chapter 9

Making Instructional Decisions: Assessment to Inform the Teacher

Martin van Reeuwijk

FREUDENTHAL INSTITUTE, UNIVERSITY OF UTRECHT

The story in this chapter focuses on teachers' methods for gathering information to inform their instructional decisions. Teachers usually plan what to do, what content to address, what pages from the textbook to cover by when, which pedagogical approach to use, and so on. During instruction, they regularly check whether students are following the intended learning trajectory and whether they need to adjust the plan. Teachers use a variety of assessment instruments to perform such checks.

To gain insight into student learning, teachers need appropriate assessment techniques that capture the learning process. Teachers then can use the information gathered through assessment to improve student learning in two ways.

- To provide students with feedback on their individual performance (so they will know how they are doing and where they need to improve).
- To make instructional decisions and adjust instruction when needed.

This chapter focuses on the formative purposes of assessment— more specifically, on assessments that inform teachers' instructional decisions. The two research questions for this study were:

- What assessment strategies and instruments do teachers use for making instructional decisions?
- How do they use these strategies and instruments?

The assessment practices of four middle school teachers were investigated, and the data show that informal methods of assessment (e.g., checking homework, class discussion, observing students' work in progress) had a significant impact on teachers' instructional decision making. Teachers used the data they gathered using informal assessment techniques as evidence to support the intuitive picture they had in mind for each student. Formal assessments had less impact on more immediate forms of instructional decision making, but affected long-term planning and informed teachers about how to improve their teaching of an instructional unit the next time.

PROJECT SETTING AND METHODOLOGY

Researchers observed four middle school teachers at two inner-city middle schools in Providence, Rhode Island. The teachers used *Mathematics in Context* (MiC; National Center for Research in Mathematical Sciences Education & Freudenthal Institute, 1997–1998) and were followed over a period of 2 years. They were visited four to five times a year for about a week each time. Each visit focused on one or two assessment moments. During these visits, classrooms were observed, teachers were interviewed, and student work on assessments was collected. Assessment issues were addressed in collaboration with the teachers: Researchers worked with teachers to design assessment tasks, discuss (existing) assessment tasks, reflect on assessment practices, score student work, and so on. Once collected, the data were analyzed with the following goals in mind:

- To build a picture of the teachers' general assessment practices.
- To document how their assessment practices changed when they implemented the MiC reform curriculum.
- To understand how teachers use assessments in their instructional decision making.

The focus of this chapter is on the third goal. The object of decision making is the instructional plan. First, how teachers plan instruction is described (what factors play a role, how teachers set their goals, and how they make an instructional plan); a sketch of the teaching situation is described in two settings (a traditional setting and a setting where MiC is used). Second, how to check the feasibility of an instructional plan is described through an examination of the instruments, strategies, and tools that teachers can use to check whether they are on track. Finally, two classroom examples are given to illustrate instructional decision making in practice.

PLANNING INSTRUCTION

A teacher who teaches a "traditional" curriculum in a "standard" way often follows the curriculum as explained in the teacher guide that comes with the textbook series. Often students complete two pages a day, and the teacher administers a quiz each week and a test at the end of each chapter. Students also might be asked to take an external (district, state, or national) test. In a traditional mathematics classroom, not much input is expected or needed from the teacher (Romberg, 1992). Instruction simply follows the plan that is outlined in the teacher guides and textbooks for the curriculum. Traditional textbook series are not designed for flexibility of use; rather they are based on the assumption that all teachers, students, classes, and schools are essentially the same. Filling out the weekly lesson plan is quite easy: The teacher simply can copy information from the teacher guide, cover two pages a day, and give a quiz at the end of the week. Of course, this description of a traditional mathematics classroom suggests a very passive role for the teacher. Indeed, traditional teacher guides and textbook series are designed to minimize the teacher's influence on student learning.

In MiC classrooms, teachers are not expected to be passive if they use the materials in the ways they were designed to be used. Such teachers need to actively set goals for a lesson, chapter, semester, or other unit of instruction. They need to use the content objectives (e.g., goals, standards, benchmarks) presented in the accompanying teacher guides, then interpret, actualize, and adjust these objectives to match the specific situation in their classroom. In other words, a teacher needs to adjust her curricular plans to match her own classroom situation. Whereas traditional mathematics curricula are not designed to be adjusted to a teacher's needs or to be aligned with a specific classroom situation, the MiC materials provide the teacher with ample opportunities to tailor the curriculum to her specific needs and requirements. To design lessons that fit specific classroom situations, use the flexible materials effectively, and take an active role in instructional planning, teachers must be able to claim ownership of the curriculum: They must have a thorough understanding of the MiC curriculum that they are putting into practice, and they must understand the origins, purpose, and objectives of the problems.

In summary, an MiC teacher is not completely on her own: Student and teacher materials that are part of the MiC curriculum provide guidance. Examples and suggestions for lesson plans and methods for teaching are included, but a teacher can use the curriculum flexibly. An MiC teacher is expected to use all available sources to create a set of goals and expectations that lead and direct instruction. Such a set of goals and expectations can be called a hypothetical learning trajectory (Simon, 1995): The teacher has a certain path in mind for the students to follow.

CHECKING THE PLAN

When the teacher has an instructional plan, she needs to check periodically to see whether students are on track and whether the plan is feasible and realistic. The teacher then can use the results of these checks to adjust the plan or to confirm that students are following the path and that no change is needed. There are various ways to perform such a check. Actually, each check is a moment of information gathering and thus assessment. In our study, we distinguished two kinds of assessments that are relevant to instructional decision making: formal and informal.

Formal assessments include instruments such as tests, quizzes, and other "tasks" that have been planned as assessment moments. *Informal* assessment strategies include observing students' work, collecting student work, checking homework, and conducting class discussions. Informal assessment strategies are often part of the daily classroom discourse. They are not always anticipated in the lesson plan, and they do not always give an honest picture of each individual student. A student may have a thorough understanding of the mathematics, but if he rarely does homework and does not participate in class discussions, his understanding will not show up through informal assessment.

A teacher often uses both informal and formal assessment strategies to get a picture of students' learning, gauge whether students are on track, and determine whether the plan should be adjusted. The teacher often uses the information gathered through informal and formal assessment strategies and instruments to provide feedback to students as well as for instructional decision making.

CASE STUDIES

The following two examples illustrate some of the aspects that play a role when a teacher designs an instructional plan and wants to check whether the plan should be adjusted. These examples show the kinds of decisions each teacher had to make, the situations she had to face, and what she decided.

Both case-study teachers—Ms. Greenfield and Ms. Nielsen—used MiC. For a teacher using MiC, it is important to realize that mathematical concepts are introduced in one chapter, revisited in other chapters, and sometimes not formalized until 1 or 2 years later. It is therefore crucial that a teacher knows where an activity is leading and what stage of conceptual development it is targeting. This helps the teacher set feasible and realistic goals and expectations for her students. Because it may take a few years for teachers to take ownership of the MiC curriculum as intended, MiC provides teachers new to the program with suggestions for planning and sequence.

Ms. Greenfield: Assessing Students' Knowledge of Statistics

Classroom norms in Ms. Greenfield's seventh-grade class changed during the half-year after she started using the MiC curriculum. Students learned to explicate their thinking, discuss their findings, clarify which strategies they had used to solve a problem, and so on. The teacher no longer considered the "textbook" answer to be the only relevant outcome for a given problem. Participation in class, the method or strategy used by a student to arrive at an answer, and the way the student showed his work had become aspects of the classroom that Ms. Greenfield looked at and considered to be important. When her classroom was observed, Ms. Greenfield was teaching Dealing with Data (de Jong, Wijers, Middleton, Simon, & Burrill, 1998), an instructional unit on descriptive statistics, statistical measures, and graphs. Students had worked with box plot, number-line plot, stem-and-leaf plot, minimum, maximum, range, median, mode, and mean. The teacher's instructional plan for the unit included the following goals:

- Students should learn the various statistical measures and graphs.
- Students should learn how to use the various statistical tools in solving problems.
- Students should learn how to decide which tool to use.

While students used measures and graphs to solve problems in the second-to-last section of the unit, Ms. Greenfield walked throughout the classroom. She had discussed homework with the class and had gotten the impression that students were doing well and had learned what she had outlined in the plan. She was not sure, though, and she needed evidence beyond the informal information she had gathered from walking through the classroom and talking with the students. To check her impressions, she gave a test. The problems on the test were straightforward and similar to the problems in the unit that the students had been working on. A table with the average life-spans of 25 animals was presented, and students were asked to construct a stem-and-leaf plot and a histogram. They also were asked to describe what kind of information is provided in a stem-and-leaf plot but not in a histogram. They were asked to use the graphs to estimate the average life-span of all animals and to use the table to calculate the overall average. The last question asked students to come up with the average life-span of humans and explain what would happen to the average that had been calculated earlier.

While the students were working on the test, Ms. Greenfield discovered that a majority had difficulty with the problems. Although the topic had been taught previously, a little over half of the students did not know how to construct a stem-and-leaf plot or a histogram. They could not tell how histograms and stem-and-leaf plots were different, and they had a hard time relating the graphs to the statistical average. Ms. Greenfield had thought that this was a "standard" assessment with problems that would be routine for most students; however, she let the students work on the problems for one class period before collecting their work. When she examined the work, she was shocked by how poorly her students had performed. What she had thought were standard problems turned out not to be trivial after all. Students did not have the skills to construct graphs themselves and were not able to make a connection between the measures and the graphs. Ms. Greenfield used a formal assessment tool (the test) to check whether her students were "on track." When she discovered that her informal assessment was not accurate, she had to adjust her plan and make unanticipated instructional decisions.

Ms. Greenfield concluded that she needed to spend more time on the skills and level of understanding listed in the goals and that her students probably needed more structure and practice time to master the skills. Her analysis of the unit, Dealing with Data, revealed that the unit focuses on interpretation and the use of graphs and measures. The unit does not provide many situations or problems in which students make graphs or compute measures. Because the students had not spent time on these skills (making graphs, computing measures), they had not yet developed all the necessary skills at a routine level. However, her analysis did not explain why students could not relate graphs to measures or tell the differences between the graphs.

Instead of continuing with the next (and last) section in the unit (which includes problems that reflect on the entire unit), she decided to explicitly address the students' issues with the unit and give them extra practice to develop a deeper understanding of the underlying statistics. She made up an activity in which students were asked to construct graphs and calculate statistics. Students worked in groups of four on the following activity:

MAKING CENTS

Each group has 40 pennies. Answer the following questions in your group:

- Find a way to organize your pennies to record their dates (years).
- Make a stem-and-leaf plot for the years of your pennies.
- Make a number-line plot with your pennies.

The students organized the data (the pennies) and made graphs. While they were working on the activity, the teacher also encouraged them to use a box plot in order to "force" them to find the median and quartiles. Each group drew its graphs on an overhead transparency. After about 15 minutes, Ms. Greenfield started discussing the problems with the whole class. Each group explained what it had done, while Ms. Greenfield displayed its transparency. In the discussion, she explicitly paid attention to the graphs, their attributes, and how to calculate averages and other statistical measures. In the discussion, the median was mentioned in relation to the box plot, and students gave the following explanation: "Divide in two equal halves to get the median . . . and then divide [the] first half again in halves to get [the] lower quartile." Ms. Greenfield asked if anybody could tell what the mode was. Rosa answered, "Mode is most, so . . ." Then she looked at the number-line plot and said, "Aha, it is 1998."

After each group's transparency had been displayed and discussed, students discovered that although the scales of the graphs were different, they all had the same shape. From the graphs, students could see the median, mode, and average as balancing points. The properties of each statistical measure and how to calculate it were summarized, and after 15 minutes of discussion, it seemed that all of the students understood the mathematics. Ms. Greenfield was pleased, and she decided to skip most of the last (summary) section of the unit. Instead, she picked one problem from this section and asked the students to work on it for extra practice.

Looking back at Ms. Greenfield's instructional decision making, she used the "making cents" activity as a summary to reflect on the statistics that students had learned earlier. The sequence of instructional decision-making steps Ms. Greenfield went through can be summarized by the following events:

- The teacher had a plan; she knew what she expected from her students.
- The teacher had a feeling (through informal assessment) that things were going okay, but she was not sure.
- The teacher felt the need for a second opinion, so she administered a test.
- The test results were different from (worse than) what she had expected.
- An analysis of the results on the assessment and a closer look at the unit, Dealing with Data, clarified what had gone wrong: Students had not gotten enough opportunities to construct graphs and calculate measures for themselves, and they had not yet developed an understanding.
- Based on the test results, the teacher adjusted her instructional plan by adding an extra activity.
- The teacher checked the students' results on the extra activity to see whether they were back on track.
- Students demonstrated that they understood and could use the mathematics to solve problems, so the teacher was able to proceed to the next section.

One activity and a class discussion about the activity helped the students understand how the graphical representations relate to each other, what the (dis)advantages of each representation are, how the statistical measures relate to each other, and where the measures can be seen in the graphs. The discussion—especially the presentation of student work on the overhead—contributed much to students' understanding of the unit goals.

Ms. Greenfield decided to use only one problem from the last section so that students could practice what they had just learned. She skipped the rest of the section and concluded that she would ask students to work on other statistics problems later in the year. Ms. Greenfield was able to make this decision because she had a plan in mind, she knew what her students had learned in the unit, and she knew what her students needed to learn before they could progress to the next unit. She was pleased because she fulfilled the goals of the unit.

Ms. Nielsen: Reinforcing Students' Statistical Skills

All of Ms. Nielsen's eighth-grade students had used MiC in seventh grade, so they had been used to the new classroom culture for a while. Ms. Nielsen was teaching the unit, Insights Into Data (Wijers, de Lange, Shafer, & Burrill, 1998), which deals with such "advanced" statistics as regression and with the critical use of statistics. In this unit, students solve problems and build arguments using statistical graphs and measures that have been introduced and developed in earlier MiC statistics units. Explicit attention is paid to concepts such as representative, sample, and bias, and students learn to look critically at statistical information. The major goals of the unit include the following:

- Students should learn what linear regression is and how it works.
- Students should learn to solve problems about linear regression and other statistical measures and graphs.
- Students should develop a critical attitude toward the use of statistics (including sampling).

In addition to the goals of the unit, Ms. Nielsen had some other goals and expectations. Her eighth-grade students were scheduled to take the state test a couple of weeks later. She knew that there would be statistics on the test and that her students would be asked to demonstrate their understanding of and ability to construct statistical graphs and measures. Because this is prerequisite knowledge for Insights into Data, it was also an implicit goal of the unit. For Ms. Nielsen it was an explicit goal, and she added it to her plan of instruction.

- Students should be able to understand and construct statistical graphs and measures.

Ms. Nielsen didn't know whether students had learned these skills yet, but the unit offered ample opportunity to find out because it asks students to use a variety of statistical graphs and measures to solve the problems. While the students worked on problems from the unit, Ms. Nielsen walked around and informally gathered information through observation—asking questions of individual students and looking at their work. She found that students were easily able to read and interpret histograms, line graphs, scatter plots, and box plots. From the graphs, they were able to estimate the mean, median, and mode.

The students had difficulty, however, when they were asked to construct graphs or calculate statistical measures. Students had a passive understanding of the statistics (reading and interpreting), but could not actively construct and calculate statistical measures and graphical representations. Ms. Nielsen decided to change the focus of the unit for a while from using, interpreting, and being critical about statistics to constructing and calculating statistical graphs and measures. She used problems from the unit and adjusted them to reinforce students' graphing and calculating skills. Here is an example.

Use the data you collected for your group on the growth of bean sprouts.

- Make a box plot for the final lengths.
- Make a histogram for the data.
- Calculate the mean, median, and mode.
- What is the difference between the information you can see on a histogram and the information you can see in a box plot?
- Compare your graphs with those of another group in your class.
- Which graph makes comparing easiest? Why do you think so?
- Compare your mean, mode, and median with those of the other group. Which measure do you think is best to use? Explain why.

Ms. Nielsen collected and corrected student work on this activity. Based on the work she collected, she concluded that the students were able to make graphs and calculate statistical measures when explicitly asked to do so. Most students organized the data in a list from small to large; indicated halfway (median), the 25% point, and the 75% point; and made the requested box plot. For the histogram, students had to choose a class width. Different groups of students came up with different numbers of classes. Because they had compared their graphs with those of other groups, students realized that different class widths are possible and thus histograms can be different. Box plots, however, are fixed and should be the same for all groups. Computing mean, mode, and median was not difficult, although some students had to look up the definitions. Again, in the discussions between the groups, students became aware that there is not one best measure, but that the reason for using a specific measure is more important.

To make sure this success was not incidental, Ms. Nielsen decided to practice the same kinds of activities during the few weeks remaining before the test.

Ms. Nielsen used Insights into Data to find out whether students were ready for the state test. She also used problems from the unit to better prepare her students. Here is the sequence of Ms. Nielsen's instructional planning and decision making.

- The teacher had her own goals and expectations in addition to those of the unit.
- Through informal methods of assessment (walking through the classroom, talking with students), the teacher noticed that her students needed extra time to work on developing and practicing specific skills.
- Because she was quite clear about the skills she was looking for, she felt confident about the information she had gathered and did not seek additional confirmation.
- The teacher adjusted instruction to meet her own goals.
- The teacher gave students the opportunity to practice making graphs, using problems from the unit.

Ms. Nielsen had a clear plan in mind and gave priority to students' performance on the upcoming state test. Rather than put the existing curriculum aside in pursuit of this goal, Ms. Nielsen adjusted it to match her own objectives. She used existing problems from the MiC unit and added questions to the problem situations. For example, where the unit asked students only to interpret a presented scatter plot about the body lengths of babies, she asked them to make a histogram and box plot, and to compute mean, median, and mode. In another problem from the unit on the lengths of fish in which students had to do linear regression, she added questions about calculating mean, mode, and median, and making a histogram to represent the data graphically.

Insights into Data assumes that students have completed the prerequisite MiC statistics units in which graphing skills are developed and students learn to calculate statistical measures. While most of the students in Ms. Nielsen's class previously had studied some statistics, Ms. Nielsen was not sure whether they were still able to use the skills they had developed in previous years. She felt responsible for her students' performance on the upcoming test, so she decided to spend extra time on these skills. As illustrated above, she embedded the practice of these skills into problems from the unit, so students were asked to think about sample, representation, and bias, and to adopt

a critical attitude toward their use of statistics. And in the same contexts, students could practice the skills of making and computing
statistical graphs and measures.

Reflections on Ms. Greenfield's and Ms. Nielsen's Plans

Although both of these teachers knew what they wanted and had
a plan in mind, they had not written it down either for themselves or
for their students. When asked about their plan, however, they were
able to make explicit their goals and expectations. Both teachers worried that their students were "lacking" certain skills needed to make
statistical graphs and calculate statistical measures, and both teachers
felt that their students needed extra practice. Ms. Greenfield's informal assessment gave her the impression that things were going well,
but a more formal assessment showed that things were not going as
well as she thought initially. Ms. Nielsen also gathered information
informally, but her methods provided enough evidence that she did
not need to conduct a more formal assessment.

These two examples of assessment focus primarily on providing
the teacher with information to answer an explicit question related
to instructional decision making. The purpose of the assessment was
not to provide students with feedback or to collect grades, but to inform the teacher. (Note that in both examples the teachers' decisions
were about the "mastery" of skills. This is not by accident; many
implementation issues deal with mastering skills, and teachers worry
about students' mastery of basic skills. Especially during the first years
of implementation, teachers do not yet have a good overview of the
curriculum, do not recognize that topics will be revisited in later units,
and therefore do not realize that students need not master a topic completely the first time it is introduced.) During interviews, both teachers indicated that it was sometimes hard to judge whether the class
was on track and whether the track they had in mind for their students was the right one. Ms. Nielsen and Ms. Greenfield often provided one another with advice, and they both expressed that it was
important to have a colleague—someone to talk to, share experiences
with, and receive support from.

RESULTS

Although these two case studies focus on informal assessment practices, they also provide examples of how the teachers used formal as-

sessment to guide their instructional decision making. Interviews, field notes, and student work confirm that these case studies represent typical assessment practices.

All four teachers in the study were "good" teachers. They were motivated, inspired, and open to reform. Although the two teachers in the case studies had worked with a traditional curriculum before their implementation of MiC, their teaching practices were not passive, and they used both informal and formal methods of assessment within the boundaries of the more traditional textbooks. In the traditional situation, however, the teachers did not have to make many instructional decisions because of the prestructured teaching–learning sequence. Over a period of 2 years, these teachers underwent a transition from the traditional way of managing a classroom to more professional, flexible, and responsible ways of teaching and making instructional decisions. In the beginning of this transition, the teachers felt insecure because they were more responsible for the teaching–learning process than they were used to. They had to decide what to do, what to skip, and what to focus on. The curriculum materials and teacher guides helped, but required more input from the teachers than they were used to. It was not possible to anticipate every situation that could possibly occur in the teaching–learning process. The teacher guide could not contain every possible action for teachers. Especially with a reform curriculum like MiC, in which teachers act as flexible guides through learning processes, there was no script for teachers to follow.

After 2 years, the teachers had taken ownership of the curriculum. They knew what they expected from their students, and they had set clear goals for their classes. The four teachers in the study used mainly informal assessments to gather data when they needed to know whether they had to adjust instruction. Although the teachers rarely needed formal evidence to justify their instructional decisions, they were not always confident about the decisions they made and would have liked an easy way to find out whether they were on the right track. Discussions with colleagues played a critical role in helping teachers become more comfortable with their own decision making.

DISCUSSION AND CONCLUSIONS

What assessment strategies and instruments do teachers use to inform their instructional decision making? How do teachers use these strategies and instruments? Based on the field notes, student work, and interviews gathered from four teachers' classrooms, teachers use a variety of informal and formal assessment instruments and strategies. To make short-term or immediate decisions, teachers often use informal strategies or small, easy-to-design formal assessments (e.g., quizzes; see case study of Ms. Greenfield's classroom). If information gathered informally is not convincing or seems biased, however, a second opinion may be sought—often through formal assessment.

For instructional decision making in the short term, informal assessments are used more often than formal assessments, such as end-of-chapter or end-of-unit assessments. When information gathered through formal assessments is used, it is mostly to make decisions for the long term. Teachers use information from formal assessments mostly for changes in instructional planning for the next time they teach the unit (usually the next year), because formal assessments often are used at the end of a period of instruction to bring a closure to a sequence of lessons.

Increased responsibility may be a problem for teachers who implement a reform, less prestructured curriculum. With a reform curriculum such as MiC, teachers have more freedom to adjust instruction to the needs of their classroom. A consequence of the increased freedom can be that teachers lose the overview and feel less secure about what they are doing. From the study, we learned that making the goals and expectations (the instructional plan) explicitly available as an outline for instruction can be a helpful support. Such an outline helps teachers make decisions on the spot about what to do and what to skip; what is important and what is not. Performing regular checks (informal and formal) to see whether students are still on track helps too. It may take 2 or more years for teachers to take ownership of a curriculum, to use it as a flexible guide rather than a script, and to take full advantage of the range of classroom assessment opportunities that reform-based materials provide.

Another conclusion from this study—although not much elaborated on in this chapter—is the finding that teachers feel more secure when they share experiences with colleagues. Talking about classroom experiences with another teacher is an effective way to reflect on one's teaching. Reflective discussions often support intuitive findings that a teacher has gleaned through informal assessments, and this makes instructional decision making more grounded.

Chapter 10

Enriching Assessment Opportunities Through Classroom Discourse

David C. Webb
UNIVERSITY OF WISCONSIN—MADISON

In spite of the critical role of instructionally embedded assessment in the teaching–learning process, studies that document teachers' classroom assessment practices have offered little evidence about the ways that teachers use assessment to inform instruction. Teachers accustomed to assessing student learning of skill-oriented mathematics curricula often struggle with interactive assessment practices to inform instructional goals aligned with reform mathematics curricula. So that teachers can recognize and take greater ownership of classroom assessment practices that support instructional decision making, case studies of the ways in which teachers use classroom discourse to support student learning and guide instruction are needed.

DISCOURSE-BASED ASSESSMENT PROCESSES

Gathering evidence and providing feedback are two assessment processes that often are embedded in classroom discourse. When teachers prompt students to share, explain, and justify their problem solutions, teachers provide all students with an array of mathematical representations against which they can contrast their own conceptions. Verbal feedback (from either the teacher or the students) can be seamlessly integrated into the flow of instruction when teachers place a priority on sense making, explanation, and justification.

Teachers regularly gather evidence to assess students' prior knowledge, level of engagement, interpretation of tasks, and disposition toward mathematics. Whereas classroom discussions present an ideal opportunity to explore student understandings and inform instructional decisions, waiting until the next quiz or chapter test yields information too late. Assessment of students' conceptions therefore is best accomplished at the site where student learning develops, through classroom discourse in which the teacher can simultaneously monitor student interpretations of the task, solicit additional information from students, and communicate expectations for mathematically valid representations. The medium of classroom discourse provides a supportive context for students to share partial understanding and misconceptions, and instructionally embedded assessment allows teachers to gather information about students' partial understanding or misconceptions and to further investigate students' intended meaning through additional probing, guiding, and reframing of questions.

Mathematically substantive feedback provides students with contrasting information to improve their responses to mathematical tasks and their articulation of mathematical principles. Feedback can be oral or written, formal or informal, private or public, geared toward an individual or a group (National Council of Teachers of Mathematics, 1995). Feedback can be directed to frame initial reactions to an unfamiliar problem, highlight changes in student conceptions over time, and juxtapose current performance with hoped-for performance (Wiggins, 1993). Feedback can be withheld (e.g., continued observation of student progress), offered indirectly (e.g., eliciting responses from other students), or provided as a direct response to one or more students.

Students receive feedback from a variety of sources, including verbal feedback from teachers and peers, that provide a coherent portrait of classroom norms and expectations. Classroom discourse can be used to provide confirming and relational feedback from several directions, giving students the opportunity to share and critique the explanations, arguments, strategies, and responses of other students. The ongoing use of classroom discourse as a source of feedback also promotes assessment of students' own and one another's work. Black and Wiliam (1998) argue that self-assessment cannot be treated as "an interesting option or luxury; it has to be seen as essential" (p. 21). Ideally, classroom assessment practices should contribute to students' internalization of performance criteria so that students can negotiate teacher expectations and engage in meaningful self-assessment. To accomplish this requires an instructional environment in which performance criteria are open, students have opportunities for reflection, and student self-assessment is modeled and valued.

CASE STUDY OF DISCOURSE-BASED ASSESSMENT: MS. KOSTER

The following case study of one teacher's discourse-based assessment practices is part of a series of studies conducted by the Research in Assessment Practices (RAP) study group. (For more details of this case study, see Webb, 2001.) The instructional goals and practices of teachers selected for this particular study were aligned with the assumptions regarding how classrooms promote learning for understanding (Carpenter & Lehrer, 1999). Because these learning objectives require greater use of written and verbal language, teachers needed to complement their use of time-restricted, paper-and-pencil quizzes and tests with more discourse-based assessment techniques. Overall, teachers recognized classroom discourse as a critical aspect of their assessment practice.

The primary research question guiding this study was, What assessment practices do mathematics teachers in the middle grades use during instruction to gather evidence of student learning? Data sources were selected to provide a record of verbal and visual teacher–student interactions and to record teachers' conceptions of and struggles with discourse-based assessment practices. Teacher interviews, classroom observations, and video recordings were used to develop a record of teacher–student communication and to chronicle how teachers utilized the instructional activities in each unit of *Mathematics in Context* (MiC; National Center for Research in Mathematical Sciences Education & Freudenthal Institute, 1997–1998). Three semistructured interviews (each approximately 60 minutes long) were administered according to a protocol developed to follow assessment-related constructs that emerged during classroom observations: one interview prior to the 6-week period, a second interview after 3 weeks, and a third interview at the conclusion of the 6-week period. Teachers' discourse-based assessment practices were documented through daily observations and videotape of each lesson. Using audio equipment, we were able to record whole-class, group, and individual teacher–student interactions. Classroom observations and field notes focused specifically on teacher–student interactions that potentially could be used for assessment purposes.

Ms. Koster was selected for in-depth study as the result of discussions with Design Collaborative researchers who noted her use of classroom discourse in observation reports and described her instructional practice as a rich source of evidence for investigating discourse-based assessment. Data gathering for this case study was initiated while Ms. Koster was using several algebra units from MiC. Ms. Koster had been teaching elementary and middle school students for over 20 years and, at the time of this study, had a seventh-grade mathematics and language arts teaching assignment. The classroom in which this study took place was characterized as an "accelerated" seventh-grade class. Ms. Koster was an experienced teacher whose love for language was evident in the way she presented mathematics to her students. She used mathematics as an opportunity for students to engage in logical reasoning and use precise, specialized vocabulary. The use of realistic contexts and language in MiC supported her underlying instructional goal, which was to demonstrate to students that the study of mathematics involves more than just finding a correct answer. Beyond routine procedures and problem solving, mathematics also involves appropriate use of language (i.e., communicating of mathematical principles, explaining solution strategies, and justifying the validity of proposed methods). As she explained, "I can't teach anything without the importance of language—to use the right words for the right spot. Or if you don't know [the words], at least a verbal flexibility to try and explain what you want to get across" (Koster, interview, May 6, 1999).

In Ms. Koster's class, the spoken word was used as the primary medium to communicate mathematical thought, and "depth of thought" was established as the goal for students to strive toward when sharing an explanation. Ms. Koster felt that she gained the most reliable information about student understanding through her interactions with students. She viewed the context of instruction as an effective forum for communicating her expectations and for providing guidance and feedback on student responses to problems. Ms. Koster's comfort with and dependence on students' verbal responses influenced how she selected and used tasks with MiC and led her to take an instructional stance where she could quickly adapt lessons according to students' prior knowledge and degree of interest. Ms. Koster demonstrated a strong ethos of respect for her students and honored her students' unique talents and idiosyncrasies. When asked to describe her conceptions of assessment, she replied, "It goes to the heart of respect and caring. It's not our job to get 'em and point out that we got it and you don't" (Koster, interview, May 6, 1999). Rather than using assessment as a means to highlight students' shortcomings, Ms. Koster portrayed projects, presentations, and written tests as "opportunities for students to showcase their learning." Her understanding of the various ways in which students learn mathematics motivated her to adopt a broad view of classroom assessment and to develop methods to elicit representations of student learning that were more authentic.

PRINCIPLES AND PRACTICES
OF DISCOURSE-BASED ASSESSMENT

Ms. Koster viewed student engagement as an essential aspect of instruction and assessment. To motivate student engagement with the problem context, Ms. Koster argued that she had to first "hook the students" and reel them into a problem situation. Capturing and maintaining student interest was an important instructional goal reflected in many of Ms. Koster's lessons, and these instructional hooks allowed her to promote and sustain classroom discussions, which she then could use to assess student learning. During the beginning lessons, Ms. Koster often asked students a series of unexpected questions that were laced with humor and creativity. As an example, for the growth charts problem in the MiC unit, Ups and Downs (Abels, de Jong, et al., 1998, pp. 14–16), in which students are asked to graph and interpret growth charts for young children, the text included a photograph of an infant being weighed on a doctor's scale. Ms. Koster decided to introduce this problem context as follows.

> [Ms. Koster is in the front of the class, facing the students who are seated in groups of three to four. Ms. Koster has just turned to page 14 of the teacher guide. (Time stamps for the videotape are noted in the left margin.)]
>
> 13:55 *Teacher:* Cute baby on page 14! [Students in unison, "Awww."]
> 14:05 *Teacher:* Please turn to 14. [Waits for students to quiet down.]
> 14:22 *Teacher:* Look at the baby. Roger, name the baby.
> *Roger:* Wow! Name the baby?
> *Teacher:* Sure, name the baby.
> *Roger:* Brian.

Teacher: This is Brian?—Julie, name the baby.

Julie: Ah—ah—Judy.

Teacher: Judy! [Laughs.] We had a discussion about this name earlier this morning. Name the baby.

Oliver: Habib.

Teacher: Charles, name the baby.

Charles: Bob.

Teacher: Bob, the baby. Alysha, name the baby.

Alysha: Rover.

15:26 *Teacher:* Rover? [Students laugh.] Hector, why bother?

Hector: What?

Teacher: Why bother? Why fool around with naming the baby?

Russ: 'Cause it's fun.

Teacher: Yeah, 'cause it's fun.

Christina: Because when it gets older you can't just call it "It."

Teacher: Okay. Backup. Rewind. Look at page 14. It's a whole page of statistics—research and statistics. And if you are not careful, what happens when you research and write down statistics? You lose all connection to the fact that what you are really trying to understand is a human. We want to know if this baby is thriving. We want to know if this baby is growing and developing the way it is supposed to. So perhaps if I suggest to you, fool around and think of the baby as a human rather than as a chart full of statistics, those of you who go into research and read charts full of statistics stuff will remember to keep your humanity with you. So, look at the chart full of statistics. This baby is weighed how often?

(Koster, video transcript, March 10, 1999)

Along with other techniques that Ms. Koster often embedded in her lessons, this excerpt demonstrates how she used instructional technique and light humor to capture her students' attention. As you may have noticed, this interaction includes no discussion of mathematics content. Rather, Ms. Koster used the problem context to evoke student interest and establish a purpose for what her students were about to do. This use of contextual, instructional hooks is a pattern of practice that was noted in at least one third of the observed lessons. During an interview that took place 3 weeks into the unit, Ms. Koster elaborated on this instructional goal.

It is my style, so I don't know that I consciously think of this, but I need to convince them that this is worth thinking about. I need a hook. I need to tell them I ran a marathon. I need to say, "Hey buddy, I want to rent a motorcycle." I think through how I am going to hook them. "We gotta give a name to this baby before we can measure this baby." That, to me, is the big deal. Reel them in a little bit. (Koster, interview, March 26, 1999)

Ms. Koster argued that to motivate student engagement with the problem context, she had to first "hook the students" and reel them into the situation. Capturing and maintaining students' attention was an important goal reflected in many of her lessons. Ms. Koster's attention to student engagement promoted and sustained classroom discussions, which then could be used to assess student understanding. Clearly, Ms. Koster understood student engagement to be a prerequisite for discourse-based assessment.

Discourse-Based Assessment Techniques

Analyses of videotape and field notes revealed three distinct patterns of discourse-based assessment that elicited qualitatively different student responses and provided unique opportunities for instructional assessment: (1) "temperature taking," (2) funneling responses, and (3) probing assessment.

A majority of the observed discourse-based assessment opportunities represented what Ms. Koster later called *temperature taking*. When asked to characterize how she assessed student learning, Ms. Koster remarked:

I am not big on calling a question and waiting for waving hands in the air, and so you will see me use a stack that has their names on them. My attempt is to call on every kid once a day. To at least hear them say, "I don't know" or "I get it" or "Could you explain it again?" or "246"—whatever it is. That is the temperature taking. I walk around and look over shoulders (Koster, interview, March 2, 1999).

During whole-class discussion, Ms. Koster asked temperature-taking questions at a brisk pace, offering little or no feedback. Her instructional stance during temperature taking was strictly to solicit information and, instead of offering feedback, ask students to judge the validity of their responses. After eliciting a response, Ms. Koster either asked different students the same question or moved on to a new problem.

This technique included choral responses, visual gestures, and instances in which Ms. Koster asked the same (or closely related) questions to several students. Even though temperature taking provided only superficial evidence of student learning, according to Ms. Koster it was a fundamental process for making instructional decisions.

With the *funneling responses* technique, Ms. Koster used a series of questions or statements to lead students to a particular response. She used hints, suggestions, and sequential questioning to elicit the "correct response." With this approach, Ms. Koster often used student responses to emphasize a specific procedure, make a point, or instruct. The manner of closed questioning used with this technique restricted the range of student responses, which resulted in limited representations of student knowledge. Student responses were used to display and reinforce information rather than reveal alternative representations or solutions.

With the *probing assessment* technique, additional questions or statements were used to probe the meaning of students' initial responses. Observers identified three variations on this probing technique.

- *Restate*. Prompt students to restate their response in a different way or clarify their response.
- *Elaborate*. Prompt students to share their interpretation of a problem, often by explaining a strategy or justifying the validity of a solution strategy.
- *Inquiry*. Use counterexamples, another interpretation, or alternative representations to shift teacher–student interaction to the sustained inquiry of a problem context or concept. Often, new questions were used to prompt the deliberation of previously elicited student (mis)conceptions.

Whereas temperature taking helped Ms. Koster sustain student engagement and informed her choice of appropriate follow-up questions, probing assessment revealed more substantive representations of student knowledge. Using relational questions, Ms. Koster was able to assess the extent of students' conceptual connections. Answers elicited without elaboration indicated the potential for student understanding but did not provide substantive evidence to assess the meaning of a student's response.

The reactions and responses of the students during temperature-taking activities often were used as a basis for instructional adjustments. When student engagement was in short supply, Ms. Koster would ask new questions, draw a different representation, make connections to a novel students had read (in language arts), or share an experience from her childhood. When student engagement was sufficient, temperature taking was used to reveal opportunities for further instruction or additional probing of student responses. These instructional decisions were based largely on intuition or interest in exploring a student response.

> So much of it is a gut level. It's, "Okay, you got it!" And some of it is, "Is this you struggling or is this everyone struggling?" And some of it is, "That's a good thought. Let's go even further. Let's make it a bigger world." (Koster, interview, March 2, 1999)

In many cases of temperature taking, multiple answers for the same question were solicited from a random sample of students. The following excerpt from Ms. Koster's classroom details the style of teacher–student interaction that was observed during these episodes and highlights the type of student responses that preceded a shift to other discourse-based assessment techniques:

> [In Ups and Downs (Abels, de Jong, et al., 1998), students read about the accomplishments of Joan Benoit, who won the women's marathon in the 1984 Olympics in a time of 2 hours, 24 minutes, and 52 seconds (p. 29). On the next page, students are told that a marathon runner "will lose about 1/5 liter of water every 10 minutes." Problem 5 asks students, "How much water do you think Joan Benoit lost during the women's marathon of the 1984 Olympics?" Ms. Koster begins asking students questions from the front of the classroom.]

> 17:15 *Teacher:* Question 5 asks, "How much fluid do you think Joan Benoit lost?" And you were given the amounts to use for your calculations in the paragraph above. Anthony, what did you come up with?
> *Anthony:* About 17 liters.
> *Teacher:* Excuse me?
> *Anthony:* About 17 liters.
> *Teacher:* About 17 liters she lost? Wow, that's a lot.
> [Many students grumble, indicating disagreement.]
> *Teacher:* Hang on. Hang on. Mike, what do you have?
> *Mike:* About 2.8.
> *Teacher:* About 2.8, 2.9. We're talking liters. All right. Kirk, what do you have?

      Kirk: Ah, 5.2 liters.

17:52 *Teacher:* 5.2 liters. Wow, we are all over the map here. Julio, what do you have?

      Julio: 2.9 something.

      Teacher: 2.9 something?

      Julio: Yeah.

      Teacher: Brenda?

      Brenda: 2.8 liters.

      Teacher: Okay. John Eaton?

      John: I did, I think I might have done the calculations wrong. Actually, I definitely did. I got 72.5 liters. [Muffled laughter from students]

18:10 *Teacher:* That's a lot of liters!

      (Koster, video transcript, March 18, 1999)

With regard to assessing student understanding, temperature taking allowed Ms. Koster to assess the extent to which a sample of students successfully solved the problem. When students' answers diverged significantly from her expected response, Ms. Koster shifted to a combination of funneling and probing assessment techniques to reveal students' interpretation of the problem.

      [After coming to a consensus that Joan Benoit finished the race in approximately 140 minutes, Ms. Koster asks students to share how they found the liters of sweat lost during the race. Ms. Koster leads the discussion from the back of the classroom.]

22:25 *Teacher:* You know how much she loses every 10 minutes. How much?

      Student: One-fifth. One-fifth.

      Teacher: A fifth of a liter. About how many minutes are we going to calculate for her? Key word here, "about." [No response from students. Ms. Koster shifts to a funneling responses approach.] Kids. Look right here. How many minutes is she running?

      Students: [Choral, mixed] 135. 140. 145.

      Teacher: Somewhere between 135 and 145. Are we happy with, let's say, 140? Let's say you forgot to subtract that first 10 minutes when she really wasn't losing anything yet. So let's say we've got to figure out how much she lost for about 140 minutes. And we know how much she

loses every 10 minutes. How do you set that up? What
does it look like?

John: Um—

Teacher: [To John] Go set up.

John: [Walks up to chalkboard.] I agree with the 140. Or I did
145 into groups of 10. So then I had 14.5 groups of 10—
then I got those into groups of 5 'cause that would equal
1 liter since it's one-fifth for every 10 minutes. And then,
5 goes into—um—I just rounded [14.5 groups] to 15, and
5 goes into 15 three times. And so, I knew that I was
going to be a little less than 3, so I said, like, it would be
a little less than 3 liters.

Teacher: And look. What's the acceptable range?

[A student volunteers to explain his strategy and then forgets
what he was going to say. Ms. Koster proceeds to write a
ratio table on the board. Alex volunteers to share his
solution method.]

Teacher: Speak really loudly, Alex.

25:30 *Alex:* One-fifth of water for every 10 minutes. So to get
1 liter, it would be 50 minutes. So, I multiplied 145 and
then divided by 50. And that came up with 2.9.

Teacher: That's kind of cool. What you did is you figured out
how to make this a whole number. So he said, "For every
1 full liter, that is—" How many minutes?

Students: Fifty.

Teacher: Fifty. Because if it's 5 times this, it would also be 5
times the number of minutes. That's a different way to
think about it. What you have to see is if this figures for
10 minutes, how are you going to determine the
unknown for about 140 minutes?

(Koster, video transcript, March 18, 1999)

In addition to monitoring student engagement, Ms. Koster used
temperature taking to reveal a need for further clarification, explanation, or instruction. When Ms. Koster shifted from temperature taking to other discourse-based assessment methods, there was a noticeable
difference in the cadence of teacher–student interaction. Students
required more time to articulate their solution strategy, and more-
complex approaches often needed to be clarified. To maintain the pace
of the lesson, Ms. Koster guided the discussion to emphasize particular aspects of the problem. In the excerpt above, students wanted to

deliberate the length of time for perspiration. After two students shared their method for finding the minutes of perspiration, Ms. Koster positioned the discussion to focus on the next part of the problem and bypassed further deliberation of what she perceived to be a moot point.

In addition to students' choral responses and group gestures, Ms. Koster also used student enthusiasm and responsiveness to questions as evidence to gauge whether students were ready to continue with the lesson. When student engagement and responsiveness were high, Ms. Koster increased the pace of the lesson and briefly addressed answers to tasks, sometimes questioning students immediately after the question was first read from the text. In contrast, when students were overtly disengaged or did not produce written work for an assigned problem context, she asked additional questions or modeled problem-solving processes to lead students to a point where they could more successfully engage in the problem context.

Students Responding to Other Students

To promote student self-assessment, teachers need to give students opportunities to engage in processes of assessment, such as interpreting responses and providing feedback. One way in which Ms. Koster encouraged student self-assessment was through peer assessment. The following selection is an example of how Ms. Koster deferred the interpretation of one student's unexpected response to other students for further interpretation and feedback. This exchange demonstrates how Ms. Koster and her students contributed to instructionally embedded assessment by listening to one another and articulating their interpretations of one another's thought processes. In this excerpt, students are midway through the review of a homework assignment related to a problem from the Ups and Downs unit (Abels, de Jong, et al., 1998), in which the problem context asks students to find the growth factor of an aquatic weed. Previous problems in this section involved whole-number growth factors. This was the students' first investigation of a situation that involved a decimal growth factor. Table 10.1 was written on the board during this class discussion.

> The aquatic weed *Salvinia auriculata* also spreads by an annual growth factor. The first time it was measured, in 1959, it had grown to cover 199 square kilometers. A year later, it covered about 300 square kilometers. In 1963, the weed covered 1,002 square kilometers of the lake. The factor is not two, but another number. Use your calculator to find this decimal growth factor. (pp. 41–42)

Table 10.1. Table on the chalkboard during a homework discussion in Ms. Koster's class.

1959	1960	1961	1962	1963
199	300			1,002

[Ms. Koster is at the board asking students to describe the method they used to find the growth factor. Alexia has already shared that she found a growth factor of 1.5 but could not explain why it worked. Ms. Koster now shifts her attention to Kirk.]

Teacher: Kirk, what did you do?

Kirk: Actually, I got a whole different answer.

Teacher: Okay.

Kirk: I thought [the growth factor] was 0.5—because you're only adding half of that number to get 300. So I don't see why you need 1.5, 'cause if you times it by that much it would be, like, 500.

Teacher: Stop a minute. Where did you get the half a number, the 300 bit?

Kirk: [From his seat in the back of the classroom, Kirk points to a table on the board.] 0.5. [Kirk has puzzled look on his face.] Er, wait. Half—no, I took 199, half of that, which is the yearly growth, which is about 99.5. Which would equal 298, and that's about 300.

Teacher: [Writing the numbers on board, with arrows labeled with 0.5 leading from number to successive numbers] Is this what you're saying?

Kirk: Yeah.

Teacher: [To the class] So he's thinking the growth factor is 0.5. [Addressing Kirk] Am I understanding you correctly?

Kirk: Yep.

(Koster, video transcript, April 9, 1999)

As more students gave Kirk their attention, he became flustered and restated an incorrect account of his method. Instead of sharing her own interpretation of Kirk's method, Ms. Koster allowed Kirk to articulate it for himself. Even though Kirk gave a procedural explanation, established norms for student articulation (which emphasize student communication of thought processes) allowed other students to interpret and respond to Kirk's proposed strategy.

Teacher: Jacob, did you get 1.5 as your growth factor?
Jacob: Um hmm.
Teacher: Do you have any clue as to why or why not this [pointing to Kirk's method on board] stands as correct—or not?
Jacob: Well, I think it's incorrect. 'Cause if you do it on your calculator it doesn't work.
Teacher: So, you punched in this. And multiplied it by this. And what did you get? [Jacob mumbles.] And while he's figuring, here's part of the strategy of a successful thinker. [Ms. Koster moves away from the board to front center of the classroom to address all students.] Can you try to understand what he's saying so you can point out what maybe he needs to rethink? Or are you sitting there saying, "Whatever. It's Kirk." [Smattering of laughter] Try to understand his way of thinking. [This comment to Kirk is meant in jest. As the self-nominated class clown, Kirk takes the comment in stride and smiles.] Linda, help us out here. Guys, don't forget what you're going to say.
(Koster, video transcript, April 9, 1999)

Ms. Koster has now made the purpose of this interaction explicit and presented it in terms of a challenge. Ms. Koster's effort to have students respond to Kirk's method reflected her goal of having students appreciate the perspective of others and demonstrated an approach that she regularly used to include students in providing feedback to others. By leveraging Kirk's misinterpretation of growth factor, she provided a timely learning opportunity to reinforce the process of finding an exponential growth factor and how it should be represented. In the exchange that followed, the combined perspectives of Linda and Rudy provided other connections to the decimal growth factor that might not have occurred if Ms. Koster had corrected Kirk's method herself.

Linda: I don't think he's saying that you multiply it by 0.5; you add 0.5. Because when you multiply something by 1.5, all you're doing is—you're adding half the number that you multiply.
Teacher: Where did the 1 go?
Linda: The 1? If you multiply something by 1, it's the same number.
Teacher: [Turning to Kirk] Did you try this?

Kirk: Yeah, well I thought it was—um, I—adding 99—er—0.5 to it. Sort of. So— [Kirk does not appear to be persuaded by Linda. At this point in the lesson, the discussion moves on to another errant method for finding the growth factor. After 80 seconds, the discussion is redirected back to Kirk's method.]

Teacher: Interesting thinking, Kirk. Can you see why your way makes sense initially but probably doesn't work?

Kirk: Um, yeah. Um, no. Sort of.

Teacher: Okay. Then let's keep going. Rudy?

Rudy: If you just added 50% of the number you add, wouldn't it be the same way as thinking what Kirk was doing?

Teacher: Give me numbers to what you're saying.

Rudy: Alright. He was thinking about adding about half of 199. So, if you just added 50% of 199 onto 199, it would equal about 300.

Teacher: Okay. Take it the next step.

Rudy: And then if you keep doing it you'll eventually get to the answer. Just add 50% of 300 to 300, you'll get the next number.

Teacher: Whatever—it's just Rudy. Or do you understand what he's saying and can you put it into a different way of speaking? Hang on, Linda. Go, David.

David: If you times something by 0.5 doesn't it get smaller?

Teacher: I don't know. Do you have a calculator? [Many students are talking. Ms. Koster picks up on what Keith announces over the other students talking.] [To class] Pause in your mumbling. [To Keith] Say that again.

Keith: You have to add the 1 to the 0.5 so you keep the same number and then you add the 0.5. Otherwise, you make the number smaller.

Teacher: You've got the idea of what you're adding on. What you have to hang onto is what you already have. And how do you hang onto what you already have?

Students: [From many students] You add a 1.

(Koster, video transcript, April 9, 1999)

By devolving the interpretation of Kirk's response to other students, Ms. Koster used student–student interaction to provide feedback to Kirk's misconception of growth factor. A byproduct of this exchange was additional evidence of students' conceptions of growth factor. By deferring student misconceptions to other students, Ms. Koster was able to generate contrasting student responses, providing additional mathematical connections to the problem context that otherwise would not have been introduced.

CONCLUSIONS

Ms. Koster's skill in generating rich classroom discourse allowed her to use it for classroom assessment. Her instruction depended on effective discourse-based assessment. From her years of teaching experience, Ms. Koster trusted her intuition to read whether students were "getting it" and to make appropriate on-the-fly adaptations to her instruction. Her knowledge of mathematics and of student learning allowed her to make informed decisions about the adaptations she should make. By design, her lesson structure was open and flexible, and she expected additional learning opportunities to emerge from student input. Because her teaching style was, by nature, practical inquiry (Richardson, 1994), she approached the implementation of a new mathematics curriculum as a chance to learn along with her students, with eyes and ears wide open.

This selection of vignettes demonstrates that instructionally embedded assessment is more than asking good questions. Student engagement is a necessary prerequisite to assessing student understanding. Without full engagement in a problem context, students' responses may underestimate their understanding of a mathematical concept or principle. As shown in the exchange between Kirk and his classmates, collaborative engagement in a problem context can create opportunities for peer assessment and sustained deliberation and sense making of a common misconception. Even within the scope of a teacher's questioning techniques, questions have different purposes in relation to assessment. Temperature taking allowed Ms. Koster to take a quick, albeit superficial, glance at "where students were." In contrast, students' responses to Ms. Koster's range of funneling and probing techniques elicited more substantive evidence of student understanding, while, at the same time, offering other students an alternative perspective on the same problem.

Importantly, Ms. Koster's perspective on assessment was formed prior to using MiC. Her willingness to experiment with new activities and curriculum was due, in part, to her comfort with dealing with the unexpected. As an experienced teacher, she had grown accustomed to developing lessons with a minimal amount of planning and preferred to construct instructional paths on the fly. I would argue that Ms. Koster, over time, acquired a dependency on discourse-based assessment to guide lessons, and her confidence in responding to students' needs as they emerged heightened her attention to student verbal communication during instruction. Even though this was her first time teaching the unit, when the interviewer asked how much of her planning was left to student reactions to the problems, Ms. Koster replied:

> Ninety percent. Having taught almost 20 years and not being floored by things going wrong, I trust myself to do that. I think to a new teacher or to a teacher who needs to be really overly planned, I would seem almost incompetent to them, knowing that I sort of trust that, "Okay, let's see what happens with this." I remain tuned in enough to know where to take it, or at least to take a best guess about where to take it. That's a large, large part.
>
> I don't think I am worth much if I have an agenda. . . . So, do I take a lot of prep time? Quite frankly, no. The time shift is at the back end when their stuff comes in and I take a look at it. The time in wandering around and looking over shoulders. And when I get really stumped with how we are doing. I know a couple of times I said, "Okay, look at the next one. Write down what you think. I am coming to look over your shoulders." Because—I don't know— I need a dipstick right now. (Koster, interview, March 26, 1999)

By observing students' work in progress, Ms. Koster was able to assess the pitfalls that students encountered. By interacting with students while they faced these challenges, she was able to assess whether students' struggles were related to the wording of the problem, contextual features of the problem, or limitations in their understanding of the mathematics required to complete the task.

To use discourse-based assessment, teachers must be sensitive to the social fabric of their classroom and be able to encourage interaction and participation, while at the same time respecting each student's confidence and comfort with sharing his or her knowledge, insight, and perspective. To effectively develop the learning environment required for classroom assessment, teachers must be sensitive to student affect and the need to promote and maintain productive relations among students.

When instruction is not supported by discourse-based assessment techniques, teachers overlook critical opportunities for student learning. Discourse-based assessment provides teachers a more substantial field for determining which features of mathematics problems challenge

students. It allows teachers to evaluate which times students are prepared to engage in tasks and activities without instructional support.
Student–student communication, adeptly facilitated in a principled
manner, is more apt to shed light on prevailing student misconceptions, which then can be turned into timely learning opportunities.
By leveraging student misconceptions in this way, teachers can use
contrasting student responses to reinforce mathematical connections
that otherwise would not be available through less flexible forms of
classroom assessment.

In her final comment from the third interview, Ms. Koster recognized that her method of instruction, while seemingly natural for her,
could pose challenges for teachers who require a high degree of pre-
dictability in their lesson structure.

> Let me phrase this delicately: If you don't think on your feet well,
> I think this is very threatening and difficult. We talked about this
> a bit yesterday: If you find yourself four and five times saying, "Well,
> that might work," then eventually, if I were a student in that class,
> I'd think, "This lady doesn't know what she's talking about." She
> can't say, "Great, you got it." "No, it doesn't work, can anybody
> tell us why?" And that's asking a lot [from teachers with different]
> teaching styles, to be very quick. Not even very quick. [To be] com-
> fortable with "you don't have a lecture prepared" or "you don't have
> a presentation prepared." You kind of have to wing a lot of it based
> on what the kids bring back. For me, that's fun. Plus, I trust enough
> of my senses trying to figure out what the kid's saying or to guide
> the discussion so I can figure out what the kid's saying. (Koster,
> interview, May 6, 1999)

To realize higher aspirations for student understanding in inquiry
mathematics, teachers will need to address not only their conceptions
of assessment but also their conceptions of teaching and learning. The
discourse-based assessment practices exemplified by Ms. Koster were
consistent with her conceptions of teaching, her respect for student
learning, and her instructional goals. To initiate the development of
teachers' discourse-based assessment practices, teachers need opportunities to reflect on their conceptions of evidence for student learning
of mathematics and to deliberate the validity of such evidence with
other teachers. Teacher experimentation with curricula designed to
elicit student explanation of strategies, along with the support of professional collaboration, also can be used to initiate the process of "professional problem solving." By observing other teachers through the

lens of discourse-based assessment, teachers can improve and develop formative assessment techniques to accommodate increased student communication and different representations of student understanding. We hope that Ms. Koster's thoughtful articulation of her assessment practices will offer teachers a starting point for exploring discourse-based assessment, which fundamentally is based on ongoing communication between teacher and student to promote learning with understanding.

Chapter 11

Collaborative Partnership:
Staff Development
That Works

Ann Frederickson
SAVANNA OAKS MIDDLE SCHOOL, VERONA, WI

Michael Ford
UNIVERSITY OF PITTSBURGH

Who says you can't teach an old dog new tricks?

That's the saying that kept coming to mind when, as a veteran teacher of 16 years, I decided to start working with the Middle School Design Collaborative at Verona, Wisconsin (VMSDC; Romberg, Webb, Burrill, & Ford, 2001), a collaborative between staff from the University of Wisconsin–Madison and Verona middle school teachers.[1]

In response to the national and state standards, our district was looking into updating our curriculum in both math and science. Our middle school math department was interested in spreading algebra concepts across sixth, seventh, and eighth grades. The goal was to eliminate the enriched sixth- and seventh-grade math classes and the accelerated eighth-grade algebra class, thus allowing us to infuse algebra into one curriculum for all students rather than for the 25% who were receiving algebra instruction at the eighth-grade level at that time. In response to our invitation, Tom Romberg, director of the National Center for Improving Student Learning and Achievement in Mathematics and Science and coordinator of the VMSDC based in the Center, offered to work with us on revamping our curriculum.

In 1997, when I was given the opportunity to participate, I was eager but somewhat skeptical. I had participated in other service programs that offered curriculum change with classroom support. Unfortunately, that support was minimal and did not last long enough to allow for changes to produce results or for the discussion of obstacles encountered on the way. As a result, curricular changes were soon abandoned, and we continued our former practices.

The VMSDC proved different. First, we were promised support for 3 years. Second, taking part in this collaborative offered me opportunities that I couldn't afford to pass up. To address our algebra concerns, we were encouraged to try the prealgebra units from *Mathematics in Context* (MiC; National Center for Research in Mathematical Sciences Education & Freudenthal Institute, 1997–1998); to address the teaching of the physics of motion, we were offered training in use of the software program Boxer (diSessa, 1997).

I was excited to look at and try the MiC materials and Boxer. The use of Boxer software would not only allow my students to experience programming but would also connect my math and science curriculum in ways that had not existed before. Previously, we had run experiments that let students explore various science concepts, write observations, and draw conclusions—but we hadn't taken the time to look for mathematical patterns in their observations. With this model, however, students would be able to graph acceleration and look for patterns in their data tables. They would be encouraged to find ways to express mathematically the patterns they observed, and they would be able to create visual representations to model the conclusions they drew from their observations. Although I was to teach a motion unit introducing physics concepts, the physics of motion was an area in which I had no expertise. Unlike typical curricular units, this motion unit did not specifically determine student activities, and I felt ill prepared to deal with this open-endedness on my own. With staff from the Center available to help, though, this seemed like the prime time to design a unit.

Taking into consideration all the opportunities offered, I felt I needed to take a chance and participate. Most staff development opportunities take place outside the classroom. Generally, we are presented with ideas to take back to our classroom: We reflect on what was presented, think about how we can effectively put those ideas into practice within our classrooms, and then try them out. Most of the time I tried those ideas but later let them fall by the wayside. Despite my efforts to stay current with changes taking place in educational practices, I knew my classroom more or less reflected a traditional math classroom, with instruction delivered through lecture and demonstration. For a while, I had been somewhat frustrated with student performance. Although students were mastering concepts, I felt their mastery was minimal. Students were not performing as well as I would have hoped on an application level. Students could imitate, but they didn't seem able to extend their thinking or look for their own methods for solving problems. When, for example, students were asked to find 25% of 36, they did so easily. But when I put the problem into a context, such as finding the price of a $36 sweater when 25% is taken off, students were not able to recognize and apply the strategies they had already "learned."

The best way to get at this issue, I felt, was to have someone come in to observe my teaching practice. But having people I didn't know very well come in and evaluate my teaching style, felt threatening. I needed first to trust that group of people. At the time, I couldn't have predicted the benefits of sustained professional growth and support over a period of years.

THE FIRST YEAR (1997–1998)

Changing the Role of the Teacher

During my first year with the project, I integrated two MiC algebra units into my curriculum. The first unit I introduced was the Expressions and Formulas unit (Gravemeijer, Roodhardt, Wijers, Cole, & Burrill, 1998). I was amazed by the content of the unit and surprised at what students were able to accomplish. Prior to teaching this unit, during a typical lesson, I did a short warm-up to review the previous day's lesson, demonstrated examples of skills from the daily lesson on the board, and then asked students to work on problems like the ones they had seen demonstrated. The MiC materials were set up in such a way that I needed to change how I delivered a lesson. First, the lessons did not concentrate on any one particular skill. Second, the skills were woven into a context, requiring students to apply skills in solving a problem situation. Third, problems were set up in a scaffolding fashion, leading students through the lessons. It wouldn't be possible merely to show students how to do a particular problem and then ask them to solve another like the one I had shown them. Instead, I had to allow students to read through and try problems on their own. I had to let go of being the sole instructor and the demonstrator of my way of solving problems.

The first time I taught the Fraction Times unit (Keijzer, Van Galen, et al., 1998) proved to me that I needed to let go. Early on, we were working on the following problem:

Lea found the information on dog ownership very interesting. She decided to take a survey to find out how many pets people have. She randomly called 30 people and found the following information:
- $^1/_8$ have no pets;
- $^1/_2$ have one pet;
- $^1/_6$ have two pets;
- $^1/_{15}$ have four or more pets.

How many of the people Lea called have two pets? (p. 8)

My concern was that students at that point wouldn't have enough background knowledge to solve this problem. My instinct was to demonstrate that we could take this group of 30 people and divide them by the denominator, but I resisted the temptation to show them and instead allowed them work time. As I walked around, I was amazed by the strategies that many students were using. One student, Brian, showed me that "you could think of it as making two equivalent fractions, $^1/_6 = {}^?/_{30}$. The answer must be 5 because it was like two equivalent fractions—you are multiplying the denominator 5 times, and so you must do the same to the numerator to keep it equal." Another student, Sara, said: "I know it's 5, too, because it's like when we did those tables in Expressions and Formulas—one would be 6, two would be 12, three would be 18, four would be 24, and five would be 30." I had not anticipated that students might go back to using two strategies that had been introduced earlier in the year. I might not have given students the opportunity to figure it out on their own if I had first presented a strategy and solution.

Over the year, with the help of my colleagues from the university, I began to feel more comfortable that my role of presenter was changing to a role of director or coach, and that first year of participation brought many positive changes to my classroom.

Changing the Role of the Students

The MiC materials were well suited for students of all skills and all abilities, and I found myself excited by the enthusiasm of the students to work on math and amazed at the ability of these sixth graders to solve problems that I knew eighth graders would not be able to solve.

With these materials, students could extend themselves by depth of explanation or by further exploration of an open-ended problem. Those who previously had struggled with math could suddenly grasp a problem that others were not seeing and could shine as they explained and helped their peers.

I was excited about working on another MiC unit but knew I needed to work on some of the logistics involved in instruction of this material. I wanted to do as I had done before—follow the book page by page, discussing each problem with my students, but the lessons were taking longer than I had expected. Many students saw their ways of solving a problem as different from their peers' ways and were excited about sharing their own strategies. But this seemed to mean that we spent too much time going over problems. I saw improvement in my students' abilities to discuss math, yet I needed to find a way for students to evaluate strategies to see if theirs were really different from other solutions that had already been presented. Their presentation of solutions also needed to key in on essential ideas, and they needed to keep a clear record of notes to use as a reference when they worked through problems at home.

A visit by teachers who were already teaching MiC materials was arranged, and time was given to me to discuss concerns with colleagues at school and with university partners. This process helped me come up with other routines, which helped me feel better prepared to teach the MiC unit, Comparing Quantities (Kindt, Abels, Meyer, & Pligge, 1998). In this unit, students are asked to solve two- and three-variable equations. I decided to introduce the unit at the end of the year because one of the sections would provide students with an accelerated understanding of algebra. Again, students' abilities amazed me. All of the students were not only motivated but able to pick up on a strategy for solving the problem.

Discussions were rich, and I began to see students improve in their articulation, both written and verbal, of the mathematics being practiced. Early in the year, written explanations had been short and incomplete. One of my students, David, always looked for short ways to write up his thinking. His favorite answer was, "Well, I just got my answer." A typical written response from his work would have sounded like his answer to this particular problem from the Expressions and Formulas unit (Gravemeijer, Roodhardt, et al., 1998), in which students are given an arrow string with the output listed and the following question: "What should Pat give as the input? Explain how you found this number" (p. 30). David wrote his answer and explained, "I did a backward arrow string."

Throughout the unit, we talked about what an answer like his meant. We then discussed how he could make it more complete. By the end of the year, his answers sounded more like the one he wrote in answer to this problem from the Comparing Quantities unit (Kindt et al., 1998).

> Monica and Martin are in charge of the school store. The store is open all day for students to come and buy supplies. Unfortunately, Monica and Martin can't be there all day to take students' money, so they start an honor system. Limited quantities of pencils and erasers are available for students to purchase using this honor system. Students leave the exact change in a small, locked box. Erasers cost 25¢ each and pencils cost 15¢ each. . . .
> On another day there is $1.50 in the locked box. Monica and Martin cannot decide what was purchased. Why?

David's response this time was more complete.

> There are a lot of different ways they could have made $1.50. One combination could be 3 erasers and 5 pencils. Another combination could be 10 pencils. You could also sell 6 erasers. Since there are so many combinations, no one could be sure what was sold unless you kept count of the items that were there before.

As the year went on, I found that my students were increasingly able to handle a level of mathematics that I hadn't thought possible. They were becoming highly motivated, and I saw improvement in their abilities to communicate their problem-solving techniques. What really surprised me is that these changes seemed related to their rich discussions of their own different strategies rather than my presentation of correct solution strategies.

Changing Classroom Assessment

As I experimented with students working in small groups on the problems, listening in as they solved problems together, I was astounded by the strategies they came up with and with their ability to articulate their understanding of problems when they interacted or presented their solutions to the class. I no longer saw their answers as just right or wrong, but began to look for a way of assessing their level of understanding of the problems through classroom activities.

As my students were working through the Fraction Times unit (Keijzer, Van Galen, et al., 1998), I gave this particular problem as an informal assessment: "Find the fractions that are the same as each of the following decimal amounts: (a) 0.24; (b) 0.125; (c) 0.375" (p. 22). As I looked over Amber's paper, I saw .24/100 = 0.24. At one time I would have marked that as a wrong answer in my grade book. This time, I asked Amber to explain her answer to me. As she rewrote it on the board, she caught that she had put in a decimal point and said, "Wait, I don't need that decimal point because the fraction and the decimal are the same. It's just a different way of writing it." She then took out the decimal point, saying, "I know the denominator should be 100 because it is like place value, and I think of two places behind the decimal like 10 to the second power, which is 100." Listening to her answer gave me insight into her understanding of equivalence and place value. Because Amber was a shy student and generally did not offer answers or explanations unless asked, I might have missed her level of understanding if I had just gone with her written answer.

Gradually as we went over problems in class, I began to feel that the way I was grading problems and tests was no longer adequate. I was still grading the traditional way: I marked problems correct or incorrect and then gave the percentage for the number correct over the number possible. As I evaluated student's notebooks, however, I noticed that students did not necessarily give a right or wrong answer. Instead, their answers showed a level of understanding, and I came to feel that the assignments and tests should be graded in a way that reflected their level of understanding.

At one of our monthly meetings, we graded assessments using a rubric developed by our university partners. I was surprised at the ease of grading with the rubric and felt as though this was the tool that could help me evaluate my students' level of understanding. Experimenting with rubrics seemed like the way to go but, having no experience in using them, I wasn't sure where to start. Eager to learn as much as possible about using rubrics, I participated in summer scoring institutes at the university. This gave me more practice but, importantly, it also provided me the opportunity to talk with other classroom teachers about how they wrote rubrics and the ways they used them in their classrooms.

THE SECOND YEAR (1998–1999)

Changing the Role of the Teacher

Feeling pretty good about the changes I'd made in my math instruction, I was eager to attack my science curriculum. Many of our science units were already developed for us. We presented concepts and had many activities at our disposal that further illustrated those concepts. Students were given a question and asked to use their observation skills as they followed prescribed steps. They were asked to memorize content without knowing the reason for memorizing it and were evaluated on what they recalled. I was looking for curriculum that would encourage students to solve and discuss science problems in much the same way that they were already attacking their math problems.

As I had learned to do the first year in working with math, I decided to take on one unit at a time—in this case, motion. Through the collaborative project, we were introduced to Boxer, a software program that allows students to experiment by writing programs to control simulations. In this unit, students first are given simple tasks and then are asked to make observations and draw representations of their observations of particular motions: a ball free-falling, a book shoved across a table, and a ball rolling off a table. As I taught the unit, I began to notice that my lessons were becoming more student-centered and less teacher-directed. The unit allowed students to have rich discussions, and it improved my assessment of their understanding.

Changing the Role of the Students

Before I started teaching the unit, I could see the students drawing the motion of a ball, but I couldn't have predicted what actually happened in the classroom during this unit. Initially, I was afraid students would simply see a ball falling to the floor, recognizing that the ball's speed increases as it falls, until it hits the ground. I did not expect to hear students talk about misconceptions (e.g., that the ball would slow down before it hit the ground, that the ball would move out, then down). Students truly had rich discussions about what they saw and the best way to represent it.

After students drew their own representations of these motions, they were put in groups of four and given a sheet of paper to draw one representation for their group. Next, groups presented this drawing to the entire class, with the class then deciding which drawing was the best representation of the ball falling. I began the class discussion by asking groups where they believed the ball was moving the fastest and how their drawing showed that. Before long, students took over the discussion. They were questioning each other about their observations and asking one another why they chose to illustrate what happened the way they did. They also made an effort to explain what they saw. After discussions of each motion, students were asked to program a simulation of each motion using Boxer. This programming was followed by students critiquing one another's work, telling which simulation appeared most realistic, and giving their reasons. After this work on the computer, we went back to the classroom and made new visual representations of the motions discussed earlier. Students were more invested and involved in their learning. They were eager to participate and seemed to actually understand what they were learning.

Changing Classroom Assessment

In the second year of the project, I added two more MiC units and switched my focus to working on rubrics for the new units and the units I previously had taught, such as a rubric used for a problem in the Fraction Times unit (Keijzer, Van Galen, et al., 1998, p. 5). Students were given survey results from two classes of different sizes: one with 20 students, the other with 30. Students were asked to cut out from an activity sheet two bars with the same number of segments and use them to show the data, in this case, in equal-size pie charts. The rubric looked like this:

WORK

- Doesn't show understanding.
- Has minor errors.
- Shows complete understanding.
- Includes the use of fractions to represent a part–whole relationship (0, 1, 2).
- Includes the use of various strategies to compare fractions with unlike denominators (0, 1, 2).

We still used the traditional A–F letter grades in our district, and the work of translating rubrics to A, B, C, D, or F was an ongoing task. In the meantime, though, I wanted to "grade" students' understanding, and creating and using rubrics made that seem possible. It also helped me see students and their abilities in new ways.

Building Professional Community

Through the collaborative, I was fortunate to be able to meet with the designer of Boxer, Andrea diSessa, and talk with him about the work he did with students in their motion club, and I had access to the videotapes of my lessons to look back on. But importantly, I also began to meet weekly with another sixth-grade teacher who had taught the same unit at the same time. A university partner with strong background knowledge in this area came into both our classrooms to observe, collect student work, and model questions to help us direct discussions. Not having a strong background in physics, I was unsure about the benefits and how much I had accomplished. As I discovered with math, changing the delivery of instruction had further implications that needed to be examined. I wasn't sure what the student work was showing me in terms of students' understanding of physics and how much I could expect students of this age to understand. But I felt we had a good beginning for a unit and looked forward to working with my colleagues on improving it.

THE THIRD YEAR (1999–2000)

At the end of the second year, I felt that the use of the MiC units and the changes I had made in delivering instruction had had a significant impact on student motivation for learning and on student performance. As a result of that experience, I decided to change over to a total MiC curriculum. As I began my third year of working with the collaborative, however, I wasn't sure how much more the project itself could offer me.

Although my instincts indicated that student performance had improved, I began to wonder what improved performance meant. I needed once again to reflect on what I wanted students to know and how I would know whether they had learned it. I began to look at student work in a new way. I wanted to know what the work told me about their levels of understanding, but with 50 students and three different class preparations, I knew I couldn't do this with every piece of student work. Instead, I needed to identify core performance tasks and look at work that showed growth in understanding, a task that is difficult enough when I assess work in which I have strong prior knowledge.

Although I still struggled with deciding how much I could expect students to gain in knowledge and with finding ways to translate mastery of that knowledge to a traditional A–F grading system, I was able to make improvements in assessment as I taught a unit with my entire class and could articulate more clearly students' strengths and weaknesses.

WHAT I EXPERIENCED

Time to reflect, discuss, and plan further is essential in order to change classroom practices. This project was unique in that it offered a team approach in the classroom, and I was fortunate enough to have an administrator who supported us by giving us the time we needed to meet and work with others. University colleagues worked side by side with us in the classroom, offering us support and encouragement. The discussions that followed visits were a valuable means of effectively changing practices and curriculum in the classroom. Monthly meetings allowed us to help set agendas and allowed me to reflect and build on changes that were taking place in the classroom. The opportunity to visit other classrooms allowed me to see other teachers model a technique I was hoping to put into practice in my classroom. Preparing to present this work at a national conference of teachers helped me reflect and share with my colleagues all that we had learned from this project.

As the project came to a close, I realized that there is more to learn in the changing world of education. But change doesn't come easily— especially when a teacher, even an experienced one, is expected to change without any support. In my experience, bridging the gap between classroom educators and education researchers has been the most effective means of professional development. I never would have predicted or imagined the many benefits I gained from being a participant in this collaborative. I found a new way of delivering instruction that has been beneficial and motivating to both my students and myself.

- I no longer see the teaching of math or science as the instruction of individual skills by showing students one way of solving problems. Instead, I now recognize the importance of weaving math and science concepts inside the contexts in which they will be used and of giving students the opportunity to discuss what they are learning and to draw conclusions based on their own observations.
- I've learned that when planning units and lessons, the focus starts with what I want my students to know and how I can best get them there. Students learn best when they are being directed or are discovering on their own.
- I've seen an improvement in student performance. Both in class activities and in individual assessments, students have shown that they retain information, can see connections to other subject areas, and can apply their knowledge in interdisciplinary projects.
- I recognize that the need for discussion is as important at the teacher level as it is with students in the classroom. Especially important is the time given for meeting and planning units in collaboration with other teachers who are teaching the same content.

In an ideal world, administrators would encourage continued teacher learning by approving time for teachers to work with other teachers. Experienced teachers and beginning teachers would have mentor programs to support one another in learning. Teachers and researchers would work side by side in the classroom, discussing lessons, student performance, and education research. I leave speculation on the downsides of that system to the administrators and the politicians.

NOTE

1. Although co-authored, this chapter is written in the voice of teacher Ann Frederickson.

Chapter 12

Retracing a Path to Assessing for Understanding

Teresa Her
SAVANNAH OAKS MIDDLE SCHOOL, VERONA, WI

David C. Webb
UNIVERSITY OF WISCONSIN–MADISON

To what can we attribute primary credit for the instigation of a major change in educational perspective or practice? What patterns or paths exist to facilitate successful learning and growth in practicing educators? What catalysts can we identify to motivate and support pedagogical reform?[1] These are critical questions for any who are invested in the classroom experiences that shape student learning, and the simplicity of an anecdote can provide powerful insight toward potential solutions. This chapter retraces my experiences and experiments with developing assessment tools and practices consistent with my goal to teach for student understanding. I hope that these reflections on the process of change in practice can reveal potential models for practical pedagogical change.

A DEVELOPING PERSPECTIVE ON THE ROLE OF ASSESSMENT

As a preservice teacher, I was inundated with books and articles about "new assessment" techniques (which primarily emphasized the use of portfolios) but was still unprepared for actually assessing and assigning grades to my first class of students. Student teaching experiences in elementary school exposed me to a variety of report forms that were multicategorical and descriptive, unlike the single letter grade and prewritten comment I was expected to select as a middle school teacher. While I disregarded the elementary format as time-consuming and subjective, I had no solid framework of my own from which to build an assessment system. I did not have the time, energy, or confidence as a first-year teacher to deviate from the norm. As a result, initially I relied on the system used by my colleagues that converted total points in each of five categories (tests and quizzes, homework, classwork, participation, and behavior) into percentages that were weighted and averaged for a final percent-based grade. The district grading scale completed the process, translating the percentages to letter grades. Assured that I was in good company with this grading procedure, I tried to ignore the uneasiness I felt while completing each grading sheet with a single letter to summarize a student's entire quarter of work and learning.

During my second year of teaching, I transferred to a newly created position in a seventh- and eighth-grade class of 25 at-risk students. The feelings of resentment and failure that students brought to my class, coupled with my uneasiness with my grading practices, motivated me to find ways to rekindle student interest in learning through innovative changes in assessment. After much debate and research into successful "at-risk" teaching practices, my teammate and I sought to engage our students through an assessment model that used student conferences to negotiate individual goals, and portfolios to demonstrate progress toward those goals for a pass-or-fail grade. This attempt had mixed results: Some students thrived in the freedom of a gradeless environment and made honest attempts to attain their goals; others manipulated the system by resisting goal setting from the start or by producing empty tokens of achievement to meet minimum portfolio requirements. In addition, setting individual student goals (and the accompanying individualized instruction) presented a significant challenge. The class was disbanded after a year, and I spent the summer preparing to teach 80 sixth graders again.

Unwilling to return to sixth grade with the same assessment practices, I sought the help of our school's learning resource coordinator, who enrolled me in conferences and showered me with books and articles. She also served as a sounding board and critical evaluator of ideas and solutions, while at the same time encouraging me to learn from experience. For example, one such attempt at changing practice found my teammate and me experimenting with portfolios and goal setting as a means to determine grades. Rather than averaging a collection of scores, we required students to document attainment of mutually agreed-upon goals in a portfolio format for a pass-or-fail grade. We found this approach had similar mixed results.

More than anything, I wanted to be fair and honest with the students and respectful of the work that they were doing, honoring progress as well as finished products. During the school year, I had open discussions with students to ask what they thought about school, grades, and report cards, and what they would like to see changed. I was eager to use their ideas to increase their sense of ownership. I wanted to create a unique assessment system that combined aspects of goal setting and self-assessment with more uniform standards of achievement. Inherent in this system was the recognition of learning as a process and greater attention to student improvement. Improvement and growth were measured by comparing scores on a single assessment piece for each unit, administered first as a pretest and again as a posttest.

Despite noticeable progress in garnering student interest and learning, the progress-based system began to lose its appeal after the first year of implementation. For one, I recognized that I still depended primarily on percentages. The goals that students set were arbitrary in that they were number amounts rather than actual items or skills they wished to learn or improve. Furthermore, this approach did not detail where the students had improved, nor did it provide adequate feedback to parents, students, or myself.

I remained dissatisfied.

AN OPPORTUNITY TO RETHINK CLASSROOM PRACTICE

Some of my colleagues, who both followed and challenged me in my ongoing search for alternative grading and instructional practices during the previous year, were involved with a university design collaborative whose aim was to improve student understanding of and performance in mathematics at the middle level (Romberg, Webb, Burrill, & Ford, 2001). After piloting new instructional materials and meeting with project staff, colleagues shared their successes and encouraged me to join their discussions. As a result, I attended several meetings and was introduced to *Mathematics in Context* (MiC; National Center for Research in Mathematical Sciences Education & Freudenthal Institute, 1997–1998). I spent the summer evaluating the materials and comparing them with the district scope and sequence for my grade level to identify overlaps or gaps in content. I found that MiC adequately covered the required content and often went well beyond grade-level expectations. I was intrigued with the unique problems that were designed to emphasize questioning, reasoning, and communication. Inherent across MiC units were opportunities to use students' informal knowledge as scaffolding to develop well-connected understanding of formal knowledge and algorithms. I decided to use MiC the following year.

During my fifth year of teaching, I grappled with the changes in pedagogy necessitated by a curriculum that emphasizes teaching for understanding. Through frequent observations, one-on-one discussions, and small-group meetings, colleagues and university researchers constantly posed questions that compelled me to defend, rethink, explain, or define what I was doing and why I was doing it: What evidence of student learning is available during the lesson? What questions could be asked to gather evidence of student understanding? What is the purpose of asking students to explain their thinking? What is a good explanation? And so forth.

During monthly meetings, we struggled through challenging mathematical problems and were encouraged to develop an appreciation for student representations and mathematical communication. Teamwork, communication, and rich conversations moved from being simply "warm and fuzzy" teaching methods to being valued as necessary components in the construction of students' understanding of mathematics. We also came to view classroom discussions as a legitimate opportunity for classroom assessment.

Several members of the research team also challenged the tacit limitations I had established for student achievement. The questions and problems I routinely used, assessed students' recall knowledge but were insufficient for assessing students' conceptual understanding. The researchers encouraged me to increase the quality and complexity of the content that I introduced, even as they taught me the mathematics necessary to do so. I was equally affected by the uniqueness of the assessments in MiC in terms of the ways that they documented student achievement and assessed student progress in understanding algebraic concepts. Getting together with colleagues and researchers to discuss our interpretation of student responses was a learning experience that deeply affected my concept of assessment. Rather than being marked right or wrong, individual problems or related problem sets were evaluated for overall understanding, and results were assigned a value according to problem-specific rubrics. It was the first time I had been encouraged to give points for something beyond just a correct or incorrect answer. The scoring rubrics that we used defined point values for student communication and progress toward algebraic understanding, sometimes in spite of the minor computation errors that students demonstrated. We also used strategy code rubrics to categorize the various strategies that students used for particular problems.

FROM GRADES TO ASSESSMENT

These collective experiences and experiments in practice eventually led me to seriously contemplate the role that informal assessment techniques should play in instructional planning and classroom assessment. I searched for alternative ways to collect information from students and tried to become more efficient and selective with the information I recorded and my methods for recording it. In part, this shift was motivated by a desire to ease the burden of evaluating and recording every task I required of students. Research staff as well as veteran colleagues made convincing arguments that a greater quantity of scores does not guarantee a greater understanding of students' knowledge (although it can guarantee greater headaches). *I came to realize that I was not morally obligated to assess every task.* The concept that some tasks could be simply "learning tasks" (i.e., tasks used to gather information about students without scoring or grading) was a difficult concept for me to grasp. I needed to let go of the fear that students would feel cheated or let down if the work they had done was not evaluated. If I truly wanted students to own and value their *own* learning, I needed to start practicing the same thing by devoting more time to learning from students instead of giving so much attention to evaluating them.

I also realized that up to this point my questions about assessment had focused not on collecting information but on reporting grades. Until I began caring more about what students actually could do and what they actually knew, I never questioned whether scores and points could tell the story I wanted to tell about each student. My interest in teaching for understanding necessitated a change in what I collected because it reoriented what I valued, what I expected students to show, and what I wanted parents to know. Yet I still held on to prior methods for assigning student grades and, for a time, maintained dual records: one for the abilities that students were able to demonstrate and one for points so that I could compute a grade. If, however, I wanted to find out what students understood and where they were struggling in order to inform my instruction, then why did I need to collect another data set in the form of points? Looking back,

I realized the redundancy of assessing students twice was a manifestation of my unresolved conflict between assessment and grading.

The final catalyst to yet another change in assessment practice was my frustration with a computerized grading program that I had been using to record and calculate student grades. Although it saved time every grading period, it was more difficult to modify for situations in which points did not "add up" to tell the whole story. For example, I refused to give an F to a student who was working hard, making progress, and learning to the best of his or her ability, regardless of what the points added up to. To me, an F represented failure to learn or make progress. In the grading program, though, an F was assigned to any student who attained at or below 69%. What did the 69% mean? I had no recollection of what the points stood for. If I had added a few more easy items to a particularly challenging test, a larger base of possible points could have boosted the overall percentage. It all seemed so arbitrary! I was growing frustrated with adjusting points to tell a more honest and complete story. When I began changing my instruction to teach for understanding—and, by necessity, began wanting to capture students' understanding—I recognized that the percent-based scoring method was the source of my problem. By the end of each grading period, the total points that students had earned told me little about their understanding. Theodore Sizer, in the foreword to *Authentic Assessment in Action* (Darling-Hammond, Ancess, & Falk, 1995), put my struggle into words when he wrote:

> The quality of that feedback must be incisive and apt. Telling the kid, "You got a 57 on Friday's test . . . you gotta do better. . . ." is not much help. Indeed, that 57 may tell us more about the test than the test taker. Understanding that one has not done well on a test is the barest beginning of why one did not do well. The learning is in the substance and barely in the score. (p. vii)

Points and percentages could be assigned and earned so arbitrarily (e.g., correct answers on work that had nothing to do with unit objectives, extra credit, completion of a worksheet, good behavior with a sub, a reward for classroom jobs). Points also could be lost just as arbitrarily (e.g., too much time spent in the bathroom, a simple mistake on a test, a penalty for late work). I was aware of several teachers who routinely subtracted anywhere from 10 to 50% of the total points for assignments that were a day late, regardless of student performance. The final percentages rarely told an accurate story about the mathematics concepts that students actually knew. A student who had little experience with a concept and struggled on quizzes, but through test retakes, after-school tutoring, and hard work managed to learn the material and demonstrate it on the final test, might still receive a low grade because the one high score was not enough to raise the collection of low scores.

Furthermore, the computerized printouts that listed possible and earned scores for every task left me constantly haggling with parents and students over scores on assignments and tests that were weeks or even months old. The discussions all seemed to revolve around getting enough points for the desired grade and rarely centered on what actually had been learned. When I realized this, a second and more powerful realization was not far behind: If a parent *had* asked what his or her student actually understood or needed help with, I wouldn't have been able to answer. At that point, my growing need and desire to assess what students understood, replaced my need to simply assign a grade for what they had done.

ASSESSING FOR UNDERSTANDING

When I stopped wanting points and started wanting information, I hit a wall. I was learning and applying new ways to gather such information but how could it possibly be recorded? I wanted something simple and efficient that I could use in a typical teaching day. It also had to be accessible to students and to parents because I felt that their involvement was critical.

After a long day of teaching, I sat in a student chair and tried to harness all the assessment-related ideas and frustrations that were swirling in my head. As I corrected a set of tests, I found I could see what the students understood by studying their answers, work, and patterns of correct and incorrect responses. When I attempted to put all of those insights into a composite numerical score, however, the insights and meaning were lost. So I began to wonder: Why combine? Why not eliminate the combining step and retain the distinct insights? If the process of aggregating scores on all the responses together causes the reporting to be meaningless, then why aggregate? I recalled the assessments designed by the university design collaborative that used points, not to total a cumulative score, but to indicate performance of separate skills. I realized I wanted a similar way to use scores to note the skills and concepts that students understood on any given test. To do that, I needed to identify the particular skills, concepts, and "understandings" I was looking for. That thought begged the question, "What *should* I be looking for?"

I turned to my experience on the district Standards and Assessment Steering Committee (SASC). One very useful result of this committee was that each staff member received a list of specific academic standards for his or her subject areas and grade level. While we shared rubrics, watched videos, and studied various epistemologies and methods, we discussed effective and desirable ways to communicate student progress.

As I struggled to pull these pieces into a unified program, I was aided by the listening ear and creative thinking of the co-author of this chapter—a university collaborative project assistant with a passion for assessment who allowed me to think through my ideas verbally and provided additional materials, ideas, and suggestions. We identified other methods that seemed practical and useful: a colleague who marked student work according to a three-point scale of 0 for "clueless," 1 for "getting it," or 2 for "nailed it"; a model for unit planning that had shared in a recent SASC meeting and emphasized beginning with standards and designing assessments to guide task selection and instructional decisions; the RME trilevel assessment pyramid that served as a model for the collection of tasks that should be used for assessing students (see Figure 1.3 in Chapter 1); and the three-tiered list of unit objectives at the beginning of each MiC teacher guide, which outlined the tasks that could be used to assess each level of the model assessment pyramid (Figure 12.1).

I combined these components to produce a system that met the following goals for my latest method of assessment:

- Identify objectives for three reasoning levels, drawn from standards and unit content, to provide appropriate challenge for a wide range of student abilities.
- Allow for both informal and formal assessment results to be recorded separately for each objective, using marks for "not yet," "in progress," or "demonstrated."
- Permit students to make multiple attempts at improving and demonstrating understanding; do not give definitive marks until several opportunities have been offered.
- Base letter grades on a performance rubric, not percentages.
- Empower students and parents by making the content objectives as well as the marking and grading process explicit.

I spent a good deal of time fine-tuning a grading system that would transcend percentages by defining the meaning of each letter grade, so that an A truly represented high-level achievement, a C matched

Figure 12.1. Objectives for the More or Less unit. From "More or Less" (pp. xvi–xvii), by R. Keijzer, M. van den Heuvel-Panhuizen, M. Wijers, J. Shew, L. Brinker, M. A. Pligge, M. Shafer, & J. Brendefur, 1998, in National Center for Research in Mathematical Sciences Education & Freudenthal Institute (Eds.), (1997–1998), *Mathematics in Context*, Chicago: Encyclopædia Britannica. Copyright © 1998 by Encyclopædia Britannica. Reprinted with permission.

In the *Mathematics in Context* curriculum, unit goals, categorized according to cognitive procedures, relate to the strand goals and to the National Council of Teachers of Mathematics Curriculum and Evaluation Standards. Additional information about these goals is found in the *Teacher Resource and Implementation Guide*. The *Mathematics in Context* curriculum is designed to help students develop their abilities so that they can perform with understanding in each of the categories listed below. It is important to note that the attainment of goals in one category is not a prerequisite to attaining those in another category. In fact, students should progress simultaneously toward several goals in different categories.

Conceptual and procedural knowledge

1. Use estimation strategies to multiply fractions and decimals.
2. Multiply fractions and decimals.
3. Use number sense to multiply two decimal numbers.
4. Find a percent of a number.
5. Calculate discount and sale price.
6. Compute the total cost with tax.

Reasoning, communicating, thinking, and making connections

7. Relate percents to fractions and decimals.
8. Find an original price using the sale price and the percent discount.
9. Develop number sense.

Modeling, nonroutine problem solving, critically analyzing, and generalizing

10. Solve percent increase and decrease problems.
11. Explore percents as operators.

---

average performance on grade-level work, and an F was reserved for cases in which the student failed to demonstrate any learning or progress. This redefined grading system combined elements of de Lange's trilevel assessment pyramid and reasonable expectations for student work habits.

I tested the new system with a representative sample of 15 students. I piloted the "rubric system" concurrently with the "total points system" to compare the final grades from each. This way, I could decide which system yielded a more accurate portrait of student achievement. I also hoped to work out any unforeseen kinks before introducing the new system to all of my students.

I was pleased with the results. Students who received As in the new system because they understood all the material and had pushed themselves "above and beyond" in their learning also received As in the total points system. Students who received As because they had accumulated enough points or were well behaved but did not demonstrate a high degree of understanding, however, received a slightly lower grade in the new system. Conversely, very few of the students who previously had received Fs based on total points received Fs in the new system because so few fit the new definition. Moreover, when student performance was inconsistent and did not fit neatly within the confines of one grade category, I circled the components of each definition demonstrated by that student and assigned a grade that fell in the middle of the range. Even though I would much rather have let the circled definitions tell the story themselves and not have been bothered with trying to pick a letter grade in the middle, I was still required by the district to give a final grade to summarize student achievement. At least, I reasoned, with the rubric attached to the report card, parents would have a clearer picture of what contributed to the grade received. By having a list of objectives, parents and students could pinpoint the mathematics skills and concepts that required additional attention.

Satisfied with the results of the pilot, I began to create a list of objectives for the next MiC unit. I notified parents of the new grading system and explained to students the rationale behind my decision. Most students were interested in giving the new system a try. They enjoyed seeing up front the concepts that they would be investigating, and the process for determining their grades was now demystified. Some students were motivated to set personal goals and familiarize themselves with the requirements for earning the grade that they desired. Each student was given a copy of the unit objectives and the grading rubric, so students could keep track of their progress throughout the unit (goals they had demonstrated, what remained yet to be demonstrated, and their current grade). An example of the student record sheet is shown in Figure 12.2.

I organized my grade book by main content objectives, with space to record student performance as 0 (not yet), 1 (in progress), or 2 (demonstrated). I heeded caution to keep the assessment load manageable by limiting the number of times I formally assessed each objective (one or two tasks or opportunities per objective), especially as I had made a commitment to trust in-class observation and other informal assessment strategies as valid information. Also built into the system was the opportunity for retakes or "prove-its," which were opportunities for students to conference with me about what was incorrect and to redo a similar task to prove that the concept was understood. This approach placed more of the burden of proof on the student to change unsatisfactory performance and less on me to test each item repeatedly for progress.

IMPACT AND CHALLENGES OF IMPLEMENTATION

Once the system had been implemented, the students and I continued to dialogue about its impact on their learning so that minor adjustments could be made if or when they were needed. David Webb sought additional student responses by conducting a series of confidential student interviews. David and I also continued to share observation notes and discuss the progress and changes that I was experiencing both in the classroom and in time spent planning, preparing, and grading. Based on these discussions, interviews, and observations, I identified six areas of major impact related to the implementation of this new system.

1. Increased student involvement, accountability, and self-advocacy.
2. Change in the content and quantity of teacher–student communication.
3. Raising of the academic "bar."
4. Increased attention to planning instructional units.
5. Major revisions in the design and content of formal assessments.
6. Ongoing adjustments to the goals and methods of in-class instruction.

I describe these changes in more detail in the sections that follow.

Figure 12.2. Student record sheet for the More or Less unit.

More or Less Student Record Sheet

0	1	2
Not yet demonstrated	In progress	Demonstrated

Basic Skills Level (Recognize, recall, identify, accurate use of basic rules)

1. Reasonable estimations (multiply fractions and decimals)	0	1	2
2. Accurately multiply fractions and decimals	0	1	2
3. Find the percent of a number	0	1	2
4. Calculate discount and sale prices	0	1	2
5. Compute total cost with tax	0	1	2

Application Level (Reason, communicate, connect, apply, solve)

6. Articulation of estimation and calculation strategies	0	1	2
7. Relate percents to fractions and decimals	0	1	2
8. Work backward to find starting price or discount	0	1	2

Analysis and Extension Level (Interpret, analyze, draw, and justify conclusions, construct informed opinions, extend and generalize)

9. Compound interest (rule of 72)	0	1	2
10. Refuting common misperceptions with percent	0	1	2
11. Finding a percent of a percent (forward and backward)	0	1	2
12. Extended thinking	0	1	2

Work Habits				**Participation**			
Timeliness	0	1	2	Math chats; class discussion	0	1	2
Quality	0	1	2	Readiness	0	1	2

Grading Rubric

A	B	C	D	F
• All basic skills demonstrated; most applications demonstrated	• All basic skills demonstrated; most applications at least in progress	• Most basic skills demonstrated	• Most basic skills at least in progress	• No evidence of any progress or understanding at any level
• Some extensions at least in progress; work habits and participation are exceptional	• Work habits and participation are consistent	• Work habits and participation are somewhat consistent	• Work habits and participation are inconsistent	• Work habits and participation are nonexistent

211

Increased Student Involvement, Accountability, and Self-Advocacy

One immediate benefit of shifting from an emphasis on grades to an emphasis on assessing understanding was the impact it had on student communication and involvement. The student record forms, progress reports, and class conversations about assessment played a major role in increasing student fluency in the language of mathematics so that students were able to communicate the specific skills that they were learning and the concepts that they did not understand. They also were able to communicate what they were learning to parents and others. Even without the benefit of the forms in front of them, many students were able to articulate a clear understanding of and appreciation for the assessment process. The student responses in the following interview excerpts illustrate some student perceptions of this approach:

Interviewer: Describe how things have changed between the old system and the new system.
Student: In the old system, she would like give you sheets and stuff to work on, and then she would score it. So if it was late, you would still get a point off whether or not everything was right on it. And now she is looking for how well you have demonstrated your skills. . . .

Student: Sometimes before, in math, I would—like—not understand things . . . I would understand them but I just didn't understand the problem or something. But now, if I mess up on something, and she already knows that I have proved it, and she knows that I can do it, it is not going to reflect badly on the rest of my stuff.
Interviewer: It is just sort of one mistake.
Student: One mistake. Our old grading system was like—the whole thing was like earning certain points, and then you see how much you can get, and then it ruins your score if you mess up on something.

Student questions like, "What is my percentage today?" or "How many extra credit points do I need to get an A?" were replaced with, "When can I demonstrate that I now can subtract fractions with unlike denominators?" or "How can I extend my thinking to go beyond the basic skills?" Parents stopped calling to haggle over points for lateness or lower-than-expected test scores. Students started advocating for themselves more, and they wanted to learn and demonstrate specific skills. As one student remarked, "We are more concentrated on learning and not on getting a good grade."

Change in the Content and Quantity of Teacher–Student Communication

The student self-advocacy mentioned above was one unexpected but much welcomed change in teacher–student communication. Another was the increase in communication necessitated by students' desire to receive help and to demonstrate the objectives they missed on formal assessments. Previous quests for points or percentages never elicited the requests that I received from students to demonstrate learning goals. As a result, I decided to institute "math chats."

Similar to the fun book chats my language arts teammate had developed as a more interactive alternative to regular book reports, math chats were organized during the mandatory tutorial period or after school as informal opportunities for students to demonstrate achievement of learning goals and verbalize higher-level thinking. During a session, I would sit with a small group of students to discuss either an area of mathematics they were struggling with or an enrichment activity they wanted to explore further. Students established the goal of the session. Sometimes students selected the math problems they wanted to discuss, and other times I would select "brain stretchers" to push students to extend and apply their mathematical knowledge in new ways. I quickly found that math chats gave me additional insight into students' math thinking, abilities, struggles, and comprehension in lieu of constant test writing and grading. Math chats also were an opportunity to try out questioning techniques and instructional strategies to help students overcome challenging content, techniques that I would use in later lessons. For example, for a group of students who were struggling with addition of fractions, with only a few questions I found that their struggle was due to a limited understanding of the meaning of numerator and denominator. After briefly discussing a fair-share activity with sub sandwiches, students had a better sense of why denominators could not be added. This principle of briefly reviewing fundamental concepts was used in later lessons and other classes to the benefit of other students. Surprisingly, math chats became a popular "hangout" for many students, and most students attended them at least once a week.

Although the move to incorporate math chats into my day amounted to an additional investment of time, often cutting into my prep and lunch periods, it was an instructional opportunity that held great benefits not just for the students but also for me as their teacher.

The small size of the group led to a style of communicating that was much more personal and revealing than in whole-class discussions. The additional time spent with students formed bonds that enhanced instructional time with the whole class. Not only did I get to know the students' math needs better, informing my instructional decisions, questioning, and pacing, but I got to know students better as people. I found that students were more connected with me and with the material I was teaching, and the improved behavior in the classroom was a testament to the increased respect that had grown out of our time together. Likewise, I felt a greater sense of connection with and understanding of their concerns, struggles, strategies, and successes, and I was able to incorporate them into class discussion for a richer dialogue and more personalized instruction.

Raising the Academic Bar

Although increased student involvement and a positive rapport with students contribute to a productive learning environment, students' interest in learning challenging material gave me further motivation to raise the academic bar for all students. Once I determined the three levels of reasoning I wanted to address, I was obligated to plan tasks and activities that could elicit such thinking. I was required, as a result, to raise my own awareness and knowledge of math content so that I could offer challenging analysis-level extension tasks to students who wanted to press beyond basic grade-level requirements. Students continuously rose to meet these challenges and attempted and achieved more than ever before.

Interviewer: What is the difference between a basic skills question and an extension question?
Student: Basic skills is where you have to know it and it is something that the unit is spending a lot of time on. And an extension question is [where] Miss Her has just briefly touched it or there has been a question on the test to see if you did it. An extension is beyond what she expects but for people who want something to challenge them. I think everybody should at least try the extension question because you might surprise yourself, like I did.
Interviewer: And so you tried extension problems?
Student: I always tried them. I didn't get compound interest but then I wanted to show her that I understand it now. . . . With extensions, I think everybody should try them because the ones I didn't think I could get, it turns out that I did understand it.

Significant Change in Planning Instructional Units

Beginning unit planning by listing the desired objectives and outcomes may sound like a reasonable and organized approach, but, to be honest, I was not in the habit of doing it. As a preservice teacher in college, I remember being required to list objectives for the lessons I designed, but more often than not those objectives were filled in after the bulk of the lesson had been designed, so that they would define and support the tasks that had already been chosen. Not long into my first year of teaching—having spent long nights writing out every single lesson with separate purposes, methods, and activities—I chose to forego the tedious lesson-planning process and rest in the assurance that I knew generally what I was teaching, what the district expected, and the outcomes I wanted. I also felt that I could produce this information on demand. The shift toward naming the skills and objectives of a unit before choosing the activities—with the intent of directing all efforts and activities to the end goal of developing or mastering these objectives—marked a significant change in my practice. The front-end work (i.e., research and preparation prior to the teaching of any lesson) was time-consuming and daunting. The first unit I tried with this new assessment-driven planning method was the More or Less unit (Keijzer, van den Heuvel-Panhuizen, et al., 1998), a number strand unit that emphasizes the application of percentages, fractions, and decimals. In this first run, the knowledge and support of the research team were instrumental in my selection of assessment items to address the three levels of objectives reflecting district and state standards. To my great surprise and pleasure, however, once under way, the days of instruction and assessment flew by smoothly with very little maintenance, and evenings were almost completely devoid of concerns over planning the next day's lesson.

Planning additional units by articulating the learning goals up front was easier the following year. I was more familiar with the curriculum and standards, had a better idea of how students might respond to problems, and had completed the process for several MiC units. I also spent time during the summer making minor adjustments to the previous year's unit goals and collaborated with another sixth-grade teacher to plan other units using this system. In comparison, I noticed that many of the supplementary lessons I taught under the "old system" of planning and assessment no longer met the recently identified goals and objectives. Some key concepts were not addressed, so I included activities to ensure that students had the opportunity to learn important unit goals. In most cases, the lessons I eliminated involved busywork projects, repetitive skill-building tasks, and nonessential problems from the unit. Lessons or tasks that needed to be added to what I previously had taught were primarily extension activities and challenges that students needed to demonstrate in order to earn higher grades.

Major Revisions in the Design and Content of Formal Assessments

Formal assessments took on a new look. At the top of each quiz or test, I indicated the objectives that were being tested. Because single questions often offered the opportunity to demonstrate more than one objective, distinguishing the objectives from the questions was an important organizational step and made recording much easier. It also helped to have the unit objectives identified up front so students could connect what they had been learning to what the assessments were asking for. As a result, the purpose of the assessments became clearer than ever—both for the students and for me. I found myself re-evaluating and rewriting assessments to focus on key concepts, to offer legitimate extension problems, and to eliminate any tasks that did not fit the desired objectives. This process made most of my "old system" tests much shorter, more focused, and more concise. It became possible to assess and record precisely what I valued in terms of mathematical content and process, and because the assessment criteria were available to all, students knew ahead of time exactly what was expected (see Figure 12.3).

Ongoing Adjustments to the Goals and Methods of In-Class Instruction

Knowing my objectives clearly from the start focused my instructional decision making so that it was more certain and purposeful. I was able to more quickly assess and choose the most productive paths of discussion, debate, and exploration because I had a better understanding of the core skills and concepts for the unit. This knowledge served as an interpretive background for making instructional decisions. I found myself asking and able to answer such questions as these: Will this sidebar or line of questioning help further our goals? Will this lead to or lay groundwork for future skills? Will further exploration of this question distract us from our primary goals? How can I redirect or use this line of thinking to connect it with concepts emphasized in this unit or with bigger mathematical ideas?

My increased desire for informal indicators of understanding also affected the instructional period. I sought less to give answers and more

Figure 12.3. First skills list for the More or Less unit.

Primary Strand(s): Number operations and relationships (Strand B)

Standards:

Grade 6—Mastery

- Add, subtract, multiply, and divide whole numbers and decimals.
- Use a variety of estimation strategies to solve and check reasonableness of results of computation problems with whole numbers, fractions, and decimals.

Grade 7—Introduction

- Multiply and divide decimals, fractions, and mixed numbers.
- Use proportional reasoning to solve mathematical and real-world problems (e.g., unit rates, equivalent fractions, equal ratios, constant rate of change, proportions, percentages).

Grade 8—Introduction

- Understand how different algorithms work for arithmetic computations and operations. Use appropriate computational methods (e.g., mental, paper and pencil, calculator, computer, spreadsheet) for situations with rational numbers.
- Perform operations on rational numbers (add, subtract, multiply, divide . . .). Understand the concept of proportion and the applications of proportional reasoning (e.g., scale, similarity, percentage, rate).
- Apply proportional thinking in a variety of problem situations that include
  ➢Ratios and proportions (e.g., rates, scale drawings, similarity).
  ➢Percents, including greater than 100% and less than 1% (discounts, rates of increase and decrease, sales tax).

Curricular Goals and Objectives:

Basic Skills Level
1. Reasonable estimations (multiplying decimals and fractions).
2. Accurately multiply fractions and decimals.
3. Find the percent of a number.
4. Calculate discount and sale prices.
5. Compute total cost with tax.

Application Level
6. Relate percents to fractions and decimals.
7. Work backward to find starting price or discount.
8. Articulation of various estimation and calculation strategies.

Analysis and Extension Level
9. Compound interest (Rule of 72).
10. Refuting common misperceptions with percentages.
11. Finding a percent of a percent (forward *and* backward).
12. Extended thinking.

---

to hear strategies and approaches in the hope of identifying students' discoveries and struggles. Conversations and student-led justifications and explanations became more than occasional practices employed for the sake of variety. Instead, they became my primary methods for gauging and documenting student understanding.

REFLECTIONS AND FUTURE IMPLICATIONS

Let me state, first and foremost, that I do not in any way wish to promote the product described herein as the definitive assessment system. Rather, this chapter recounts a journey of experimentation with assessment models and practices that is by no means over. Assessing for understanding and teaching for understanding both rely on dynamic interaction and construction of meaning rather than static procedures and formulas. No system can be canned and reproduced without inviting the resentment from teachers that might result from top-down directives. The process described herein, which involved years of questioning, trial and error, experimentation, conversation, readings, failures, successes, and communication with parents, students, administrators, and colleagues, was driven by a personal quest to assess student understanding.

If it is not desirable to replicate a product, then how might one replicate the process? Although it is difficult to isolate one catalyst as the primary factor for the change outlined in the path I have retraced, I believe I can identify at least three critical contributing components.

Dissatisfaction with the Status Quo

A recurring theme throughout my years of teaching has been continuous experimentation with change motivated by regular re-evaluation of and reflection on what led to a sense of frustration or dissatisfaction with the methods I was using. Prawat (1989), in his writing on teaching for understanding, observes that "[students] must first be dissatisfied with their preconceptions before being receptive to alternative explanations" (p. 321). I would take this observation a step further to assert that for any of us to be receptive to alternatives to the status quo, we first must be dissatisfied with it. Encouraging other teachers to examine their practices critically and engage in active reflection, so as to desire change, is by far preferable and more likely to be maintained than for someone else to be dissatisfied and require teachers to change something that they may be comfortable with. Inherent in this, is the issue of ownership; the intrinsic desire for change that results from personal discovery will always outperform the extrinsic motivation of a top-down mandate.

A Philosophy of Respect for Students

Because true educational reform above all should benefit students, a desire to improve the learning opportunities for students will not be made willingly unless one is motivated by a concern for their welfare. It takes little effort as a teacher to maintain teacher-centered practices. Student-centered teaching and assessing, however, require great effort and perseverance. They also require the willingness to take risks. Unless teachers see improved student performance and engagement as valid rewards, they will have little reason to take on the extra work concomitant with changing familiar practices.

Presence of Support Systems

Even the most motivated teacher can become quickly and easily burned out when attempting to innovate practice in isolation. In my own story, I acknowledge four key aspects of outside support without which I would still be dissatisfied with the status quo and desiring to do better by my students, but trapped in old and unproductive methods of teaching and assessing.

1. *Administrative support.* The administration provided valuable support, granting me permission to experiment with assessment systems, albeit in the confines of my own classroom. Such flexibility was necessary fertilizer for innovative growth. The money and time to attend various conferences and workshops inspired me and fed my ideas for reform.
2. *Collegial support.* Many of the ideas that collided to create my most recent system of assessment were borrowed or built using the advice and work of admired colleagues. Fellow teachers with a love for students shared rubrics they had created or spent time listening to my ideas and sharing their experiences and wisdom. Others who took similar risks and advocated for departmental reforms in tracking, grouping, and instruction inspired my efforts further. Darling-Hammond and colleagues (1995) acknowledged the power of peers when they witnessed that resistant or skeptical faculty were "won over to innovative practices by three factors: the improved quality of student learning and performance they have witnessed; the persuasive arguments of a critical core of peers; and opportunities to collaborate with colleagues" (p. 266).
3. *A "big brother" or, in this case, university support.* The role of the university collaborative in my later efforts at reforming practice was invaluable. Videotaping and personal observations were instrumental

to my growth, making it possible to view my practices with a critical and curious eye. The university research assistants who worked closely with the teachers also provided critical support. Through the mathematics problems they introduced and encouraged us to solve, through their availability to answer questions over the phone and in person regarding the content and skills promoted in MiC, we grew in our knowledge of content and knowledge of student learning—two critical perspectives needed when teaching and assessing for understanding (Ball, 1993). A final benefit of the university collaborative's involvement was the ability of its staff to show us the "big picture" by connecting us with articles, research, and other examples of reform in the mathematics community. As outsiders, they also helped set limits and reasonable goals in order to avoid the dangers of burnout.

4. *Curricular support.* Although quality materials are not a panacea for improvements in math education, they definitely support change in classroom practice. The open-ended and well-designed tasks in MiC lent themselves to richer discussions and explorations than might have been possible with more traditional materials. By modeling and requiring students to make use of alternative strategies and nonroutine problem solving, the materials helped to create an environment that encouraged teachers to do the same.

For me, the quest to change classroom assessment was a complex journey requiring a great deal of reflection, planning, and experimentation. There were potholes and dead ends along the way. The journey was not overnight, but one that spanned many years and continues to unfold. And while others might be willing to brave such an adventure solo, in my experience it would be wise to consider sharing the journey with interested colleagues, who can provide alternative perspectives for proposed ideas and offer insight on practical ways to put those ideas into practice.

NOTE

1. Although co-authored, this chapter is written in the voice of teacher Teresa Her.

PART V

GENERALIZING THE APPROACH

Too often, interesting stories based on research end up in volumes like this, but are never acted upon in new sites with other teachers. Because changed classroom assessment is a key component in the current reform movement in school mathematics, this summary chapter describes a current research project designed to see whether what has been learned can travel to teachers at other grade levels and be used with other reform curricula.

In Chapter 13, Classroom Assessment as a Basis for Teacher Change, by David C. Webb, Thomas A. Romberg, Truus Dekker, Jan de Lange, and Mieke Abels, the authors suggest a professional development strategy based on the standards-based assessment practices examined in the previous chapters. They describe a current project in which teachers focus on assessment design, interpretation of student work, and instructionally embedded assessment with respect to hypothetical learning trajectories in specific mathematical domains. The authors demonstrate that the program is generalizable to teachers at other grade levels and those using other reform materials. The potential of this approach to professional development and reform in the teaching and learning of mathematics is an exciting consequence of the research reported in this volume.

Chapter 13

Classroom Assessment as a Basis for Teacher Change

David C. Webb
Thomas A. Romberg
UNIVERSITY OF WISCONSIN—MADISON

Truus Dekker
Jan de Lange
Mieke Abels
FREUDENTHAL INSTITUTE, UTRECHT UNIVERSITY

In this chapter, we outline some of the important features leading toward a professional development program focused on reform-based assessment practices that we believe will help teachers make the necessary transitions. We then describe the Classroom Assessment as a Basis for Teacher Change (CATCH) project, where we are studying the potential of an assessment-driven professional development effort in two urban school systems.

As teachers move toward teaching for understanding, they also need to begin to assess for student understanding. To do so, teachers need to critically examine their classroom assessment practices and the familiar conventions of testing, scoring, and grading—practices that have been developed largely to monitor student mastery of skills and procedures. In this book, researchers and classroom teachers describe the teachers' struggle in making the transition from traditional instruction toward teaching mathematics for understanding. When teachers use a reform curriculum, with its potential to promote student understanding, initially they are often unaware of the need to reconsider their current assessment practices in light of the rich evidence generated through complex, real-world mathematics problems. However, as portrayed in Chapters 2, 3, and 4, and particularly in Chapters 11 and 12 by teachers Ann Frederickson and Teresa Her, considerable instructional conflict is generated when teachers use a limited range of assessment practices to assess more substantive learning goals. Getting teachers to shift their assessment practices toward assessing student understanding has the potential of invoking real instructional change, which is key to reaching the overall reform goals for school mathematics.

Although research supports the contention that formative assessment benefits student learning and can be used to facilitate learning with understanding, many mathematics teachers (as described in several chapters here) show limited understanding of the ways in which formative assessment can be incorporated into their classroom practices. As a result, teachers often have difficulties in making didactical decisions based on their students' work and therefore defer instructional decisions to the sequence of activities in a textbook. Students in such classrooms are often left with incomplete information about their progress. They frequently find themselves at a loss to self-assess what they know or don't know, and they continue to apply and reinforce faulty mathematical conceptions.

Both the literature and our experience indicate that assessing for understanding is a critical component of teaching for understanding. Authors of the chapters in this book have suggested a number of design issues that teachers should consider when assessing for student understanding: What is the purpose of an assessment task? What type of response format should be expected from students? Does the problem context support or impede student problem solving? Does the current assessment program allow students opportunities to demonstrate understanding as well as procedural competence? The insight stories in this book have noted particular aspects of teachers' classroom practice and their role in teaching for understanding.

SUPPORTING CHANGE IN TEACHERS' CLASSROOM PRACTICES

The standards-based reform approach to instruction assumes that teachers will use evidence from several sources to inform instruction, but in order to do this effectively, teachers require support in developing their ability to monitor student progress. In the studies reported in this volume, we found that teachers needed technical assistance with assessment design and that they sought tools and methods to further develop their capacity to assess student learning. The studies also showed that teachers could learn to use such practices in their classrooms, that they needed the support of appropriate professional development to do so, and that, as a result, their students' achievement improved (Fennema & Nelson, 1997; Webb et al., 2001).

The assessment methods used by teachers at the sites initially were grounded in practices that focused on mastery of skills and procedures. Despite the efforts of research staff to promote alternative assessment practices, we found that in the absence of additional on-site support, teachers faced difficult challenges in selecting appropriate assessment tasks and adopting the questioning techniques intended by the developers of *Mathematics in Context* (MiC; National Center for Research in Mathematical Sciences Education & Freudenthal Institute, 1997–1998). Teachers saw a need for change in their own assessment practices only after they saw the quality of students' work (including students' ability to construct reasonable justifications for their assertions) that was not being captured by conventional quizzes and tests. Over time, teachers developed a more comprehensive view of assessment as an ongoing process and regularly began to use a wider range of assessment tasks and strategies. The increased attention given to student learning via assessment motivated teachers to study further the relationship among mathematics content, instruction, and the evolution of student understanding as students progressed from informal to formal reasoning in mathematical domains.

Teachers' concerns about assessment are not strictly an issue of resolving problems related to tests and quizzes. Emerging research of teachers' instructionally embedded assessment practices has revealed that teachers are interested in exploring the use of assessment in a variety of instructional contexts (Webb, 2001). As described by teacher Teresa Her in Chapter 12, more purposeful instruction emerged after she restructured and redefined her grading system. These changes motivated her further study of the students' ways of representing and communicating their understanding of mathematics *during* instruction. It follows that when teachers explore and reflect on their own ways of formally assessing student understanding, their inquiry is likely to influence the instructional activities they choose, the questions they ask students, and the content of the classroom discussions they guide. Teachers' motivation to explore student thinking also may require giving additional attention to classroom norms so that students can safely share their emerging conceptions.

Such changes, however, mean risk taking, with consequences that seemed at best uncertain to the teachers in these studies. To influence and support change in teachers' assessment practice, we identified four components that need to be in place or developed as part of a professional development program.

1. *Collaboration with other teachers.* Teachers value discussing rubrics and grading systems as well as their own views (e.g., "Don't score and grade everything"; "Include multiple opportunities for students to demonstrate what they learn"; "A few good tasks can be used to demonstrate understanding—You do not need 20+ items").
2. *A "lifeline" to technical support.* Teachers do not want the research staff to dictate what they should do, but they do want researcher expertise available as needed.
3. *Time.* Change is not easy, but as teachers set aside time to work through the curricular materials and discuss the mathematical goals of the activities, they gradually become comfortable with the instructional process and, in turn, the assessment possibilities.
4. *Support for experimentation.* Teachers need administrators and other teachers to value their efforts to make changes. Much of this support can be supplied by the implementation of a relevant, ongoing, interactive professional development program over which the teachers themselves have considerable control. Some of it can be supported by the growth of external professional networks that such programs can generate (e.g., Newmann & Wehlage, 1995; Webb, Heck, & Tate, 1996).

THE CATCH PROJECT

With these components in mind, we decided to design a professional development program in collaboration with two groups of teachers at different sites to further investigate how the principles and practices would "travel" to other school districts committed to standards-based reform. For a given school district, what kind and level of administrative support, technical knowledge, and professional community are necessary to establish local capacity for teacher learning toward self-sustaining assessment practices that support teaching for understanding?

For a group of teachers, what kind and level of resources and professional development activities are needed to promote teacher interest, inquiry, and reflection toward the development of principled methods for assessing student understanding? Our effort to investigate these and other related research questions was realized as the CATCH project.

In 2001, we implemented the CATCH project in two school districts (Philadelphia, PA, and South Milwaukee, WI) to investigate further how principles of classroom assessment could be disseminated to a significantly larger group of schools and teachers. The research questions that we sought to address were largely questions of professional development and change in teacher practice, coupled with the effect of such changes on student performance. Our work included (1) the identification of materials to initiate teacher inquiry and to support the development of teachers' assessment practices, and (2) the documentation of features of school context that supported teacher change. Our documentation involved gathering information about teachers' conceptions of assessment, teachers' instructional decision making, change in teacher practice, and the relationship between teachers' assessment practices and student achievement. In particular, we were interested in answers to such questions as: How do teachers make decisions about what assessment tasks they use? What reasons motivate their choices? What kind of approach is needed to assist teachers in shifting their instructional focus (as reform curricula require) from covering topics and helping students master a collection of skills to fostering student learning with understanding in specific mathematical domains? How do teachers' assessment practices change as a result of their participation in this professional development program? How are changes in teachers' assessment practices reflected in their students' achievement?

The CATCH professional development program is designed to initiate teachers' critical examination of conventional assessment practices and support integration of teachers' assessment methods and instructional goals. Teachers are introduced to a framework for assessment design to evaluate and critique commonly used classroom assessments. An essential design principle that underpins professional development in CATCH is the pyramid model for assessing three levels of student thinking (see Chapter 1). The three levels in this model, as suggested by the three layers of the pyramid, are described as:

- Level 1: Reproduction, procedures, concepts, and definitions.
- Level 2: Connections and integration for problem solving.
- Level 3: Mathematization, mathematical reasoning, and generalization.

The relative size of the three levels in the pyramid exemplifies the number of items at each level that are required in order to assess student understanding. Assessment tasks used to describe student performance should, over time, fill the pyramid.

As teachers compare their own classroom assessments with the pyramid model, they quickly recognize that most of the assessments that they are using consist of items to assess basic skills, facts, and routine procedures (Level 1), often in multiple-choice or short-answer format. Teachers find that they rarely use problems designed to deepen student knowledge and understanding; more often, students learn how to use basic skills and routine procedures in unfamiliar contexts or choose appropriate mathematical tools to solve problems (Level 2). Nonexistent in teachers' classroom assessments is the use of questions to encourage generalization, mathematical reasoning, and argumentation (Level 3).

Through CATCH institutes and related activities, teachers concluded that they were not giving students opportunities to gain ownership of the mathematical content and were only asking students to reproduce what they had been practicing. Teachers who strive to teach for understanding find that they need to design tasks to assess goals at Levels 2 and 3 in order to assess for understanding. As teachers operationalize this assessment design model, they begin to rethink the learning objectives of their curricula and the questions that they use during instructional activities. Worth noting, these design principles have been applied successfully on large-scale assessments in the Dutch national alternative assessment used in conjunction with the Third International Mathematics and Science Study (Kuiper, Bos, & Plomp, 1997) as well as in the Programme for International Student Assessment (Organisation for Economic Cooperation and Development, 1999).

Underlying the design of resources and the organization of professional development experiences in CATCH is the emphasis on reconnecting formative assessment and teachers' instructional decisions to the development of big ideas in mathematics and assessment of student understanding over time (Shafer, 1996; Shafer & Romberg, 1999). To promote change in teachers' beliefs about assessment, teachers must experience authentic, nonroutine problem solving and need examples of tasks that promote mathematical thinking and reasoning. Achieving student learning with understanding, however, requires more than a collection of engaging classroom activities or thought-revealing assessment tasks. Rather, instructional activities need to be considered in relation to students' current conceptions of mathematics and related activities to further develop those conceptions. The mapping of instructional activities and assessment tasks onto a learning sequence for specific mathematical domains is based on the concept of *hypothetical assessment trajectories* (de Lange, 1999), which are loosely sequenced sets of performance benchmarks for student learning in a content domain. The notion of learning lines within content domains is used as an organisational framework for teachers to select, adapt, and design assessments. There are practical issues teachers must consider, however: Tools and practices used by teachers are limited by the extent to which they can reasonably assess individual and collective learning within a classroom setting. (For additional examples of using learning trajectories as an organizational tool for instruction, see van den Heuvel-Panhuizen [2001], Fosnot and Dolk [2002], and Romberg, Carpenter, and Kwako [in press].) As demonstrated by Ann Frederickson and Teresa Her, when teachers view student learning in terms of learning and assessment trajectories, they are more apt to organize and sequence classroom activities that build from students' prior knowledge.

Attention to content goals and students' mathematical reasoning in the selection and design of classroom activities permits rich opportunities for formative assessment. As teachers broaden their conceptions of classroom assessment, use assessment trajectories to select and design assessment tasks, and make greater use of instructionally embedded assessment, they become better prepared to base their instructional decisions on the student thinking that they listen to and observe. As argued by Kilpatrick, Swafford, and Findell (2001) in *Adding It Up*, "Learning with understanding involves connecting and organizing knowledge, learning builds on what children already know, and formal school instruction should take advantage of children's informal everyday knowledge of mathematics" (p. 342). By improving the alignment among student thinking, instructional decisions, and classroom assessment, learning activities will more likely result in improved student achievement (Bransford, Brown, & Cocking, 1999). Whereas conventional classroom assessment focuses primarily on student outcomes and student recall of formal knowledge and procedures, assessing for student understanding requires that teachers attend to students' incoming knowledge and the way in which evidence for student thinking emerges through informal, preformal, and formal representations. As students learn, teachers must continue to monitor their progress, not in terms of correct or incorrect answers on some percentage scale, but in the broader and deeper sense of their conceptions of mathematical content and their growing ability to adapt what they understand to solve unfamiliar problems embedded in new contexts.

PROFESSIONAL DEVELOPMENT PROGRAM

To support teachers' efforts in implementing new assessment instruments and practices in their classrooms, the professional development activities for CATCH include opportunities for teachers to collaborate with district administrators and engage in shared planning of future professional development activities. During the introductory CATCH institute, teachers and district administrators engage in a range of assessment activities and discuss characteristics of assessment tasks. As part of the institute, teachers and administrators later identify the salient aspects of classroom assessment that require change and begin to prioritize and plan local professional development initiatives to support such changes.

Over a 2-year period, attention is given to supporting implementation of new classroom assessment tasks and practices and to developing the leadership capacity of teachers. After the initial CATCH institute, teachers implement new assessment tools and share the results with their district team. These resources and lead teachers' experiences in developing principled formative assessment methods form the practical basis that district teams use to organize and conduct local CATCH institutes for a new cohort of teachers, beginning with colleagues from the schools of lead teachers. *Framework for Classroom Assessment in Mathematics* (de Lange, 1999) serves as the theoretical basis for these institutes, and *Great Assessment Problems* (Dekker & Querelle, 2002) provides practical examples to promote teacher discussion of design principles for classroom assessment. (An outline of *Great Assessment Problems* is available online at http://www.fi.uu.nl/catch/products/GAP_book/intro.html.)

Underlying the organization of CATCH activities are four related goals for teacher engagement to support the assessment of student understanding. These categories are identified as *initiate, investigate, interpret,* and *integrate.* Figure 13.1 portrays these four interrelated categories of teachers' formative assessment practices as a *professional development trajectory,* noting for each the objective, activities provided, and intended outcomes for students and teachers. It is important to note that this trajectory does not represent a lockstep sequence of activities. The collective beliefs and interests of participating teachers in each district inform the design of professional development activities and the categories of formative assessment that need to be addressed. The intent of Figure 13.1 is simply to highlight the shift in program emphasis as a teacher cohort grows in understanding and practice.

Figure 13.1. Professional development trajectory.

Initiate	Investigate	Interpret	Integrate
Initiate teacher understanding and critique of conventional assessment practices	Engage teachers in selection and design of principled assessment instruments	Support teachers' principled interpretation of student work	Support teachers' principled instructional interventions

Tools & Activities

Initiate	Investigate	Interpret	Integrate
• Critique of "expert" assessments (i.e., common standardized tests) and common classroom assessments • Experience with other assessment methods (i.e., informal classroom assessment, use of Level 2 and Level 3 tasks, and other example from *Framework for Classroom Assessment* and *Great Assessment Problems*)	• Assessment pyramid • Teacher use of *AssessMath!* and other assessment resources • Examples of Level 1 and Level 2 tasks • Technical support for design and adaptation of assessment instruments	• Domain-based scoring institutes • Teacher design and use of analytic and holistic scoring rubrics • Teacher collaboration on rubric design and scoring student work	• Investigation of domain-based assessment trajectories • Use of student verbal and written reasoning • Use of student misconceptions to guide instruction • Discussion of video case studies • New development cycle of balanced assessment materials • Analysis of student representations to discern student capacities and address the needs of more students

Outcomes

Initiate	Investigate	Interpret	Integrate
• Teacher dissatisfaction with current methods • Teacher classroom experimentation • Teacher use of other formative assessment methods • Teachers developing a sense of the pros and cons of using other methods in *their* classrooms • Beginning of student learning with understanding	• Teacher categorization of tasks • Teachers designing Level 2 and Level 3 tasks • Teachers designing and using classroom instruments to assess a wider range of student thinking • Teacher development of nonconventional assessment instruments • Teachers gaining classroom experience with Level 2 and Level 3 tasks • Students learning to reason mathematically, use mathematical models, and generalize	• Teachers learning to interpret student reasoning and use different student work as starting point for instruction (i.e., teaching for student understanding) • Increased use of student argumentation • Student opportunities to "show what they can do"	• Greater instructional flexibility • Student understanding, rather than just reproduction, of mathematical content • Greater student involvement in the assessment process • Greater use of peer assessment • Opportunities for student self-assessment • Increased use of student argumentation • Increased learning opportunities for lower-achieving students

Initiate

Professional development activities in this category are oriented toward initiating teacher understanding and the critique of conventional assessment practices. Teachers critique "expert" assessments, such as commonly used standardized tests and conventional classroom assessments. Teachers also engage in other assessment methods, as students, and respond to tasks that require Level 2 and Level 3 reasoning and to other examples provided in *Framework for Classroom Assessment in Mathematics* (de Lange, 1999) and *Great Assessment Problems* (Dekker & Querelle, 2002). The expected outcomes for this category are teacher dissatisfaction with current assessment methods and reflection on the pros and cons of their own assessment methods, both of which lead to experimentation with formative assessment techniques. As teachers change their classroom assessment goals, an expected outcome is students' shift toward learning mathematics with understanding.

Investigate

Professional development activities in this category are designed to engage teachers in the investigation, selection, and design of principled assessment techniques. Using a model for categorizing tasks and examples of Level 1, 2, and 3 questions (for example, see *AssessMath!* [Cappo, de Lange, & Romberg, 1999]), teachers develop practical expertise in selecting assessment tasks and experiment with designing tasks and balanced tests to assess student understanding. The *AssessMath!* software includes an interactive collection of assessment tasks classified by content, competency levels, and grades. As teachers design and adapt assessment instruments to assess particular content, they receive technical support from colleagues and the research team. Expected teacher outcomes for this category include teacher classification of tasks, greater use of Level 2 and 3 tasks, design and use of assessments with a greater balance across reasoning levels, and use of other assessment instruments (e.g., two-stage tasks, projects, writing prompts). The expected student outcome is that students will learn to reason mathematically, use mathematical models, and generalize.

Interpret

Professional development activities in this category support teachers' principled interpretation of student work. Teachers' development of shared knowledge is promoted through scoring institutes, design and application of holistic and analytic scoring rubrics, and discussions of student representations. To support domain-based formative assessment, activities are structured to promote teacher discussions of student work (e.g., scoring student work). Through these activities, teachers improve their ability to interpret student reasoning and begin to use student work as a starting point for instruction (i.e., teach for understanding). This leads to increased use of student argumentation and the opportunity for students to "show what they know and can do."

Integrate

Professional development activities in this category are designed to support teachers' principled instructional interventions. Teachers investigate student representations with respect to hypothetical assessment trajectories. Video selections of classroom practice are used to broaden teachers' awareness of assessment opportunities such as instructionally embedded assessment. For example, the *Modeling Middle School Mathematics* (Bolster, 2002) video series provides useful examples of teacher–student interaction in classrooms using middle grades reform curricula. Teachers investigate ways to devolve a greater share of the assessment process to students, through principled use of peer and student self-assessment. Workshops and monthly meetings offer opportunities for teachers to further develop domain-based assessment trajectories. By integrating assessment and instruction and investigating ways to use student written and verbal thinking to inform instruction, teachers develop an informed basis for making instructional decisions and eventually show greater adaptability in their lessons, transcending the textbook's lesson to address connections among mathematical concepts in students' terms. These developments lead to greater student understanding of mathematics and improved student achievement.

ENDING NOTE

Our experience shows that teachers benefit greatly from exploring such tacit features of classroom assessment as the design of assessment tasks, the interpretation of students' written and verbal responses, and strategies for eliciting or responding to student ideas during the course of instruction. Yet changing teachers' assessment practice requires more than providing them with a new set of assessment tasks or a new scoring rubric. Teachers must be motivated to change.

- They must recognize the limited information their current assessment practices provide.
- They must realize the necessity of using tasks and practices that can reveal student understanding.
- *And* they must view teaching for student understanding as an important goal.

In the Research in Assessment Practices study, we found that teachers could learn to use formative assessment practices as a consequence of appropriate professional development and, over time, both develop a more comprehensive view of assessment as an ongoing process and use a wider range of assessment strategies. We also have found that administrators and teachers essentially agree on the value of a professional development program oriented toward improvement of classroom assessment. Those involved in our studies see the CATCH project as an opportunity to promote student-centered practice and improve student understanding of mathematics through the project focus on interrelated principles of assessment design, interpretation of student work, and instructional decision making.

In the CATCH program, professional development activities are grounded in the theory and practice of classroom assessment. Teachers developed a broader view of assessment and used guiding principles for teaching for student understanding in their selection of assessment tasks, instructional activities, and the questions they asked during instruction. Teacher inquiry of student understanding, through the exploration of classroom assessment principles and practices and supported by ongoing collaboration with colleagues, provided teachers the beginnings of a theoretical foothold to construct classroom assessment practices more conducive to student learning. CATCH teachers and administrators also participated in regular discussions of practical ways to monitor the implementation of their district curriculum standards and developed reasoned ways of judging and interpreting student performance on district assessments and state-mandated standardized tests. We note that the administrators and teachers involved in CATCH were *motivated* to make those changes.

To replicate this type of assessment-based professional development program, teachers and administrators must be receptive to a long-term, collaborative endeavor that focuses on assessment design, interpretation of student work, and formative assessment practices to support student learning. By *long-term*, we mean both that the program should last several years—until the practices become *self-sustaining*—and that the goals for students are long term. By *collaborative*, we mean that there is a mutual relationship between the professional development staff and the teachers and that information and resources provided by the professional development staff respond to the needs and gradual development of the teachers as they change their formative assessment practices.

Participating teachers also need to commit themselves to participating in workshops and school-based professional development activities, documenting changes in their formative assessment practices, and reflecting on the impact of these changes on other instructional practices. Teachers need to be willing to share the assessment instruments they use, participate in the development of assessment materials, and reflect on and critique their own developing practices and those of their colleagues.

As Lorrie Shepard (2000) argued in her presidential address to the American Educational Research Association, "In order for assessment to play a more useful role in helping students learn, it should be moved into the middle of the teaching and learning process instead of being postponed as only the end-point of instruction" (p. 10). Assessment, particularly when situated as a necessary component of the teaching and learning process, *can* be used to bridge the often separate processes of educational practice, but it is unrealistic to expect teachers to become spontaneous assessment designers. Teachers need appropriate professional development support. A professional development program oriented toward the study and development of classroom assessment will need to become a necessary component of any district's effort in order for teachers to achieve teaching for understanding.

References

Abels, M., de Jong, J. A., Meyer, M. R., Shew, J. A., Burrill, G., & Simon, A. N. (1998). Ups and downs. In National Center for Research in Mathematical Sciences Education & Freudenthal Institute (Eds.), *Mathematics in context*. Chicago: Encyclopedia Britannica.

Abels, M., Wijers, M., Burrill, G., Cole, B. R., & Simon, A. (1998). Operations. In National Center for Research in Mathematical Sciences Education & Freudenthal Institute (Eds.), *Mathematics in context*. Chicago: Encyclopedia Britannica.

Ball, D. L. (1993). Halves, pieces, and twoths: Constructing representational contexts in teaching fractions. In T. P. Carpenter, E. Fennema, & T. A. Romberg (Eds.), *Rational numbers: An integration of research* (pp. 157–196). Mahwah, NJ: Erlbaum.

Black, P., & Wiliam, D. (1998). Assessment and classroom learning. *Assessment in Education, 5*(1), 7–74.

Bolster, L. C. (2002). *Modeling middle school mathematics (MMM): Enhancing professional development in NSF standards-based middle grades mathematics* [On-line video]. http://mmmproject.org/index.html

Bransford, J. D., Brown, A. L., & Cocking, R. R. (Eds.). (1999). *How people learn: Brain, mind, experience, and school*. Washington, DC: National Academy Press.

Cappo, M., de Lange, J., & Romberg, T. A. (1999). *AssessMath!* Santa Cruz, CA: Learning in Motion.

Carpenter, T. P., & Lehrer, R. (1999). Teaching and learning mathematics with understanding. In E. Fennema & T. A. Romberg (Eds.), *Studies in mathematical thinking and learning: Mathematics classrooms that promote understanding* (pp. 19–32). Mahwah, NJ: Erlbaum.

Clarke, B. A. (1995). Expecting the unexpected: Critical incidents in the mathematics classroom. *Dissertation Abstracts International, 56*(01), 125A. (UMI No. AAT 9510289)

Clarke, D. M. (1993). Influences on the changing role of the mathematics teacher. *Dissertation Abstracts International, 54*(06), 2081A. (UMI No. AAT 9318612)

Covey, S. R. (1989). *The seven habits of highly effective people: Restoring the character ethic*. New York: Simon & Schuster.

Curwin, R. L. (1976). In conclusion: Dispelling the grading myths. In S. B. Simon & J. A. Bellanca (Eds.), *Degrading the grading myths: A primer of alternatives to grades and marks* (pp. 138–145). Washington, DC: Association for Supervision and Curriculum Development.

Darling-Hammond, L., Ancess, J., & Falk, B. (1995). *Authentic assessment in action: Studies of schools and students at work.* New York: Teachers College Press.

de Jong, J. A., de Lange, J., Pligge, M. A., & Spence, M. S. (1998). Ways to go. In National Center for Research in Mathematical Sciences Education & Freudenthal Institute (Eds.), *Mathematics in context.* Chicago: Encyclopedia Britannica.

de Jong, J. A., Querelle, N., Meyer, M. R., & Simon, A. N. (1998). Tracking graphs. In National Center for Research in Mathematical Sciences Education & Freudenthal Institute (Eds.), *Mathematics in context.* Chicago: Encyclopedia Britannica.

de Jong, J. A., Wijers, M., Middleton, J. A., Simon, A. N., & Burrill, G. (1998). Dealing with data. In National Center for Research in Mathematical Sciences Education & Freudenthal Institute (Eds.), *Mathematics in context.* Chicago: Encyclopedia Britannica.

de Lange, J. (1987). *Mathematics, insight, and meaning.* Utrecht, The Netherlands: Vakgroep Onderzoek Wiskundeonderwijs en Onderwijscomputercentrum, Utrecht University.

de Lange, J. (1995). Assessment: No change without problems. In T. A. Romberg (Ed.), *Reform in school mathematics and authentic assessment* (pp. 87–172). Albany: State University of New York Press.

de Lange, J. (1999). *Framework for classroom assessment in mathematics.* Madison: National Center for Improving Student Learning and Achievement in Mathematics and Science, Wisconsin Center for Education Research, University of Wisconsin.

de Lange, J., Burrill, G., Romberg, T., & van Reeuwijk, M. (1993). *Learning and testing mathematics in context.* Pleasantville, NY: Wings for Learning.

de Lange, J., Roodhardt, A., Pligge, M., Simon, A., Middleton, J., & Cole, B. (1988). In National Center for Research in Mathematical Sciences Education & Freudenthal Institute (Eds.), *Mathematics in context.* Chicago: Encyclopedia Britannica.

de Moor, E. (1999). *Van vormleer naar realistische meetkunde* [From the study of shapes to spatial reasoning]. Utrecht, The Netherlands: Freudenthal Institute.

Dekker, T. (1997). *Enquiry project: Assessing realistic mathematics education.* Utrecht, The Netherlands: Freudenthal Institute.

Dekker, T., & Querelle, N. (2002). *Great assessment problems.* Utrecht, The Netherlands: Freudenthal Institute.

diSessa, A. (1997). Open tool sets: New ends and new means in learning mathematics and science with computers. In E. Pehkonen (Ed.), *Proceedings of the 21st conference of the International Group for the Psychology of Mathematics Education* (Vol. 1, pp. 47–62). Lahti, Finland.

Feijs, E., de Lange, J., van Reeuwijk, M., Spence, M. S., & Brendefur, J. (1998). Looking at an angle. In National Center for Research in Mathematical Sciences Education & Freudenthal Institute (Eds.), *Mathematics in context*. Chicago: Encyclopedia Britannica.

Fennema, E., & Nelson, B. S. (Eds.). (1997). *Mathematics teachers in transition*. Mahwah, NJ: Erlbaum.

Fosnot, C. T., & Dolk, M. (2002). *Young mathematicians at work: Constructing fractions, decimals and percents*. Portsmouth, NH: Heinemann.

Freudenthal, H. (1983). *Didactical phenomenology of mathematical structures*. Dordrecht, The Netherlands: D. Reidel.

Freudenthal, H. (1984). *Appels en peren: Wiskunde en psychologie* [Apples and pears: Mathematics and psychology]. Apeldoorn, The Netherlands: van Walraven.

Freudenthal, H. (1987). Mathematics starting and staying in reality. In I. Wirszup & R. Street (Eds.), *Proceedings of the USCMP conference on mathematics education on development in school mathematics education around the world* (pp. 279–295). Reston, VA: National Council of Teachers of Mathematics.

Graue, M. E., & Smith, S. Z. (1996). Shaping assessment through instructional innovation. *Journal of Mathematical Behavior, 15*(2), pp. 113–136.

Gravemeijer, K. (1990). Context problems and realistic mathematics instruction. In K. Gravemeijer, M. van den Heuvel-Panhuizen, & L. Streefland (Eds.), *Context, free productions, tests, and geometry in realistic mathematics education* (pp. 10–32). Utrecht, The Netherlands: Vakgroep Onderzoek Wiskundeonderwijs en Onderwijscomputercentrum, Utrecht University.

Gravemeijer, K. (1994). *Developing realistic mathematics education*. Utrecht, The Netherlands: CD β Press.

Gravemeijer, K., Pligge, M. A., & Clarke, B. (1998). Reallotment. In National Center for Research in Mathematical Sciences Education & Freudenthal Institute (Eds.), *Mathematics in context*. Chicago: Encyclopedia Britannica.

Gravemeijer, K., Roodhardt, A., Wijers, M., Cole, B., & Burrill, G. (1998). Expressions and formulas. In National Center for Research in Mathematical Sciences Education & Freudenthal Institute (Eds.), *Mathematics in context*. Chicago: Encyclopedia Britannica.

Greeno, J. G., Pearson, D. P., & Schoenfeld, A. H. (1996). *Research in cognition, learning, and development relevant to the National Assessment of Educational Progress*. Menlo Park, CA: Institute for Research on Learning.

Jonker, V., van Galen, F., Boswinkel, N., Wijers, M., Simon, A., Burrill, G., & Middleton, J. (1997). Take a chance. In National Center for Research in Mathematical Sciences Education & Freudenthal Institute (Eds.), *Mathematics in context*. Chicago: Encyclopedia Britannica.

Keijzer, R., van den Heuvel-Panhuizen, M., Wijers, M., Shew, J. A., Brinker, L., Pligge, M. A., Shafer, M., & Brendefur, J. (1998). More or less. In National Center for Research in Mathematical Sciences Education & Freudenthal Institute (Eds.), *Mathematics in context*. Chicago: Encyclopedia Britannica.

Keijzer, R., van Galen, F., Gravemeijer, K., Shew, J., Cole, B., & Brendefur, J. (1998). Fraction times. In National Center for Research in Mathematical Sciences Education & Freudenthal Institute (Eds.), *Mathematics in context*. Chicago: Encyclopedia Britannica.

Kemme, S. L., & Wijers, M. (1996). Als jonge honden op een bak met lever [Like young dogs at a bowl of liver]. *Nieuwe Wiskrant, 15*(3), 22–27.

Kilpatrick, J., Swafford, J., & Findell, B. (Eds.). (2001). *Adding it up: Helping children learn mathematics*. Washington, DC: National Academy Press.

Kindt, M., Abels, M., Meyer, M. R., & Pligge, M. A. (1998). Comparing quantities. In National Center for Research in Mathematical Sciences Education & Freudenthal Institute (Eds.), *Mathematics in context*. Chicago: Encyclopedia Britannica.

Kuiper, W., Bos, K., & Plomp, T. (1997). De TIMSS nationale optietoets wiskunde [TIMSS national alternative test in mathematics]. *Nieuwe Wiskrant, 17*(1), 39–46.

National Center for Research in Mathematical Sciences Education & Freudenthal Institute. (Eds.). (1997–1998). *Mathematics in context*. Chicago: Encyclopedia Britannica.

National Council of Teachers of Mathematics. (1989). *Curriculum and evaluation standards for school mathematics*. Reston, VA: Author.

National Council of Teachers of Mathematics. (1991). *Professional standards for teaching mathematics*. Reston, VA: Author.

National Council of Teachers of Mathematics. (1995). *Assessment standards for school mathematics*. Reston, VA: Author.

Newmann, F. M., & Wehlage, G. G. (1995). *Successful school restructuring: A report to the public and educators by the Center on Organization and Restructuring of Schools*. Madison: Wisconsin Center for Education Research.

Organisation for Economic Cooperation and Development. (1999). *Measuring student knowledge and skills: A new framework for assessment*. Paris: Author.

Prawat, R. S. (1989). Teaching for understanding: Three key attributes. *Teaching and Teacher Education, 5*, 315–328.

Richardson, V. (1994). Conducting research on practice. *Educational Researcher, 23*(5), 5–10.

Romberg, T. A. (Ed.). (1992). *Mathematics assessment and evaluation: Imperatives for mathematics educators*. Albany: State University of New York Press.

Romberg, T. A. (1997). Mathematics in context: Impact on teachers. In E. Fennema & B. S. Nelson (Eds.), *Mathematics teachers in transition* (pp. 357–380). Mahwah, NJ: Erlbaum.

Romberg, T. A., Carpenter, T. C., & Kwako, J. (in press). Standards-based reform and teaching for understanding. In T. A. Romberg, T. C. Carpenter, & F. A. Dremock (Eds.), *Understanding mathematics and science matters*. Mahwah, NJ: Erlbaum.

Romberg, T. A., & de Lange, J. (1998). *Mathematics in context: Teacher resource and implementation guide*. Chicago: Encyclopedia Britannica.

Romberg, T., & Shafer, M. C. (1995). *Results of assessment*. Madison: National

Center for Research in Mathematical Sciences Education, University of Wisconsin.

Romberg, T. A., Webb, D. C., Burrill, J., & Ford, M. J. (2001). *Middle school design collaborative: Final report to the Verona area school district.* Madison: National Center for Improving Student Learning and Achievement in Mathematics and Science, Wisconsin Center for Education Research, University of Wisconsin.

Romberg, T. A., Zarinnia, E. A., & Collis, K. F. (1990). A new world view of assessment in mathematics. In G. Kulm (Ed.), *Assessing higher order thinking in mathematics* (pp. 21–38). Washington, DC: American Association for the Advancement of Science.

Roodhardt, A., Abels, M., Clarke, B., Clarke, D., Spence, M., Shew, J., & Brinker, L. (1998). Triangles and patchwork. In National Center for Research in Mathematical Sciences Education & Freudenthal Institute (Eds.), *Mathematics in context.* Chicago: Encyclopedia Britannica.

Roodhardt, A., Wijers, M., Cole, B., & Burrill, G. (1998). Great expectations. In National Center for Research in Mathematical Sciences Education & Freudenthal Institute (Eds.), *Mathematics in context.* Chicago: Encyclopedia Britannica.

Sarason, S. B. (1971). *The culture of the school and the problem of change.* Boston: Allyn & Bacon.

Shafer, M. C. (1995). *The impact of a teacher's assessment practices on instructional decisions.* Madison: Wisconsin Center for Education Research, University of Wisconsin.

Shafer, M. C. (1996). Assessment of student growth in a mathematical domain over time. *Dissertation Abstracts International, 57*(06), 2347A. (UMI No. AAT 9631840)

Shafer, M. C., & Romberg, T. A. (1999). Assessment in classrooms that promote understanding. In E. Fennema & T. A. Romberg (Eds.), *Classrooms that promote mathematical understanding* (pp. 159–184). Mahwah, NJ: Erlbaum.

Shepard, L. A. (2000). The role of assessment in a learning culture. *Educational Researcher, 29*(7), 4–14.

Simon, M. A. (1995). Reconstructing mathematics pedagogy from a constructivist perspective. *Journal for Research in Mathematics Education, 26,* 114–145.

Smith, M. E. (2000). *Classroom assessment and evaluation: A case study of practices in transition. Dissertation Abstracts International, 61*(12), 4713. (UMI No. ATT 9996883)

Stenmark, J. K. (Ed.). (1991). *Mathematics assessment: Myths, models, good questions, and practical suggestions.* Reston, VA: National Council of Teachers of Mathematics.

Taylor, C. (1994). Assessment for measurement or standards: The peril and promise of large-scale assessment reform. *American Educational Research Journal, 31,* 231–262.

van den Heuvel-Panhuizen, M. (1995). *Developing assessment problems on percentage: An example of developmental research on assessment conducted with the MiC project along the lines of realistic mathematics education* [Internal publication]. Utrecht, The Netherlands: Freudenthal Institute.

van den Heuvel-Panhuizen, M. (1996). *Assessment and realistic mathematics education.* Utrecht, The Netherlands: Center for Science and Mathematics Education Press, Utrecht University.

van den Heuvel-Panhuizen, M. (2001). Learning–teaching trajectories with intermediate attainment targets. In M. van den Heuvel-Panhuizen (Ed.), *Children learn mathematics* (pp. 13–22). Utrecht, The Netherlands: Freudenthal Institute & National Institute for Curriculum Development.

van den Heuvel-Panhuizen, M., Streefland, L., Meyer, M., Middleton, J. A., & Browne, L. (1997). Per sense. In National Center for Research in Mathematical Sciences Education & Freudenthal Institute (Eds.), *Mathematics in context.* Chicago: Encyclopedia Britannica.

van Reeuwijk, M. (1995, April). *Realistic assessment.* Paper presented at the research presession at the annual meeting of the National Council of Teachers of Mathematics, Boston.

van Reeuwijk, M., & Wijers, M. (2002). Explanations why? The role of explanations in answers to (assessment) problems. In H. M. Doerr & R. A. Lesh (Eds.), *Beyond constructivism: Models and modeling perspectives on mathematics problem solving, learning, and teaching* (pp. 191–202). Mahwah, NJ: Erlbaum.

Verhage, H., & de Lange, J. (1997). Mathematics education and assessment. *Pythogoras, 42,* 16.

Webb, D. C. (2001). Instructionally embedded assessment practices of two middle grades mathematics teachers. *Dissertation Abstracts International, 62*(07), 2368A. (UMI No. ATT 3020735)

Webb, D. C., Ford, M. J., Burrill, J., Romberg, T. A., Reif, J., & Kwako, J. (2001). *Middle school design collaborative: Report on Year 3 student achievement data.* Madison: National Center for Improving Student Learning and Achievement in Mathematics and Science, Wisconsin Center for Education Research, University of Wisconsin.

Webb, N. L. (1993). Assessment for the mathematics classroom. In N. L. Webb & A. F. Coxford (Eds.), *Assessment in the mathematics classroom.* Reston, VA: National Council of Teachers of Mathematics.

Webb, N. L., Heck, D. J., & Tate, W. F. (1996). The Urban Mathematics Collaborative project: A study of teacher, community, and reform. In S. A. Raizen & E. D. Britton (Eds.), *Case studies of U.S. innovations in mathematics education* (Vol. 3, pp. 245–360). Dordrecht, The Netherlands: Kluwer Academic.

Wiggins, G. P. (1993). *Assessing student performance: Exploring the purpose and limits of testing.* San Francisco: Jossey-Bass.

Wiggins, G. P., & McTighe, J. (1998). *Understanding by design.* Alexandria, VA: Association for Supervision and Curriculum Development.

Wijers, M., de Lange, J., Shafer, M. C., & Burrill, G. (1998). Insights into data. In National Center for Research in Mathematical Sciences Education & Freudenthal Institute (Eds.), *Mathematics in context*. Chicago: Encyclopedia Britannica.

Wijers, M., van Galen, F., Querelle, N., de Lange, J., Shew, J. A., & Brinker, L. (1994). Reflections. Madison: National Center for Research in Mathematical Sciences Education, University of Wisconsin. (Revised and published as Reflections on number, by M. Wijers, J. de Lange, K. Gravemeijer, N. Querelle, J. A. Shew, L. J. Brinker, M. A. Pligge, & A. N. Simon. (1998). In National Center for Research in Mathematical Sciences Education & Freudenthal Institute (Eds.), *Mathematics in context*. Chicago: Encyclopedia Britannica).

About the Contributors

Mieke Abels is a researcher at the Freudenthal Institute at the University of Utrecht in the Netherlands. From 1975 to 2000 she was a secondary mathematics teacher in the Netherlands. She also worked for 3 years as a part-time teacher at the College for Primary Education and was involved in the development of textbooks in the Netherlands (Moderne Wiskunde) and in the United States (Mathematics in Context). She has conducted many professional development activities in the Netherlands, South Africa, and the United States. Her most recent work is the design of a guide for professional development in assessment, a product that was developed and tested during the CATCH project.

Jan de Lange is director of the Freudenthal Institute and a professor at the University of Utrecht in the Netherlands. His research focuses on modeling, assessment design, multimedia applications, and issues related to program implementation. Dr. de Lange was member of the National Advisory Board of the Third International Mathematics and Science Study (TIMSS) and the International Commission for TIMSS–Repeat, served as chairman of the Commission for the Development of New Curricula in the Netherlands, and currently serves as supervisor to curriculum projects in the United States, Bolivia, and South Africa. He is currently chairman of the Mathematical Expert Group of the Organisation for Economic Cooperation and Development (OECD) Programme for International Student Assessment project and was influential in the writing of the OECD Framework for Mathematics.

Truus Dekker is a senior researcher at the Freudenthal Institute at the University of Utrecht. She has over 25 years of experience as a secondary mathematics teacher. She served as chairwoman of CEVO, the Dutch national committee in charge of central examinations in mathematics, and was a member of the National Advisory Board of TIMSS.

Her recent work at the Freudenthal Institute focuses on assessment development for the Programme for International Student Assessment of the Organisation for Economic Cooperation and Development. Her international experience includes writing professional development materials for classroom assessment, and she has been a featured speaker at assessment workshops in the United States.

Els Feijs is a researcher at the Freudenthal Institute at the University of Utrecht. She has been working as a researcher and as a curriculum developer for various projects. She was involved in professional development activities for both teacher trainers and inservice primary mathematics teachers, including development of and research into courseware and video materials. Since 1991, she has been a coordinator for the middle school curriculum development project Mathematics in Context. Besides curriculum development and the design of teacher materials, her activities for this project have included conducting research into the implementation of Vision Geometry as embedded in the MiC curriculum, resulting in various presentations and publications. Other projects in which Feijs was involved include the Show Me project, the Research into Assessment Practices project, and the CATCH project, in which she focused on changes in teachers' attitudes and practices as a result of their participation in professional development activities.

Michael Ford is an Assistant Professor at the University of Pittsburgh. He recently completed his doctorate in educational psychology at the University of Wisconsin–Madison. His research focuses on classroom experiences that instill not only a respect for science through the demonstrated power of its products, but also an ability to engage appropriately in scientific practice. In his research, Ford draws on the history and philosophy of science to identify the practices through which scientists transform intuitive ideas into scientific knowledge. He then designs classroom instruction to immerse students within these practices and studies empirically how these instructional designs support student understanding of scientific inquiry and a propensity to employ scientific practices in novel situations.

Ann Frederickson is an eighth-grade math and science teacher at Savanna Oaks Middle School in Verona, Wisconsin. She has taught for 21 years. During that time, she taught eighth-grade math for 5 years, seventh-grade math for 3 years, and sixth-grade math and science for 13 years. She is involved in the staff development committee and teacher mentor program at her school.

M. Elizabeth Graue is Professor in the Department of Curriculum and Instruction at the University of Wisconsin–Madison. A former kindergarten and early childhood special education teacher, she has focused her research on kindergarten policy and practice, research methodology (particularly related to studying children), and home–school relations. She has served as associate editor of the *Review of Educational Research*, on the technical advisory board for the National Education Goals Panel, as member-at-large for the early education–child development special interest group, as chair of the American Educational Research Association (AERA) special interests group on qualitative research methodology, as a member of the AERA special interests group committee, and as a consulting editor for *Early Childhood Research Quarterly*.

Teresa Her taught mathematics at Savanna Oaks Middle School in Verona, Wisconsin, for 6 years before leaving full-time teaching to raise her son. She currently lives with her husband, son, and extended family near Madison, Wisconsin, and maintains contact with teaching as a high school mathematics tutor.

Thomas A. Romberg is Bascom Professor of Education and Professor Emeritus in the Curriculum and Instruction Department at the University of Wisconsin–Madison. He was director of the National Center for Improving Student Learning and Achievement in Mathematics and Science from 1997 to 2000. He was also chair of the National Council of Teachers of Mathematics (NCTM) Commission on Standards for School Mathematics, which produced the NCTM's standards. His areas of interest include the learning of mathematics, methods of assessing and evaluating both students and programs, and integration of research on learning, teaching, and curriculum.

Mary C. Shafer is an Assistant Professor in the Department of Mathematical Sciences at Northern Illinois University. She taught mathematics at the junior high and high school levels for 16 years. From 1996 to 2002, she was research coordinator and co-director for NSF-funded research projects on the impact of *Mathematics in Context* on student achievement. She is co-editor of a forthcoming book on the results of this research. Her publications have focused on classroom assessment and studying the impact of reform mathematics curricula. She currently teaches mathematics education courses to prospective and practicing teachers. Her research interests include studying teachers' pedagogical decisions and classroom assessment practices.

Marvin E. Smith is a curriculum consultant and developer for Brigham Young University's Bilingual/ESL Endorsement through Distance Education project. His scholarly expertise includes learning with understanding, assessment, and teacher education. He was instrumental in the development of *Assessment Standards for School Mathematics*, published in 1995 by the National Council of Teachers of Mathematics, and worked on the development of assessments for *Mathematics in Context*.

Stephanie Z. Smith is Assistant Professor of Mathematics Education in the Department of Teacher Education of the David O. McKay School of Education at Brigham Young University. After 8 years of teaching in grades pre-K through 12, she designed professional development experiences for teachers beginning to use *Mathematics in Context*. Currently she has been conducting a teaching/research experiment to teach mathematics to one class of elementary students each day. Her research interests include teachers' and children's conceptions of mathematics and the learning and teaching of mathematics for understanding.

Marja van den Heuvel-Panhuizen is a senior researcher at the Freudenthal Institute at the University of Utrecht in the Netherlands. Her research interests lie with the instruction theory for mathematics education, curriculum development, and professional development. Within this field, she has a leading role in developing expertise on assessment of students' achievements in mathematics. She has been working on a number of national and international research projects, including comparative and evaluative studies, and has experience in qualitative and quantitative research methods and in design research. She is project leader for two government-funded projects, one developing learning–teaching trajectories for primary school mathematics, and the other developing a course for inservice training of primary school mathematics coordinators.

Martin van Reeuwijk is a researcher at the Freudenthal Institute at the University of Utrecht. He was a coordinator of the curriculum development project *Mathematics in Context*. In the context of this project, he conducted research on early algebra and assessment, resulting in various presentations at international conferences and publications in journals and magazines. As a consequence, he has been involved in inservice trainings and other professionalization programs for teachers at the middle grades. Currently he is directing two projects in which applets (small computer programs that run over the Internet) have been developed, tested, and implemented.

David C. Webb is Associate Research Scientist at the Wisconsin Center for Education Research at the University of Wisconsin–Madison, and is Executive Director of Freudenthal Institute USA. His research has focused on teacher change through classroom assessment, the impact of reform curricula on student learning and achievement, and design of formative assessment tools.

Monica Wijers is a researcher at the Freudenthal Institute at the University of Utrecht. She has been a teacher, teacher trainer, researcher, and curriculum developer in the field of mathematics education since the early 1980s. She has been involved in several curriculum development projects both nationally and internationally, among them the development of the *Mathematics in Context* curriculum. One of her domains of interest is the role of mathematics in relation to other subjects. For high school, this involves the relation between science and mathematics; for lower vocational education, the relation between mathematics and the vocational subjects.

Index

Abels, Mieke, 49, 51, 53–54, 56–57, 147, 148, 173, 177, 180, 192–193, 221, 223–235
Aberson, Ms. (teacher), 101–121
Accountability, increased levels of, 212–213
Adding It Up (Kilpatrick et al.), 229
Administrative support systems, 219, 226
American Educational Research Association (AERA), 235
Ancess, J., 205, 219
Angle (MiC unit), 123–127
AssessMath! (Cappo et al.), 232
Assessment, 14–19
  assessment pyramid in, 17, 18, 207, 227–228
  case study of classroom, 60–79
  changes made by teachers and, 25–44, 51–53, 55–58
  changing classroom, 193–194, 196
  constraints of time in, 33, 48
  constraints on change in, 38–41
  creating assessment tasks, 16, 17
  cutoff point in, 98
  designing, 85–87, 104–119, 127–136
  developing perspective on role of, 200–202
  discourse-based, 169–187
  documenting learning in, 48–49
  educational change and, 200–220
  emergent changes in, 46–49
  end-of-unit. *See* End-of-unit assessments
  exemplars in, 64
  expanding practices in, 49–53
  focusing, 46–47, 54–55
  formal approaches to. *See* Formal assessment
  formative. *See* Formative assessment
  grading student performance. *See* Grading process
  of individual students, 47–48
  informal approaches to. *See* Informal assessment
  information about student learning and, 27–37, 49–51, 155–168
  interpreting and communicating information on, 37–38
  levels of student performance, 16–19
  measurement model of, 64
  observing student work, 35–37, 49–51, 58
  ongoing opportunities for, 78
  open-open. *See* Open-open assessment
  peer assessment, 180–184
  in Per Sens (MiC unit), 85–97
  perspective on role of, 200–202
  practical issues in, 97–98
  principles of classroom, 15–16
  problem context and, 30–33
  problem of simple marking in, 97–98
  problems on percentage and, 83–99
  quizzes in, 29–30, 31, 55, 56–57
  standards model of, 64
  steps in process of changing, 15
  teacher interaction with students in classroom, 33–35, 45–59
At-risk students, 201
Authentic Assessment in Action (Darling-Hammond et al.), 205

Backwards curriculum design, 76, 78–79
Baker, Ms. (teacher), 101–121
Ball, D. L., 220
Benchmark problems, 55–58
"Big brother" support systems, 219–220
Black, P., 170

Blakemore, Ms. (teacher), 49–53
Bolster, L. C., 233
Bos, K., 228
Boswinkel, N., 10
Boxer (software), 189, 195–196
Brain stretchers, 213–214
Bransford, J. D., 59, 229
Brendefur, J., 123–124, 132, 191–194,
    196, 208, 215
Brinker, L., 49, 51, 64–65, 132, 208, 215
Brown, A. L., 59, 229
Browne, L., 83
Burrill, G., 10–15, 20, 27, 29, 53–54, 56–
    57, 64–65, 78, 128, 147, 148, 159,
    163, 173, 177, 180, 188, 190, 192,
    202
Burrill, J., 225

Cappo, M., 232
Carpenter, T. C., 229
Carpenter, T. P., 58, 171
Case studies of assessment, 60–79
    comparison of MiC and traditional
        approaches in, 60–79
    discourse-based assessment, 171–184
    in formative assessment, 159–166
    goals for learning and, 65–67, 76–78,
        159–160, 163
    practices for evaluating and grading
        in, 71–73
    practices for monitoring study
        progress in, 67–70
    study design, 64–65
CATCH. See Classroom Assessment as a
    Basis for Teacher Change (CATCH)
Change. See Educational change
Clarke, B. A., 15, 49, 51, 100, 102, 138,
    139
Clarke, D. M., 15, 49, 51
Classroom Assessment as a Basis for
    Teacher Change (CATCH), 223,
    226–235
    assessment pyramid and, 17, 18, 207,
        227–228
    hypothetical assessment trajectories
        and, 229
    origins of, 226–228
    professional development program in,
        230–235
Classroom culture, 121

Cocking, R. R., 59, 229
Cole, B. R., 11–12, 27, 29, 53–54, 56–57,
    128, 190, 191–194, 196
Collegial support systems, 219
Collins, Mr. (teacher), 102–121
Collis, K. F., 61–62
Comparing Quantities (MiC unit), 192–
    193
Covey, Stephen R., 76, 78–79
Critical attitude, of students, 8
Curricular support systems, 220
Curwin, R. L., 76
Cutoff point, in assessment, 98

Darling-Hammond, L., 205, 219
Dealing with Data (MiC unit), 9, 10, 11,
    159–163
De Jong, J. A., 10, 147–149, 159, 173,
    177, 180
Dekker, Truus, 17, 221, 223–235, 230,
    232
De Lange, Jan, 3, 5–21, 9, 10, 11–
    15, 17, 20, 64–65, 76, 78, 82, 122–
    136, 123–124, 137, 138, 163, 221,
    223–235, 229, 230, 232
De Moor, E., 101
Differential trait theory, 66, 73
Differentiated instruction, 39–40
Digging Numbers (MiC unit), 11–12,
    13
Discourse-based assessment, 169–187
    case study of, 171–184
    peer assessment in, 180–184
    principles and practices of, 173–
        184
    processes in, 169–171, 175–180
DiSessa, Andrea, 189, 196–197
Dolk, M., 229

Educational change, 200–220
    assessing for understanding, 55, 56–
        57, 71, 131, 206–210
    classroom assessment and, 193–194,
        196, 223–235
    constraints on, 38–40
    and dissatisfaction with status quo,
        218
    emergent, 46–49
    impact and challenges of
        implementation, 210–218

moving from grades to assessment, 204–206
perspective on role of assessment, 200–202
respect for students and, 219
rethinking classroom practices, 202–204
role of students and, 191–193, 194–195
role of teachers and, 190–191, 194–195
supporting change in classroom practices of teachers, 224–226
support systems and, 219–220, 226
teacher motivation for, 234
by teachers, 12–13, 20, 25–44, 51–53, 55–58
End-of-unit assessments, 48, 55, 65
in Angle (MiC unit), 123–127
in Expressions and Formulas (MiC unit), 27–44, 128–131, 190–191
in Per Sens (MiC unit), 87–97
in Reallotment (MiC unit), 100–121
rules of, 131
Evaluation. *See also* Assessment
feedback to students and, 71, 72, 76
in traditional versus MiC approach to mathematics, 71–74
Exemplars, 64
Expressions and Formulas (MiC unit), 27–44, 128–131, 190–191

Falk, B., 205, 219
Feedback
in discourse-based assessment, 170–171
to students, 71, 72, 76
Feijs, Els, 82, 122–136, 123–124
Fennema, E., 225
Findell, B., 229
Ford, Michael J., 154, 188–199, 202, 225
Formal assessment, 71–73, 156, 158, 160, 166–168, 216
Formative assessment
case studies in, 159–166
CATCH and, 228
checking instructional plans in, 157
defined, 155–156

impact on student learning, 224
information about learning of, 155–168
instructional planning in, 157–158, 159–160, 165
Fosnot, C. T., 229
Fraction Times (MiC unit), 191, 193–194, 196
Framework for Classroom Assessment in Mathematics (de Lange), 15–16, 137–138, 230, 232
Frederickson, Ann, 2, 154, 188–199, 224
Freudenthal, Hans, 7, 12, 101
Freudenthal Institute, 1, 5, 10, 15, 25, 60, 83, 100, 123, 138, 156, 171, 189, 202–203, 225
Funneling responses, in discourse-based assessment, 176, 184

Goals for learning
in case studies of assessment, 65–67, 76–78, 159–160, 163
in MiC versus traditional approach, 65–67, 76–78
ongoing adjustments to, 216–218
teacher interpretation of, 123–125
Grading process, 37–38, 40–41, 48. *See also* Assessment
computation of letter grades, 75–76
for investigations, 144–145
moving to assessment from, 204–206
problem of simple marking in, 97–98
for Reallotment (MiC unit), 144–145
in traditional versus MiC approach to mathematics, 71–74
Graue, M. Elizabeth, 23, 25–44, 73
Gravemeijer, K., 12, 27, 29, 63, 100, 102, 128, 138, 139, 190–194, 196
Great Assessment Problems (Dekker and Querelle), 230, 232
Great Expectations (MiC unit), 11
Greenfield, Ms. (teacher), 159–163, 166, 168
Greeno, J. G., 63

Heck, D. J., 226
Her, Teresa, 2, 154, 200–220, 224
Hetereogeneous grouping, 39–40, 67
Homework, 71, 74, 103, 144

Homogeneous grouping, 66
Humor, in discourse-based assessment,
    174

Informal assessment, 67–70, 103–104,
    156, 158, 167–168. *See also* Quizzes
Initiation, in professional
    development trajectory, 231, 232
Innovation. *See* Instructional innovation
Insights Into Data (MiC unit), 10–11,
    163–166
Instructional hooks, in discourse-based
    assessment, 174–175
Instructional innovation, 25–44
    constraints to change in assessment,
        38–41
    with Expressions and Formulas (MiC
        unit), 27–44
    information about student learning
        in, 27–37, 49–51, 155–168
    interpreting and communicating
        assessment information in, 37–38
    with Operations (MiC unit), 55–58
    setting for, 27
    with Triangles and Patchwork (MiC
        unit), 51–53
Instructional planning, in formative
    assessment, 157–158, 159–160, 165
Integration, in professional
    development trajectory, 231, 233
Interpretation, in professional
    development trajectory, 231, 232–
    233
Investigation, in professional
    development trajectory, 231, 232
Investigations, 137–151
    features of, 146–150
    "Floor Covering" problem, 138–147,
        149–150
    from Reallotment (MiC unit), 138–
        147, 149–150
    reflections on, 145–146, 150–151
    research on, 137–138
    from Tracking Graphs (MiC unit),
        147, 149
    from Ups and Downs (MiC unit), 147,
        148

Jonker, V., 10

Keijzer, R., 132, 191–194, 196, 208, 215
Kemme, S. L., 146
Kilpatrick, J., 229
Kindt, M., 192–193
Koster, Ms., 171–187
Kuiper, W., 228
Kwako, J., 225, 229

Labeling, 66
Lehrer, R., 58, 171

Mathematics in Context (MiC). *See also*
    names of specific units
    adaptation for use in U.S.
        schools, 1
    case study in use of, 60–79
    comparison with traditional
        approaches, 60–79
    components of, 7–15
    described, 1
    development of, 1
    educational change and, 200–220
    field-tests of, 45–59
    funding of, 6
    progressive formalization in, 6, 11
    Realistic Mathematics Education
        (RME) as foundation for, 6–15,
        63, 83–99
    statistics and probability strand, 8–
        12
    traditional approach to mathematics
        versus, 60–79
McTighe, J., 78–79
Measurement model of assessment,
    64
Meyer, M. R., 83, 147–149, 173, 177,
    180, 192–193
MiC curriculum. *See Mathematics in
    Context* (MiC)
Michaels, Mr. (teacher), 53–58
Middle School Design Collaborative at
    Verona, Wisconsin (VMSDC), 188–
    199
    building professional community,
        196–197
    changing classroom assessment in,
        193–194, 196
    changing role of students in, 191–193,
        195–196

changing role of teacher in, 190–191,
194–195
first year (1997–1998), 190–194
participation in MiC, 189–190
second year (1998–1999), 194–197
summary of experiences in, 197–199
third year (1999–2000), 197
Middleton, J. A., 10–12, 83, 159
Modeling Middle School Mathematics
(Bolster), 233
More or Less (MiC unit), 208, 211, 215,
217

National Center for Improving Student
Learning and Achievement in
Mathematics and Science (NCISLA),
1, 2, 188–189
National Center for Research in
Mathematical Sciences Education
(NCRMSE), 1, 2, 5, 10, 25, 60, 83,
100, 123, 138, 156, 171, 189, 202–
203, 225
National Council of Teachers of
Mathematics (NCTM), 1, 15, 26, 35,
60, 62–67, 76–79, 170, 208
National Science Foundation (NSF),
2, 6
NCISLA. *See* National Center for
Improving Student Learning and
Achievement in Mathematics and
Science (NCISLA)
NCRMSE. *See* National Center for
Research in Mathematical Sciences
Education (NCRMSE)
Nelson, B. S., 225
Newmann, F. M., 226
Nielsen, Ms. (teacher), 159, 163–166
Notebooks, student, 47
Note taking, by teachers, 36

Observing student work, 35–37, 49–51,
58
Open-open assessment, 122–136
Angle (MiC unit), 123–127
defined, 122
degrees of openness in, 125–127
design of, 85–87, 104–119, 127–136
Expressions and Formulas (MiC unit),
27–44, 128–131, 190–191

passive assessment expertise of
teachers in, 123–125
simple but complex, 131–135
Open tasks, 14
Operations (MiC unit), 53–58
Organisation for Economic Cooperation
and Development (OECD), 228

Participation, student, 34–35, 54–58
Patterson, Anne (teacher), 27–29, 33–38
Pearson, D. P., 63
Peer assessment, 180–184
Percentage problems, 83–99
Per Sens (MiC unit), 83–99
assessment activities in, 84–97
"Best Buy" problem, 88–91
"Black Currant Jam" problem, 91–93,
94
contexts of, 84
described, 83–85
designing assessment for, 85–87
"Twax Bar" problem, 93–97
Picturing Numbers (MiC unit), 8, 11
Pligge, M. A., 10–12, 100, 102, 132, 138,
139, 192–193, 208, 215
Plomp, T., 228
Portfolio assessment, 78, 201
Prawat, R. S., 218
Probing assessment, in discourse-based
assessment, 176, 184
Professional community, 196–197
Professional development
building professional community in,
196–197
changing classroom assessment and,
193–194, 196
changing role of students and, 191–
193, 195–196
changing role of teacher and, 190–
191, 194–195
and Classroom Assessment as a Basis
for Teacher Change (CATCH),
230–235
in Middle School Design Collaborative
at Verona, Wisconsin (VMSDC),
188–199
participation in MiC and, 189–190
and professional development
trajectory, 230–233

Programme for International Student
Assessment (Organisation for
Economic Cooperation and
Development), 228
Progressive formalization, 6, 11

Quality scales, 74–75
Querelle, N., 64–65, 147, 149, 230, 232
Questioning, in teaching process, 68–
70
Quizzes
in assessing student understanding,
55, 56–57, 71, 131
progressive development of, 29–30, 31

Realistic Mathematics Education (RME),
5–21
assessment pyramid in, 17, 18, 207,
227–228
components of, 7–15, 12, 14, 19
described, 6–7
as foundation for MiC curriculum, 6–
15, 63, 83–99
mathematization of reality in, 20
Reallotment (MiC unit), 100–121
assessing student performance in,
103–104
"Creating Shapes with a Given Area"
problem, 116–118
described, 101, 138–140
designing assessment for, 104–119
differences between classes and, 101–
103
evaluation of test, 119–121
"Find the Area" problem, 109–111
"Floor Covering" problem, 138–147,
149–150
investigations from, 138–147, 149–
150
"Photo Frame" problem, 115–116
"Prices of Shaded Pieces" problem,
111–112, 113
scoring and grading in, 144–145
student work in, 140–143
"Tesellation" problem, 118–119
"Two Methods for Finding Area"
problem, 112–115
"Urba and Cursa" problem, 105–109
Reasonableness criterion, 98
Reflection (MiC unit), 64–79

Reflections on Number (Wijers et al.), 76–
78
Reif, J., 225
Report cards, 40–41
Research in Assessment Practices (RAP)
study group, 137–138, 171–184, 234
Richardson, V., 184
Romberg, Thomas A., 3, 5–21, 9, 12–15,
20, 46, 61–62, 157, 188–189, 202,
221, 223–235, 225, 228, 229, 232
Roodhardt, A., 11–12, 27, 29, 49, 51,
128, 190, 192

Sarason, S. B., 20
Schoenfeld, A. H., 63
Scoring rubrics, 42–43, 203–204, 209–210
Self-advocacy, increased levels of, 212–
213
Shafer, Mary C., 23, 45–59, 46, 49, 53,
78, 132, 163, 208, 215, 228
Shepard, Lorrie A., 235
Shew, J. A., 49, 51, 64–65, 132, 147, 148,
173, 177, 180, 191–194, 196, 208,
215
Simon, A. N., 10–12, 56–57, 147, 148,
149, 159, 173, 177, 180
Simon, M. A., 158
Sizer, Theodore, 205
Small-group work. See also Discourse-
based assessment
in assessing student progress, 57–58
assessment of student disposition
toward mathematics in, 47
informing instruction through, 51–53
math chats in, 213–214
rethinking classroom practice and,
203
student participation in, 54–58
Smith, Marvin E., 23–24, 60–79, 68–70
Smith, Stephanie Z., 23, 25–44, 73
Social-constructivist approach, 62
Spence, M. S., 10, 49, 51, 123–124
Staff development. See Professional
development
Standards and Assessment Steering
Committee (SASC), 207
Standards model of assessment, 64. See
also Assessment
Stanton, Tim (teacher), 27, 29–30, 32,
33–41

Statistics and the Environment (MiC unit), 10
Stenmark, J. K., 61
Sticking points, 54, 58
Streefland, L., 83
Students
 at-risk, 201
 changing roles of, 191–193, 195–196
 collecting student products, 28–33
 critical attitude of, 8
 differential trait theory and, 66, 73
 generating information about learning of, 27–37, 49–51
 grouping of, 39–40, 66–67
 increased communication with teachers, 213–214
 increased involvement of, 212–213
 information about learning of, 27–37, 49–51, 155–168
 levels of performance of, 16–19
 in MiC versus traditional approach, 60–79
 monitoring progress of, 14–15
 participation of, 34–35, 54–58
 peer assessment and, 180–184
 philosophy of respect for, 219
 responses to investigations, 140–143
 responses to other students, 180–184
 teacher interaction with, in classroom, 33–35, 45–59
 teacher observation of work of, 35–37, 49–51, 58
 teacher recognition of patterns of, 36–37
Student self-evaluation, 78
Summary discussions, 78
Support systems, 219–220, 226
Swafford, J., 229

Take a Chance (MiC unit), 10
Tate, W. F., 226
Taylor, C., 64, 79
Taylor, Ms. (teacher), 60, 64–79
Teacher guides, 76–78
Teachers. See also Instructional innovation; Professional development
 changes made by, 12–13, 20, 25–44, 51–53, 55–58
 changing roles of, 190–191, 194–195
 increased communication with students, 213–214
 information about student learning and, 27–37, 49–51, 155–168
 interaction with students in classroom, 33–35, 45–59
 interpretation of goals for learning, 123–125
 in MiC versus traditional approach, 60–79
 monitoring of student progress, 14–15
 motivation to change, 234
 note taking by, 36
 observation of student work by, 35–37, 49–51, 58
 passive assessment expertise of, 123–125
 recognizing student patterns, 36–37
 supporting change in classroom practices of, 224–226
Teaching style, 121
Technical support systems, 226
Teller, Dennis (teacher), 27, 30, 32, 33–38
Temperature taking, in discourse-based assessment, 175–179, 184
Third International Mathematics and Science Study (TIMSS), 228
Time constraints
 in assessment, 33, 48
 educational change and, 226
Total points systems, 209–210
Tracking Graphs (MiC unit), 147, 149
Triangles and Patchwork (MiC unit), 49–53

U.S. Department of Education, 2
University of Utrecht, 1
University of Wisconsin-Madison, 1
University support systems, 219–220
Ups and Downs (MiC unit), 147, 148, 173–174, 180–181

Van den Heuvel-Panhuizen, Marja, 14, 81, 83–99, 86, 87–88, 91, 132, 208, 215, 229
Van Galen, F., 10, 64–65, 191–194, 196

Van Reeuwijk, Martin, 12–15, 20, 82,
    103, 123–124, 137–151, 153, 155–
    168
Varso, Max (teacher), 27, 30–33, 40
Verhage, H., 17

Ways to Go (MiC unit), 10
Webb, David C., 153, 154, 169–187, 171,
    188, 200–220, 202, 210, 221, 223–
    235, 225
Webb, N. L., 59, 226
Wehlage, G. G., 226

Whole-class discussions. *See also*
    Discourse-based assessment
    in assessing student progress, 57–58
    informing instruction through, 51–53
Wiggins, G. P., 78–79, 170
Wijers, Monica, 10, 11, 27, 29, 53–54,
    56–57, 64–65, 76, 78, 81–82, 82,
    100–121, 103, 128, 132, 137–151,
    146, 159, 163, 190, 192, 208, 215
William, D., 170

Zarinnia, E. A., 61–62